Susan Blackwood Reynolds

Primordial yogic Movement

**Movement Expression
with Evolutionary Perspective**

© 2024 Europe Books | London
www.europebooks.co.uk | info@europebooks.co.uk

ISBN 9791220147521
First edition: February 2024

Primordial yogic Movement

Movement Expression
with Evolutionary Perspective

Table of Contents

Chapter 1. A View Beyond 11

Chapter 2. Perspective, from the Inside Out 25

Chapter 3. Nagerai Aquatic Life.. 37

Chapter 4. Land Dynamics 81

Chapter 5. Earth Series 123

Chapter 6. Primates to Hominins 153

Chapter 7. Mimicry, Emulation and Embodiment................................... 183

Chapter 8. Just another Species 211

In Memory of Ian Harte.
The soul is blessed by the beauty of life endowed ~ choose again to live and love

CHAPTER 1

A View Beyond

What do you do when you feel trapped in a pit of hopelessness? When days grind on endlessly in constant desultory pointlessness? Where it seems impossible for trust to be found in the world with others? Is there a place where a feeling of solidarity with life can exist? Will it ever be possible that what you see – is seen and shared by everyone?

We've beginning a second decade in the onset of the fifth millennia in recording human history. Yet with all our accomplishments, we are a species steered by ideas which simply bubble up from the froth of cultural mediums, ideas often misguided by the scum rising to the surface of the masses - so full of hot air and filled with meaningless dribble. Social media polarizes, conventional media is corporate-controlled, and the public loses to the many prominent leaders in our societies who not only accept the misinformation but spread and vote on it to perpetuate the disruption. Delusion and paranoid thinking often sway opinion because its impact is sensational enough to simply be heard louder than the rest. Discord and damage all too often triumphs… Is there a way out?

Only one way through …**IMAGINATION!**

Sure, I'll go first. Let's start with perspective, because that's an easy one. We all have it, or perhaps it's the other way around, it has us. It's like your shadow – if there's light to see, you have an individual perspective through which you see what you see. Okay, but what if we could use imagination to create scenarios in which everyone has the same perspective? Are there any that allow us all to see the same thing from their different perspectives; are you willing to try one? It's a visual exercise and you'll find it at the end of the chapter. First though - to have a perspective, we must first perceive ourselves in the world, yes? Otherwise, we wouldn't have a point of reference for having a personal perspective at all. So before you rush to the end of the chapter, and I'm going to start sounding pedantic here, bear with me:

The main avenue to feeling our existence is through physical experience. Although the European philosopher René Descartes had some validity when he said, "I think, therefore I am"; it is actually a rather weak statement since most of our thinking is subconscious, so we'll never experience the "I am" that could be. It is through our senses that we interact in a physical world. Doing anything at all in the world occurs physically, right down to the neurons that light up in the brain when sitting still with eyes closed. Although it is commonplace in this day in the information age to largely ignore our body state in preference to being in our heads; however, in the long term, it is not ideal to be so. I hope you can agree that both physical and mental health is generally better when the body and mind are integrated rather than at odds constraining. Good awareness and integration are key to trusting one's perceptions. When our physical presence is grounded in sensing the surroundings, even subconsciously, we can better recognize and access the reality of the present in order to accurately interact in it. We directly connect to the physical reality in the immediacy of events through our senses. Sensing transmits external data through neural connections, transmitting and receiving in nanoseconds. And by seeing and hearing the world around us through our individual neural-based sensing pathways, it delivers us the possibility of having a conscious awareness of it. Bada Bing! To what degree we are consciously aware does not make it any less physical, it is still neurons firing, or not, in our brains. It is fair to say that - We may think we know, but we may know only what we can. Yet, what we can know can also be a choice - what to focus on or not perceptively can be repurposed as perspective, individually. In other words – while perceptions can only be altered neurologically (in the sense that they are physical); perspectives on the other hand, although also neurologically based, can often be widened or narrowed by us. That is where this book works a principal point. Primordial yogic Movement (PyM) is an experiential primer of perceptual change through movement exercises which also carry the possibility of expanding perspective to access commonality. Changes in perspective are relatively easy. Changing perception is much more difficult. Both, however require a step back, and back again, and again further and further back… as many steps as are necessary to expand on who and what we are.

    Primordial yogic Movement is a perceptual practice, designed to provide a wide-angle lens to deepen and widen our understanding of evolution and life. It is a method to take note and survey inner perceptions in outward expression. For some, that may entail re-experiencing the body in motion and working the senses to become more comfortable with feeling physically and expressing through it. PyM is experiential meaning that we learn from the experience through physical engagement, by doing. The experiential method is highly effective as it directs muscle memory - which isn't just about the learning and storing what is learned and felt in the body, it also involves the emotions, present thinking and state of being, and how open to learning one might be. Experiential training to build change through skill typically begins with understanding how it is internalized and reaches into a visceral level. Thinking through the body with intent works well in a workout because it also helps to reduce the querulous mental activity of the mind. The comparative narratives (am I doing this right? Am I being judged? I can't do this. What if it's wrong? I can't really feel what I should be feeling?) that often runs in the mind and diverts attention. They are thoughts that wait in the wings to distract from being fully, mindfully present in doing something; and may affect clarity of spirit in action. Yeats knew it only too well:

> *God guard me from the thoughts men think*
> *In the mind alone.*
> *He that sings a lasting song*
> *Thinks in a marrow bone.*

~ **William Butler Yeats, "The King of the Great Clock Tower.**

For more than a millennium, humans thought the universe they saw in the sky was a spinning fixed tapestry, yet eternal. But we've known for over a couple of centuries just how dynamic and expanding the universe is. The timeline of the cosmos is so vast; our minds cannot consciously grasp the totality in measurable units. Even simply looking at the timeline of events in the formation and emergence of life on earth is difficult. Yet our planet is considered relatively young. Planet earth is only 4.543 billion years old and while it is hard to imagine such an age, I have found that knowing a little earth history and evolution helps to broaden my understanding of the expanse. By looking at the formative booms and busts of planetary history and its many inhabitant lifeforms, it is possible to gain a perspective on how we came to be part of the greater fabric of life as a species. So, I invite you to take the long view with me in this book - and rediscover an ancient past through the evolution of movement. At this point in our human history, there are a few simple current truths upon which all the major cultures of the world can base some tacit agreements on what we are. We are a biological species, evolved as any other species on earth and most will agree that as a mammalian species, we are fortunate to be here. This is not facile to say because all biological life on earth has more than once tipped close to the brink of total annihilation. Only recently have discoveries revealed just how compelling the story of earth's biological evolution is, a story that is still unfolding. It's a tale that chronicles how planetary cyclical changes have coolly transformed all life on earth, repeatedly challenging organisms with extreme tests in their ability to survive. There have been incredible trials in rites of passage for all forms of life as the earth transitioned from a burning cauldron to periods of cold almost as frigid as Mars, often with atmospheres as toxic as Venus. Since the first twitch of a protocell and against all odds - life on earth has managed with creativity and synchronicity to escape the final silencing, thus far. If we could but turn back the pages to witness what exquisite lifeforms that have been lost to the collective through extinction events…we would weep. Yet many a phoenix has arisen from the ashes of the extinction to carry forth multiple evolutionary legacies. Cells, once a possibility has existed will find a way again to re-emerge in new organisms, and the vitality of primordial life has repeatedly re-inherited the earth. Time and time again, those traits long pronounced dead have somehow managed to resurface, as though certain aspects in evolution had little need to be sustained by a long history of linear ascent. How life itself continues to triumph after millions of desolated years pass from cataclysmic extinctions to again reclaim dynamic roles is unknown. Whether by unrelenting persistence to survive or through the tenacity of the creative force of life or by some other irrepressible, mutative force in Nature, we cannot know. All life on earth has been cut and tailored by numerous planetary passages which to this day continues to creatively hammer change in the planet's living systems, earth composition, hydro, atmospheric and thermal flux among other factors of earth science. Given its vital creative nature - it is all the more reason to honor and celebrate the evolutionary resilience of life and its changeable nature.

What is gained from our inner nature is exact knowledge, which gives us a far reaching outlook over the earth. The many powers of inner nature are hidden in everyone, and these are identified with Wakan-Tanka.
~ Blue Thunder

We are born of the same cloth as all other creatures on earth. All life is the result of microbial beginnings, born of stardust. From the first pulse of cell life barely beyond the fertilization of our mother's egg, the imprint of how we grew as a baby, a child, an adolescent to an adult -- was set by the symbiotic synchronizations of biological programming passed down from previous generations reaching far back in time. How cells form and differentiate into different organs and body parts is a result of billions of years in the making. The creative power in the organization of microbiotic cells is uniquely expressed in the lives of all species on earth, both past and present. They exquisitely reflect the symbiotic nature of life that guides the build and functioning of each living system through evolutionary processes that were worked out billions of years ago in the evolution of organisms. It is miraculous to be sure – to be alive in the astoundingly well-evolved physical body, for it is a result of all the bodies which equally make up the billions of species which have graced the earth. All species are the result of a powerful drive in cells to work together in collaboration and conjunction in order to create all single and multi-celled life. Physicality itself is the result of a long evolutionary history and the building blocks are cells that each day, give form to life. Each living plant, ant, whale, amoeba, and human carries every trace of the deep primordial paths that rendered each organism into what they are. Seen and unseen complexities of mechanisms and forces control the biological processes -- endlessly challenging scientists, scholars, physicians, anthropologists and artists to unravel their many mysteries.

For us and throughout our hominin (early man) history, we have studied the human body depicting the human body in a myriad of ways, expressing a fascination for its intricacies, its strength, fragility, resilience, structural movement, grace and more. As humans, we are considered many things. The different perspectives through which we might view ourselves only increases with the number of facets through which the *Homo sapient* species may be viewed given the creativity we are capable of. There is the physical or biological aspect of who we are; a cultural aspect, a social aspect, an emotional aspect, a mental aspect, a learned, economic, familial and situational aspect to each of us, and all of these with varying degrees of complexity and exclusive to view. We change, seemingly always in flux from moment to moment, event to event; and as a result -- we are often flummoxed by who we are at any one time. While the complexities and variations within our own species as *Homo sapiens* are vast and intricate, we all share the same origin. We are all simply another species of hominin in the *Homo* lineage.

Nothing has existed or evolved on its own, in a vacuum.

As a species we would not be who we are without the adaptations and exaptations which have evolved earlier in other species, including non-linear precedents. The effects of evolutionary refinements, attunements, survival behaviors, random mutations and adaptations should not be minimized, but realized for what they are. There are some major mutative passages that all species share as our collective heritage forged billions of years ago. They have influenced all species to create a tapestry of the environment that has helped shape the many paths of evolution. They are the result of eons of opportunity, creativity, cooperation, happenstance, battle, struggle, growth and synchronicity in other species. Wondrous aspects of evolution born from the development of composite configurations of chemical elements, bacterial symbiosis, cell-to-cell communication, molecular chemical and mineral receptivity of cells, the chemical nature of emotive sensing, the energetic transference of cells and the evolutionary responses which have tailored the structural and neurological systems of motor control with nerves, ganglia, sense and fluid systems which course daily in physical bodies. They are the control aspects which have led to the evolution of hair, eyes, teeth, ears, lungs, skin, tissues, ligaments, tendons muscles, digestive systems, hormonal systems, reproductive organs and other organs, the rhythmic autonomy of a heart and lung breathing, the development of the spinal column, and so, so much more. All these we owe to other organisms that came before us as attributes and characteristics we share in kind. Our *Homo* lineage is just as related to their ancestors as we are to ours. Many of the creatures living around us are not only our brothers, sisters and cousins, but our grandmothers and grandfathers as well. They have informed our past and will determine our future.

Perceptual Practice

The deepest transformations in human training typically occur from engagement in the perceptual practices that reach, integrate and connect the creative dimensions of a person's being into the present, immediate world. Primordial yogic Movement is a perceptual practice designed to expand the view of what we are, and quite possibly, help to regain more insight into our species' purpose and actions. The practice begins where life itself began…in a fluid environment. In Chapter 3, we begin by exploring the first movements of life as a single cell, and continue on a semi-chronological path into our biological past to discover and experiment with other species' forms and movements as they evolved on earth. While the first movements take place in a water environment, many of the land species that are sampled are forms and movements that can be performed in quite a small space - some are practiced ideally on a soft surface such as a bed or cot. Using our finely tuned senses and innate physical and mental faculties to observe, visualize, mirror, mimic, and emulate other species - my hope is that the practice of other species' forms and movements will allow you to connect to and realign to your biological heritage. Through practice, self-perception may deepen as perspectives widen through feeling a shared history. PyM is a new approach to relationships that can color individual perceptual responses to other species. PyM is typical of the many practices followed by ancient and indigenous peoples around the world for thousands of years; ancient practices which are intended to attune each of us to being present in the immediate world.

The History of Dependency

Well before the advent of multicellular creatures on the earth, species survival depended largely on accurate sensing within the living systems of the surrounding environment, landscapes and ecosystems. All animal survival on land had to include knowledge of other species behaviors and characteristics, the properties of plants and the seasonal patterns. Sensing and observing others in an environment carried clues to behaviors to further survival in living in the world. For example, by observing the flora and fauna, several species of hominin "pre-Homo sapien could optimize food sources, anticipate defensively and capitalize offensively in preparation for seasonal occurrences and for periods of scarcity. Observations of their surroundings improved food gathering into timed, integrated nomadic lifestyle patterns to better match the flux found in ecosystems and to optimize the seasonal events, animal and insect behaviors and to plan for the annual migrations. Animal traits, their social structures and associations with other species helped shaped behaviors, methods and practices. As far back as anthropological human history goes, it is fair to say that hominins as *social species* have been infused with the observations that built on the knowledge passed generation to generation to form the basis for indigenous practices, beliefs and rituals.

A foundational signature in tribal indigenous traditions has been to honor and celebrate other creatures as givers of life. (Suzuki, D., Knudtsen, P., 1992) Tribes culturally offered up respect and reverence to other species, especially those they were dependent upon. Many indigenous practices that focus on relationships in and with the natural world were rooted in rituals and practices of a pantheistic nature. Associative connection to existence dependent on other animals and the seasonal growth of the natural world in turn were reflected in the prehistoric art of different hominin species. Pantheistic belief in the possibility of spirit in natural objects and in their surroundings can be found as far back as a million years ago. Animistic thinking then excluded what has become an assumption of our separation based on hierarchical superiority. No, the playing field for all species was essentially level in their daily life. All species existed equally under the same threat that they could be hunted as easily as they could hunt in a mutual quest for survival. Animistic thinking and pantheism diminished as numerous other belief mechanisms swept the "civilizing" world before the first millennium. Animists and indigenous practices were further disavowed with the entrenchment of nation statehood, formal religion, scientific method and the industrial revolution. (Lewis, J.,2020) (Gadgil, M., 2018) Western culture remains largely dismissive of animistic and pantheistic belief. Today, it is now more difficult to perceive what may exist beyond the pale when it has neither black nor white characteristics, and must be accessed from within each of us. The awareness that divinity can be witnessed all around us in the immediate world however, can result in more spirited and spirit-full connections – but only if there is awareness that a participatory divinity is possible in the universe. There are many ancient indigenous tribal songs, stories, ceremonies, prayers, vision quests, practices, rituals and dances of indigenous groups around the world that tap into that elusive spirituality. They are the rituals that attest to and reflect the deep connections members share in caring for the natural world of their birth. There are practices that unite participants in honor of the earth - that venerate plant and animal spirits by aligning human members in harmony with the beauty and grace in the munificence of the natural world.

From their observations, our ancestors saw a kinship of dependence; humans depending on animals and birds and insects; animals depending on insects and plants; insects depending on plants; plants depending on the earth, sun and rain… They and we, take part in creation by re-creating. When living things die, they become part of the earth, a sacred burial ground deserving of reverence. What our ancestors learned of the land, the wind, the fire and the waters, the beetles, the hawks, the wolverines and the otters is revelation. Through the high places and low, Kitchi-Manitou (Great Spirit) shows us, speaks to us…The land has given us our understandings, beliefs, perceptions, laws, customs. It has bent and shaped our notions of human nature, conduct and the Great Laws".

~ **Ojibwa native Basil Johnston, Honour Earth Mother**

Animistic reverence and celebration are today very much a part of the rituals still practiced by many indigenous peoples around the world. Some of my first memories growing up in the States came from my increasing awareness of the ongoing tradition of the native reverence for the natural world in their teachings. I came to know how indigenous tribes in North America lived for tens of thousands of years on the offerings of the North American continent as nature-based tribal societies; very much attuned to living sustainably in the abundant lands and well within the bounds of what it yielded. The eastern American tribes were found to be so full of gracious freedoms and individual expression that many of the democratic principles from the native governance principles were woven into the initial cloth of the laws governing the Constitution. Prior to the incursion of European and western acculturation, indigenous tribal language, laws, customs and most celebration traditions perpetrated tribal member participation in continuing a deep relationship to nature and creation as grounded in respect, reciprocity and honor. They included beliefs that all creatures were sentient, had conscious lives worthy of respect. Many especially revered those animals that could fight and kill as equitably as the tribes' warriors could kill them. In some Native American ceremonies – animal spirits are called upon to endow members with the powers of animal wisdom, strength, speed, agility, prowess, ferocity and other attributes. Animal spirits were thought to be complete in the divine nature of each creature. And many indigenous groups today around the world have rituals to attune to nature to share in a sense of ancestry in order to feel that completeness in nature. (Suzuki, D. and Knudtsen, P., 1992) In Pueblo Indian ritual dances, tribal members might tap into animal spirits by stepping "out of their human roles to put on the mask, costume and the *mind* of Bison, Bear, and others… and re-enter the human circle and by song, mime, and dance to convey a greeting from the other realm." (Waters, F., 1950) Representations of animals in native North American dances are meant not only to invoke certain animal characteristics but to affect a spiritual transformation within the performers.

Celebrations that access ecstatic states and visions through dance and ritual could reinforce beliefs that spiritual energy and soul within the human heart can never exist nor be divorced from the natural world.

It is entirely possible that our human ability to consciously emulate and embody other persons and species is an attribute specific to the *Homo sapient* species. There is no evidence to the contrary to show that other non-human species display more than mimicry, strategy, camouflage and learned behaviors of imitation. Humans on the other hand, may access and develop knowledge to extrapolate characteristics for expression and practice those skills experientially to emulate a wide range of species. There is a possibility to sense connection, to relate in intimate ways and realign a sense of self in reciprocity with another species.

Primordial yogic Movement

PyM is a visual, experiential health practice that draws on the knowledge of earth history and bryology to create movements which can reasonably emulate evolutionary heritage. Microbial life initiates narrowing the time gap imposed by living only a single lifetime and thus to expand our outlook. This recognition begins with evolved physicality -- because our bodies are the beginning, the middle and the end of living for all of us. Our bodies are worthy of honor, certainly worthy enough for each of us to discover the power of its potential to inform us of its wisdom - regardless of how much baggage the past might weigh us down. Trusting your body comes from a willingness to listen and a capacity to be kind to yourself. As you begin PyM practice, focus on freeing yourself from any thoughts of self-image, any comparative niggling in your mind, and banish as much as possible the narratives you live your life by, they are only constructs. Leave that baggage -- at the door. PyM will work with what is, whatever it may be, which may require old viewpoints to be dealt with along the way. Keeping focused will help you to creatively surmount the issues that arise, wrought by a particular lifestyle or personal history. Work and lifestyle, cultural habits and past life can leave some of us quite divorced from thinking through the body or of having much of a 'felt' sense internally. The Information Age can easily bury our creative ability to freely express in movement. Developing a sense of the physical ability in movement or even mimicking a posture may seem quite beyond reach. It is an unfortunate fact that the most basic sense can often be blanketed over by habits and veils of doubt, distrust, confusion, shame and contortions in reasoning. That doesn't mean that you'll never connect with your body, it can always be rediscovered and regained through trust in the body again -- we all began with it at one time or another, to a greater or lesser degree. In order to get the most out of PyM, it is tantamount to be present in the "felt experience", to allow awareness and sensation to open individual inclinations of expression.

Confidence in a workout typically improves with repetition whereupon any roadblocks are smoothed or skirted with modifications. Imagination and creativity can ultimately reveal ways around difficulties - so trust and listen to your inner voice with kindness to help you learn. Initiating body awareness may come more easily from listening in stillness (static stretches), from nurturing yourself with appreciative self-touch, from thinking and practicing energetic mudras to help to better direct the sensing paths (to complete a form posture). Build confidence by being in touch with yourself physically; it completes you on many levels and can cultivate more trust and intuition. Honor begins with your body, and by extension it can be possible to honor others.

Live a Life Connected

Intellectually we may sense we are part of a greater whole, but how can we feel that connection to nature at all times? In living day to day, is parity with wholeness in the world even possible? It is easier to see how indigenous peoples of the forest and desert live within the bounds of their lands sustainably? It is more difficult with the pressures of daily life when sustenance depends on a wage job in the city. How do we find peace in the busy bustle of a crowded city? Our human societies do not lend themselves to having constant awareness and physical attention in the immediacy of each moment. Being aware and present would be too overwhelming and exhausting. Imagine a guru making a living in the city of Las Vegas. You'd think the constant sensory stimulation from the distracting sights and scenes would be untenable for anyone to contain in total awareness. They may inwardly maintain a sense of well-being by integrating body and mind to dwell in a meditative peace from within, but how to live and maintain that attentive awareness while constantly attuning to the imbalance and artifices, the overwhelmingly transitory acculturation and accumulation amidst the unceasing barrage of media? Well-being might be attainable for a guru, but how does one live in wholeness in an artifice of life in the flux of moment to moment change? I venture to say it may happen through methods and practices which encourage skillful perception and conscious filtering to derive meaning in a commodity-based culture of appropriation.

If we indeed wish to heal ourselves, our communities and our amazing planet, a good place to begin is in how we perceive our relationships. While indigenous peoples have traditions of honor and respect, our commerce-based culture in the West does not. Few of us know where our food and shelter comes from or what structural systems they rely on. We simply don't give much thought to the processes of convenience. From hiring, picking, sorting, collecting and slaughtering, packaging and distribution, and from the clear-cutting, planting and mining to the processing and financing, most of us have little or no experience of the resources, practices or the frameworks behind the organization, distribution, and delivery of goods and products. It has all been set in the inherited cultures we cannot easily understand and far less, change in a single lifetime. So how can we possibly witness what is happening to our planet to apply what we know in order to feel connected to the nature of our birth? The Las Vegas guru may have the answer.

Remember, a guru is only a guru because he/she lives a lifestyle based on remaining open to the constant input in her or his perceptions. The yogi is a yogi by consistently expanding perspectives to incorporate all the new input skillfully. It is how he or she can retain the peace within no matter what is happening outside. Expanding perspectives help to distance and widen ourselves in the immediacy of any backdrop that is going on in life. The next chapter deals with perceptions more in detail: what they are and how we can alter and guide them.

Developing a practice of meditation can result in greater physical awareness, improve hormonal, endocrine and other health systems, internal stillness and mental resilience, and prepare the bodymind for contemplative movement. Primordial yogic Movement differs slightly in its intention as a perceptual practice although it can be a moving meditative practice also.

PyM is a body-based movement method to realign us with the past lineage of evolution in sampling movement expressions in the other species and rediscover the threads of origin we share. The practice is experiential and motion dynamic, so it's an exercise workout. You are encouraged to focus on connecting with individual species in reciprocity and on the past that is your body. There may necessarily be steps to reconcile differences that can separate; the practice is an individual process and PyM is meant to enhance wholeness which may entail addressing departures.

As you begin, simply listen to what past ancestors have to teach. Follow your own discovery and impressions in expressing. If you witness a different aspect of a creature's movement or an attribute that can better embody a creature; visualize it and internalize to let it flow from you. It will be more authentic, expressive and meaningful to you. In living systems, function ramifies form and form ramifies function.

By enacting other species, PyM seeks three epistemic functions: to integrate mind and body in honoring our past heritage; to enhance awareness of what we are and understand the creative paths forged by life in a changeable earth through the evolution of its inhabitants; *and* to bridge concepts of individual singularity so that we reconnect *as a species* in more meaningful ways. Primordial yogic Movement is a practice like others that work on perceptions: such as studying religious texts, practicing yoga or martial arts or engaging in meditation. But in PyM, you step into another's shoes; or rather... another's paws, hooves, tentacles, chitin, shell or gelatinous body. It's more fun to think outside the box by opening our narratives and attitudes to embody another species.

To get you started - the first known indication of life on earth were the first microbial protocells (not quite cells). PyM movements begin in water and move to mimic early aquatic creatures and their movements of propulsion and swim and transition into more complex species. PyM movement patterns are loosely progressive in lifeform evolution and can appear to be linear in their chronological appearance on the earth. From the earliest oceanic multicellular life to the Devonian Age of Fishes and the transition onto the land masses, where four-limbed amphibian and reptilian species evolve into the more complex notions of biomechanical lift in birds and the contralateral movements of mammals; PyM briefly journeys through periods of upheaval and extinctions to highlight some of the ingenious and complex strategies of organisms, how they morph, move and form, only to arrive at the species associated with our own *Homo* lineage. It is an honor to emulate all the species in a narrative of evolutionary heritage through posture, stretch and movement as a workout, exercising their passages handed down by nature and by extension - as gestures of goodwill expressed as reflected in us and back to honor them.

If you decide to try PyM, it will be easier to perceive how a guru living in Las Vegas can live beyond wellness into wholeness and connection. Transformation and growth is possible in each of us; however if there is no opportunity to expand ourselves from the navel-gazing into a wider perspective of who we are, we will languish as forever separated. The planet carries the story narrative of its lifeforms for you to express in form and movement. I encourage you to use the heritage of the past to enrich your stretch and workout experience. While conscious movement is key to integrating body and mind, it is your creative expression and visualization that will affect the perspectives needed to weave a better web for *Homo sapiens* in nature; and it may also enhance your acuity of a spiritual kind.

Visualization

What is perceived in this exercise is perspective seen together

    Try It: Think of where you are right now, perhaps in a room or outside. Visualize yourself in that particular place and then wrap your mind around where that place is, in the building or an area, and where it's located from a birds eye view, and yourself in it. Then, view that locale (with you) and its location in a district or a city, or on a coastline, in a desert or woodland perhaps; and yourself in the place within it. Step back a little further to view the land configuration where you are to expand outward to encompass the terrain, the county or region, and yourself there. Then visualize where in the land, coast shape it is within the nation, and where the nation is located on the continent where you are, and witness the whole of your locale in that part of the world. Then view the continent, its location on the planet, and where you are within it, there, on the earth. Then visualize the continent where you are on the planet in the solar system. And each planet in its relative position to the earth; each step you visualize where you are in it. Visualize the sun in the solar system as just one of over 100 billion stars residing there - in one of the spiral arms of our galaxy, the vast Milky Way. Our sun is just a star, a celestial body in a small cluster of 54 different galaxies which make up what is known as the Local Group. It is a small cluster of galaxies tiny in comparison to a greater grouping of galaxies, the Virgo Supercluster. Our Local Group sits on the outskirts, a mere speck in the Universe that holds you.

    Did your perspective widen outward? Did you seem smaller as your perspective expanded inclusive of your place from adding the space around you widened? This can be a good little exercise to help you gather your thoughts when something momentous happens. It can provide some often needed spacious distance from which to handle the business of the present moment; it can provide a more open perspective to moments that are painful and difficult to absorb immediately - emotions dealing with shame, disappointment, despair; whether they are the result of personal actions or by others. By widening perspective with time, space and distance; the serious gravity of the moment can seem less critical and consequential. A change in perspective can expand into a new outlook, a possibly overlooked facet in your thinking. Having perspective is seeing ourselves as we truly are. Ultimately, we are but specks and no matter what has occurred - past or present, what you do or have done in the past – none of it will change the order of the Universe.

References

Gadgil, M., 2018. Sacred Groves, *Scientific American Magazine,* December Issue.

Jean, T., 2003. *365 Days Walking the Red Road*. Adams Media: Avon, MA.

Johnston, B., 2003. *Honour Earth Mother*. First Nebraska PBk Printing.

Lewis, J., 2020. Living With the Forest, *Scientific American*, May Issue.

Suzuki, D.& Knudtson, P. (1992). *Wisdom of the Elders.* New York, NY: Bantam Books.

Waters, F. (1950). Pueblo Shaman in Ritual Dances. *Masked Gods*. Athens, OH: Swallow Press.

CHAPTER 2

Perspective, from the Inside Out

Health is individual and quite different in each of us. If we sample a cross-section of those born with a congenital disease or a physical impairment and without other associative pain, they often consider themselves comparatively healthy, although preferring not to have to deal with the difficulty. This is largely due to the ability to accommodate and carry on but can also be a general indicator of perspective on health. Similarly, there are those with no physical or mental impairments and no appreciable economic struggle who wallow miserably with hypochondria, depression, anxiety, and anguish. An individual's concept of health often boils down to self-perception. Health is also greatly influenced by others with whom we coexist, by habits and lifestyle, economics and surroundings, past history and current situations. Stress also plays a role in health and outlook, and affects the ability to live in the reality of the world. Determinant factors are too numerous and complex to cover the whole scope of the possible outlooks, yet our perspectives weigh heavily on our feelings regarding health.

No living entity exists freely in and of itself. How physical and mental health is felt is often a result of the genetic, sociocultural and economic history that preceded us and continues to influence our perspectives in daily life. Individual concepts of wholeness in health are often affected by current lifestyle and situations, but whether they allow for opportunity to exercise methods of self-care or promote healthy feelings or not; individual perspective typically on health will emanate from our self-held narratives. Research makes it clear that both what we feel and project outwardly about health is neurologically wired as a component of self-awareness, an awareness formed by perception and influenced by our perspectives.

A few decades ago, cognitive science - the study of cognitive self-awareness, and the science of neurobiology - the science of the sensory processing of neurons (nerve cells), began to merge together. The merger occurred because human cognition is neurological. Cognitive scientists agree that thought is a physically active processing of neurobiological stimulus signalling through which awareness is created in experiencing the world. How something is known relates to explicit and implicit mental representations specifically manifested in the neural structures of our brains. They are represented in the mind as neural circuitry maps daily events through perceiving through the senses. Individual neural mapping begins from infancy, in learning more and more every day, as physicality and awareness emerge. First perceptions come from those who nurture and care for us to build a context of external reality. Each day notions of the world activate individual neural circuitry repeatedly to be confirmed by assurance of consistency in events. Experiences form a sense of identity and placement in the world to provide awareness of ourselves from the inside out. Perception through internal sensing outwardly integrates psychophysically not only through experiencing individual reality but also gives us our personal viewpoints. When we look out on the world, who we are is molded by repeat activation of neurons through pathways that are reinforced by experience. The reinforcement reassures us of what and where we are in the world. (Lakoff, 2012) It is through these reinforced neural pathways that independent thoughts and actions can be trusted and are defensible to us.

Repetitive reinforcement along distinct neural pathways predisposes our inner narratives with perspectives within the context of the world to give us a firm and comfortable picture of reality from which to form individual viewpoints. They are internal narratives that carry attitudes, views, opinions and beliefs from what we sense and feel. And hominins can be quite firm on attitudes by eight years of age from sensory-supported neural connections that wire thinking. Neural mapping has plasticity and changes with experience; typically, those concepts and ideas that fit with established narratives resonate with us and seem more trustworthy to us than those that don't fit into individual views. Cognitive scientists have found that narratives that reinforce existing perspectives are more likely to be accepted as "motivated reasoning". If events don't fit well with a running internal narrative, then it has less purpose for us and is typically rejected outright or is not given much thought or conviction. And most of the filtering of what is applicable to understanding or viewpoint in our narrative, happens subconsciously.

With our thoughts, we make the world.
~ **The Buddha**

Conversely however, everyone has surprising moments of self-discovery when suddenly we're thrown off-balance and find out just how little we actually know. It can happen when confronted by something different for the first time, when perceptions are found to be fallible or no longer trustworthy, when narrative no longer supports what was known. Discovering holes in a comfortable, picture-perfect perspective on reality from an encounter that upends prior thinking can be quite unsettling, or exciting. It can happen when logical reasoning is revealed to be a crutch or unreliable enough to cause a narrative to crumble. It is when a perspective is seen from a new angle or in a different light. They are the wonderful moments when what was thought be intractable suddenly expands and opens a whole new realm of understanding and possibility.

Change in the long-running narratives in our minds happen anyway – memories and events fade, recall weakens, new events and people enter and depart from our lives. Life changes open new doors to perceptions and bring in new perspectives. Or events can serve to render us more closed. Often a closure to veracity can seem to insulate conviction from outside reality, but it can be a form of self-isolation. The important thing to remember is to see perspectives as malleable, especially when events fit in with ideas and when they do not. It is possible to guide internal narratives. Those who tame and tailor perspectives and attitudes better self-direct an internal narrative. There are methods and practices which can affect internal narratives and self-held concepts through acquiring skill in guiding thoughts, especially when habitual. (W. Wood, 2019) (Reddy, S.M.W.,2016) To skillfully change behaviors and responses as inappropriate into more desirable responses always requires practice however. Narratives thought to be engrained by habit can morph into newly constructed perspectives when replaced with new cognitive ones that, if strengthened with repetition, can alter neurologically.

Plasticity in perspective often starts with an awareness of change. School Phys Ed classes might have made you aware of your comparative skills in certain activities and formulated thoughts about teamwork. At that stage, neural circuitry was forming comparative impressions as a part of self-knowledge. Later those initial self-evaluations morphed or solidified based on subsequent experience. Most likely, earlier personal evaluation and teamwork scenarios have been replaced or expanded upon with more accurate assessments based on subsequent training and experience. When there's a struggle to identify beyond an initial self or other assessment influencing perspective, there is often a lack of opportunity to grow beyond a certain thought position or there is an imposed constriction in personal flexibility when confronted with what you know is the reality of the concept or situation. When stuck, developing self-reflection might be just the ticket to make an internal narrative alter and morph.

Particularly in western cultures, self-reflection and discernment as a practice more often occurs if it is accepted as a current cultural trend. This is not to say techniques are not available in the West to develop perception and discernment skills. But historically, practices of conduct, thought and methodology to calm the mind, to instill equanimity, discernment and right thinking, to reduce the mind chatter, and open the heart and mind began in the East. They are practices firmly accepted and steered by spiritual and community leaders, shamans, tribal counselors and governing leaders and will continue to be passed down through generations. The West has been guided more by the sciences in the arena of mental health, typically by psychiatry, psychology, social and cognitive science. These fields and other empirical sciences tend to drive the methods, tools and practices that best promulgate how we explore, attain and support mental and physical health.

Eastern perceptual practices have proven over thousands of years to be effective in effectively guiding self-awareness and perspective through practices of meditation, tai chi, breath work techniques, martial arts, qigong, and yoga – they have been established long before modern medicine arrived on the scene. Both ancient and modern science-based methods can and do enhance ability to improve outlook and construct healthy responses by developing skill in what is perceived in self-held narratives. By practicing a perceptual practice, new knowledge, insight and a skilled calmness can enhance better responses when faced with the veracity of new perspectives. Learned perceptual skills can reinforce new concepts of self-understanding and allow many old ways to whither. Overlaying and discarding old neural circuitry with newly trained responses are created and may ramify and expand.

Perception, o' shining light

Perceptions are not simply inferences made from sight, smelling, hearing, taste and touch, they're much more. They are physical-based and yet are also abstract – and none of us have exclusive claim on the objectivity of perceptions that are mutually shared because so much of felt experience is purely individual. Just as we see colors differently, we perceive from the inside outwardly and individually -- it's in our DNA. We take in outside information, extract the pertinent data, reflect it, compare it and analyze it with past information, often twist it, and extrapolate what is perceived. In other words, we reinterpret observations as we form our thinking. Plus, like a melting pot – our minds extract, analyze and interpret to refine perceptions into perspectives in the light of new experiences; and in particular, in exchanges with one another. In the previous chapter, I said it's easier to change a perspective and difficult to change perception. To illustrate, most of us have, at one time or another, been amused by a foreign product description or usage instructions included in with a product. The description as interpreted from another language may explain something that is quite ordinary in a very odd or funny way from an unexpected perspective, and is especially amusing when delivered seriously. Perspectives may seem odd to us depending on the source, angle and light through which they are seen; yet we can easily see them. Changes in perception, however is more difficult because most of what we perceive is subconscious. Perceptions and their inferences are largely automatic. We are not consciously aware of how our brains form them. (Lakoff, G., Johnson, M., 1999) As an example - during a physical workout, how much sensation you experience can be based entirely on the value and importance you give to your physical fitness. Sensing and perceiving the results from a workout varies greatly from person to person. And those views are circular, because the sensory experience of exercising itself shapes our thoughts about the basic value of exercise. We continuously, unconsciously fashion our own personal narrative in response to whether we have thoughts of aversion, pleasure, fear, desire or other attachments. Conscious rationalization can and does shape our thoughts and the impulse to frame those perceived experiences is largely subconscious. Perspectives change with the viewpoint; and neurologically-based perceptions often mix with emotions. It's too easy (and inaccurate) to say that we sense what we perceive and perceive what we sense. Perceptions contribute to internalized narratives with which we tailor our personalized perspectives. The usefulness of any perceptual practice will depend on how consciously aware of thought we are and how willing to perceptively access and mitigate our perspectives.

All that we experience is subjective
There is no sensation without interpretation
We create the world ourselves;
Only when we stop, do we see truth.
~ Taoist prose

Perceptual practices filter out the noise and pain to improve and support mental and emotional stability in daily life. All perceptual practices have three components: form, function and discipline. A perceptual practice may be as simple as, say, engaging in the art of making pottery. It takes its form from knowledge of clay, the amount of moisture needed, kneading and throwing technique, and knowledge of regulating firing; all are aspects in a form of making pottery. The discipline required in making pots involves patience along with physical and emotional steadiness; no matter what is occurring outside the potter's attention, there must be a disciplined focus. Drop attention momentarily and the form will thin unevenly, flop and fold. Lastly, the function of pottery is the skill that defines the craft and makes a potter a craftsperson. The practitioner defines the form and the form identifies the practitioner.

In meditation, the main function of a practice is to calm the mind and train equanimity, right thinking and discernment. Its form is taught and practiced as a method (transcendental, *Vipassanā*, Taoist, Buddhist). And of course, discipline comes from sitting long enough to clear the mind beyond contemplation. Perceptual practices help us skillfully learn through re-learning how to train to perceive within a new context. Especially in somatic (body-based) practices, success is first measured by how attuned and present you are in your own body.

Primordial yogic Movement (PyM) is such a perceptual somatic practice. It has form, function and discipline much like practicing meditation, but with one difference. Form in PyM is the movement expressions of organism structures and movements within the context of their evolution. Its discipline is the attention and creativity to mimic and emulate other species to build skill, kinship and reciprocity as a practice. The function of PyM is two-fold, and this is where it differs from other perceptual practices. The obvious is to improve physical and mental well-being and creativity through mind-body integration. The second function is a fourth aspect that requires practitioners to release their self-held narratives and fully witness our heritage by listening to what evolution has to teach us as a species. By doing so, the expressive collaboration is intended to consciously narrow the gap that separates us from the dynamic of living systems. Naturally PyM is fun as a workout, yet it can be more when expressed as interpretations of life from widening our perspectives on our species in the world. PyM works to resonate with other species in perceiving reciprocity.

Dynamic Participation

A crucial pillar in understanding the body and mind connection is to consider the nature of homeostasis. Homeostasis maintains the body's physical functioning autonomously (without conscious will) by daily balancing our physical and emotional responses. Homeostasis works through the endocrine and nervous systems to either stimulate physical systems. It pushes the cortisol in awakening from sleep to rush to catch a train; or to dampen with serotonin response to calm us back down in the aftermath of a stressful situation. When we sense something with anticipation or dread, for example, we become aware of its automatic and autonomous functioning when unable to directly control blushing or breaking out in a cold sweat. The built-in biochemical balancing mechanism of homeostasis always works to react to any upset in the overall balanced internal state and to thereby reestablish a normalized state. Yet homeostasis can also be guided with perceptual training. Training the mind helps homeostatic efficiency because a well-integrated body and mind make it easier for homeostasis to function when mitigating life occurrences with automatic responses. Generally, if we're in touch with how we feel, when minds are trained, we are more poised to confidently establish states of balance making homeostasis more energetically efficient. Trained self-perception helps to guide and integrate responses in the world by helping to conserve nervous energy as a method to skillfully maintain peace of mind.

Since the discovery of homeostasis as a bio-mechanism of the nervous system in the last century, researchers and teachers alike have concluded that experiential learning by *doing* is recognized as effective technique to build confidence in learning new skills. (Dewey J., 1929) Body-based practices not only train muscle memory and assist in homeostatic response but can help integrate emotions through training impulsive and reactive narrative perception.

Movement expression when integrating abstract concepts also address emotionally-associated feelings that are often attached. Perceptual training works with thoughts and emotions to trust the perception of a new perspective. Experiential training by doing instead of thinking something through is a direct process of learning and the equivocating, abstracting mind thoughts that use the higher cortices of the neocortex region are largely short-circuited, by-passed by the acts of physically expressing. It comes from being fully present in listening to the body. It is a sensing experience where responses are streamlined and are consequently often tapped down emotionally. (Damasio, A., 1999)

While the experiential nature of a moving practice helps us look beyond the abstract narratives in our minds, movement expression requires us to be present in a framework that informs us of the immediate direct experience.

In 1987, a Harvard biologist and a cognitive scientist postulated that the moment sentient beings perceptively tap into being wholly present in the immediate - they couple to a dynamic environment that is interactive and reciprocal. If all sentient beings' sensory perceptions are internal constructions of external information - then how the world is viewed subjects all participants to co-create reality as a dynamic process. The cognitive theory addresses the nature of perception as partnered in a "dance of congruity" in a dynamic world. (Maturana,H. and Varela, F.) Simply recognizing the environment as a dynamic force directly influences individual thinking and perceptions while simultaneously affecting the reality of it. How we perceive, make connections and inferences in forming perspectives vary in all of us, so change in the surrounding dynamic is unavoidable even as we look outward. Individually and as a collective, viewpoints and perspectives may be fluid or relatively stiff within the confines of conceptualization. Those concepts all affect change in a dynamic world perceived with other sentient beings. Just how we perceive other sentient beings is central to how we influence the dynamic of shared reality.

With much of the human dynamic founded in rhetoric, how we address other non-human species is part of our ability to participate in the natural dynamic directly affecting our relationships with other species.

Generally in languages referencing a non-familiar individual of any species, our own or another is simply stated as a gender or as an "it". The 'it' is essentially an objectification unless it becomes personalized and named as individual. An objectified being typically carries less meaning as it is framed only descriptively until a change is perceived as warranted. As a result, the method through which a particular species, eco-environment or geological place may be discussed in most *lingua franca* are largely reduced to a simplified singular meaning without any context given to the wider participatory dynamic. This is understandable as language has been developed largely and perhaps, primarily to name objects. Yet some indigenous, some nature-based languages have avoided this narrowing of meaning in words.

We learn to objectify at an early age as part and parcel of acculturation with use of verbal communication. Not only does language exacerbate objectification through commodity-conferred words; naming also narrows and simplifies our perception of their possible inherent complexity. It organizes and facilitates quantification, for example of living systems rather than conferring an open, qualifying description that is integral to a system that perpetuates life. This obscures the bio-centric soul that is profoundly essential to its' holistic nature. Objectification of other species is eloquently discussed in "The Grammar of Animacy" from her 2013 book, *Braiding Sweetgrass,* by Robin Wall Kimmerer. Ms. Kimmerer draws comparatively on the Ohlone native language to show how language carries an inherent arrogance towards species other than our own, simply by referring to an individual or species as "it":

"Our toddlers speak of plants and animals as if they were people, extending to them self and intention and compassion—until we teach them not to…When we tell them that the tree is not a who, but an it, we make that maple (tree) an object; we put a barrier between us, absolving ourselves of moral responsibility and opening the door to exploitation. Saying it makes a living land into "natural resources". If a maple (tree) is an it, we can take up the chain saw. If a maple is a her, we think twice.

Describing something to encapsulate the dynamic aspects of living systems is challenging, no matter the language. The vagaries of language can be complicit in distancing meaning from sensing the complexity in how they are interwoven and dependent. Language objectifies to simplify. Yet, if there's any relationship involved referring to another, typically there is no objectifying partiality. We would not refer to a pet or a family member as an "it"; for in doing so would carry intent to snub as disregarding the existence of relationship or as a witless solecism.

However, using words is a tool that *Homo sapiens* have readily used in cultural development; and languages have their own slow paced dynamic. It is far more important to keep in mind that the use of language is to communicate meanings in a meaningful way as a gateway to growth. Being aware of relationship and living systems can directly connect us. Forming attachments and relationships with other species can carry personal, valued meanings for us. It is a basis of caring for others in their fragility on the earth. We can discuss and consciously acknowledge whether "it" is in balance or not, the status of their surroundings, and whether an individual requires assistance, all by referring to it or them as an "it". However, relationships require more... in listening for parity in participation, sensing the dynamic qualities or something essential in their nature. Finding meaning and parity should not be precluded by words, they are a common resource.

In PyM, there are a few ways to deepen the experience of connection and reciprocity in a dynamic relationship. The most obvious first step is to learn of another species as a species. Next, we consider how an animal's attributes might be representative of an evolutionary aspect of the species. Study, observation and encounters in nature can help to relate more deeply and to other species to give insight into how individual characteristics might also exhibit divergence in behaviors from outside influences. If an animal's personality is somewhat known, there's more to add to express and personify. The way we see and express another species can render quite subtle aspects through visualization. The more adjectival it is in the imagination, the more enriching: a hippity-hoppity rabbit/stealthy octopus/energy-conserving shark/fuzzy-headed wallaby/cartilaginous penguin, and other expressions. It requires openness to express concepts and impressions as behaviours and blatantly anthropomorphizes -- a topic I'll address later.

Evolution in all species has forever been shaped and sharpened by the demands of the environment and world around them. There is creative will in the spirit of all healthy species. Generally, evolutionary modifications reinforce attributes and behaviors that purport to confer some opportunity or advantage in a species to exist within the bounds of its environment. The dynamics at work in habitats and ecosystems shape the way a rabbit will dart from tree to tree, characterizes how a snake may blend into foliage, the way a bird will sleep with one eye open, and how an octopus could evolve an ink cloud as a blind and informs a bear's sense of smell to detect a meal from miles away. Time, resiliency, luck and genetic adaptability have all played a role in molding a species within living systems. One species may develop a kind of warrior wisdom of inner strength to compete; another may lend itself to a more co-collaborative strategy, while another might adapt physically and thereby improve odds of survival. Other evolutionary changes seemingly confer no viable advantage or perhaps, they seemingly await for a niche to arise, fickle-de-dee! Whether a species evolves by chance, discovery, mutation, symbiosis, networking, behavioural mutuality or through a consensual relationship with another species, or some other adaptation -- evolutionary change works more successfully in an open, vital environment(rather than in a static or closed system). The ideal is in a vibrant, diverse living system. Time may favour those who develop faster, can grow bigger in size, thicker in muscle and flesh, have bigger teeth and claws, a more vicious attitude, or can attain the strength, stability, flexibility, maneuverability or can expend energy more efficiently to match the challenges living presents. No matter what they confer or take away, all participants are in a dance of interaction within the environment they live. A flowing pond will always have more health than a stagnant one. Having awareness of how we perceive living systems and their dynamic nature is an important aspect to building the skills necessary for our perspectives to encompass those species other than ourselves.

Each a Living System

Joanna Macy, a scholar of general systems theory, wrote the following in 1988:

"Living systems evolve in variety, resilience, and intelligence; they do this not by erecting walls of defense and closing off from their environment, but by opening more widely to the currents of matter-energy and information. They integrate and differentiate through constant interaction, spinning more intricate connections and more flexible strategies."

Evolution is a primary tenant in living systems which are built on relationships: molecular, cellular, genetic, organic and behavioral. The primary intent in Primordial yogic Movement also rests on these same relationships – from the primordial metabolic networks that cells cobbled together of the biochemistry of earthly substances into fully functional physical body awareness, with our individual perception, emotion, neuronal-shaped historical concepts of the world - PyM relates these and other dynamic aspects of physicality. It has been stated that all living systems are organic, mutable and communal. Living systems are alive and dynamic only because they function intrinsically through the ability of resident species to interact in their surroundings. Fritjof Capra (1996) described living systems in the *Web of Life* as: "The properties of the parts are not intrinsic properties but can be understood only within the context of the larger whole". Understanding more of the "larger whole" is the working basis of PyM.

For us to evolve sustainably as a species, a fuller perspective of ourselves as a *hominin* species is vital, especially as the planet's ability to withstand our assaults on living systems wane. As Caroline Fraser, author of *Rewilding the World* has stated "We will survive only in a world as complex and biodiverse and interdependent as the one that created us."

To choose what is best for future needs we must work together to create viable, vibrant and living systems. It requires a new way of envisioning what those true needs are and plan chosen limitations and boundaries with long-sighted, knowledgeable, expansive insights, with more cohesion and co-operative attitudes and firmly backed by enforcement. There's a need to look from singular interests and felt entitlements, historical or otherwise, and to recognize the baselines that tie human health to the health of the planet. The landscapes of the earth are complex in their life-giving qualities and are spiritually vital to us – let's find agency for living systems to thrive! Culturally we can evolve to do so with visionary leadership from the mothership.

We do much to separate and distract ourselves from feeling connected to the roots of our origin in the past, from the inherited history, and there's a real need to reverse the tide that washes us as a species in obscurity. While worthwhile to be cognizant that Primordial yogic Movement expresses our thoughts, feelings, ideas and intentions; we must recognize that our physical sensory apparatus also incline us to particular viewpoints which are organized as held perspectives in life's narratives. As complex, multi-faceted beings, we may move, stretch, dance, and sing praise to honor the earth and love all of its manifestations of life and living, but if there's little understanding or interest in why we are here or in what we share–it's tantamount to abandoning our birthright. No matter how exceptional or how powerful we think we are or how opposed our outlooks, there is an obligation, a covenant if you will, for a species to coexist with other species. No matter how self-absorbed and narrow-bore our navel-gazing may be, humans, as a privileged species will require a new perspective as active participants in the dynamic to sustain a living world.

A journey through time in PyM begins with the realization that each of us is a living system. There is a world outside you and within you to venture into and discover a past in the fullness of those that have preceded you. As the First Peoples of the Navajo Nation say… "Walk in Beauty!"

References

Capra, F. (1996). *The web of life: A new synthesis of mind and matter*. London: Flamingo.

Damasio, A. R. (1999). *The Feeling of What Happens: Body, Emotion and the making of consciousness.* New York, NY: Harcourt Brace.

Dewey, J. (1929). *Experience and Nature.* New York, NY: W.W. Norton & Co.
Dewey, J. (1985). *The Collected Works of John Dewey*. Carbondale, IL: Southern Illinois University Press.

Johnson, M. (2007). *The Meaning of the Body.* Chicago, IL: University of Chicago Press

Jung, C. G. (1977). *The Symbolic Life.* Collected Works (Vol.18). London, U.K.: Routledge & Kegan

Kimmerer, R.W., 2013. *Braiding Sweetgrass*. Milkweed Editions: Canada

Lakoff, G. (2012). Audio lecture sponsored by KPFA. [Compact Disk] Berkeley, CA: First Congregational Church.

Lakoff, G., Johnson, M. (1980). Metaphors We Live By. Chicago, IL: University of Chicago Press.
Lakoff, G., Johnson, M. (1999). Philosophy in the flesh: The embodied mind and its challenge to western thought. New York, NY: Basic Books.

Macy, J., Seed, J., Fleming, P., Naess, A., Pugh, D. (1988). Thinking Like a Mountain: Toward a Council of All Beings. New Society Publishers.
Macy, J. (1988). *Coming Back to Life: Practices to reconnect our lives, our world*. New Society: Stoney Creek, CT

Maturana, H. R., & Varela, F. J. (1987). *The tree of knowledge: The biological roots of human understanding.* New Science Library/Shambhala Publications.

Reddy, S.M.W. et. al., 2016. Advancing Conservation by Understanding and Influencing Human Behavior. From Conservation Letters, Journal of the Society for Conservation Biology.

Varela, F. J., Thompson, E., & Rosch, E. (1991). The Embodied Mind: Cognitive Science and Human Experience. Cambridge, MA: The MIT Press.

Wood, W., (2019), Good Habits, Bad Habits: The science of making positive changes that stick. New York, NY: Farrar, Straus and Giroux

CHAPTER 3

Nagerai - Aquatic Life

Evolution of life on the young, volatile, asteroid-bombarded earth 2.5 billion years ago began with the advent of cell life. The humble protocell prior to the first primordial microbial life was barely more than simplified protoplasm, a filmy membrane. The awakening occurred in chemically harsh, anaerobic conditions, yet organisms as single cell microbial life emerged in the aqueous environment. From the earliest stage in single cell development, there is much to suggest that dynamics of the natural environment may have pushed single cells to colonize together very early on in earth history. If evolution could be explained as a simple gnarly tree, single cell microbes would form the massive tree trunk at the base that over billions of years continued to widen into over a trillion bacterial species. Evolution, however does not play out in so simple a picture although the primordial tree has most certainly branches.

It is estimated that single cell microbes have been around for 4 billion years, and they still dominate as the most numerous of any species in a single family. Microbes were also were the *only* lifeforms for more than 2 billion years, enough time to figure out much about living collectively on earth, and of opportunity. New bacterial species were then as they are now formed by replication often in association with other bacteria, as traders and borrowers of RNA and later, of DNA. Synergetic and symbiotic cellular associations have formed such strong alliances and methods in order to thrive that their processes eventually led to multicellular organisms and a myriad of new phyla (plants, fungi and animals), and eventually to give rise to hominins and the *Homo* species.

It is generally accepted that the earliest forms of life were little more than gelatinous microscopic blobs of protoplasm from hydrated polymers that formed a membrane. The suspended protocells absorbed energy (not yet considered "food" at that point) from drift contact. (Hanczyc, M.M., 2003) (Pollack, G.H., 2001) The early protocells were composed of proteins from twelve basic chemicals, all proximal minerals. They reproduced by mitosis, replicating to reproduce another copy. Grouping together brought about some genetic exchange and single cell microbes began to react to chemical changes in the environment and new evolutionary pathways. Microbial life evolved, transforming to better accommodate what tended to help them survive and fortify.

An ability to sense molecular differences optimized in strategies for feeding, reproduction and survival from predation. Small genetic mutations transformed some microbes to better accommodate what tended to favour them... and what lifeform wouldn't savor a windfall if it could? - Microbes began to differentiate advantages with improvements in cell absorption, molecular manipulation, binding and transference which brought signalling and selectivity in receptor receptivity with which to moderate adverse exposures and welcome others. On a changeable planet, primordial evolution was guided primarily by adapting to changes in surroundings.

As the earth "settled" with periods of less volatility, microbial respiration and the use of photosynthesis to source energy and produce oxygen, microbes further their transformations with moving parts to morph, shimmy, whip and fling to take advantage of the energetic opportunities they might resource. Through countless generations in RNA and DNA tweaks, the external energy they resourced translated into cell movement and locomotion. However as a caveat, when energy is expended - as when a microbe moved towards a food source, energy loss incurs. Overall, microbial proficiency in movement and sensing likely came about in fits and starts, as is often typical in evolution, to eventually best meet or reduce energy cost to source food. Yet the most primitive microbes had no mechanism with which to store resourced energy, initially.

In a strictly genetic sense there are commonalities that make us all of one family. This is because the earliest form of life, the protocell, composed the same protoplasmic stuff that formed the first archaea and bacteria that formed the first eukaryote that makes up the cells of our bodies. However, our physical cellular makeup is no longer simple, each or our body's cells differentiated into different cell types as they grew into our multicellular body, just as in any and all multicellular creatures. These were and are based predominantly on their function and neat organizing regulation of their overarching genetic signatures. Basic cell composition is repeated in all multicellular organisms. Animals have evolved a much greater diversity of cell types than, say, fungi and plants. While Crisper technology has answered some questions in genetic evolution, how the great diversity of cell types emerged in multicellular bodies is not known. Yet a first step was RNA gene expression as a foundation to DNA. Indeed, the human body is a most complex organism that contains the greatest number of different cell types: four different blood cell types, and others too numerous to count that comprise our skin, bone, muscle, hormone, fat, nerve and lung cell types; all which are quite different from one another. Function leads form; but the process of single cells to differentiate for differing functional purposes within a collective body was possible even prior to multicellular organisms' proximal exchange of DNA it is thought. Yet today's research into cell biology are mere fragments of puzzle pieces which remain hidden in the indescribably numerous generations of microbial evolutionary history of life on earth.

Life is the heat of the fire and the light of the sun, the wind, rain and thunder in the sky. From the formless was born that which has form. It became involved with the self and is therefore self-created.
~ From the Upanishads, J. McCartney, 1978

The PyM Aquatic Series (Nagerai) introduces earth's first primordial lifeforms and their movements in a chronology meant to enhance human fitness. The exercises integrate the different species' appearance in earth history to grow awareness of how biological movement has evolved. The benefits of exercising in water are numerous and can be enjoyed by most who feel comfortable moving in water. *Nagerai* swim explores new possibilities in swim techniques that differ from conventional aquatics by sampling the motion expressions in animals. The baseline in PyM is to emulate different forms of life as creative expression - you are encouraged to experiment and include children in developing the practice. The more you can find on each creature to add to your catalog in the practice the more it will deepen observations of the natural world and creatively express as a body experience!

Precepts

Before beginning a session, take time to consider your connection to the surrounding medium of water. How you connect to water will be affected not only by past memories and associations, but consider its present characteristics of clarity, temperature, depth, flow and perimeter as a body of water. Your feelings may affect ease in water. If so, it's important to give yourself the time to become receptive and responsive to what you are sensing and to build confidence. Focusing intention in order to visualize and express the forms and creature movements can weigh in trusting ability. When first entering a body of water, take in not only the medium but your surroundings. Remember it is important to try to find repose in each organism form pose. If you are distracted from being easefully engaged because of nervousness or how your body feels in the water - take a moment and imagine folding inwardly to embrace yourself until you can ease up. Find the moments of fluid openness in your thought. As you proceed, check in occasionally and refresh how you sense being present in the liquid environment; try to approach PyM with the same clarity as the water that surrounds you.

Consider some exercises to warm-up. It's beneficial to focus on the "yogic" aspect of the practice by including a prayer, dedication, blessing, chant or ode to the sea to enrich the experience; it's entirely up to you. If not, feel free to go straight into the water and simply feel and attune your senses to the primordial cradle of life, water.

Liquid Engagement

We are air-breathing, aerobic organisms. The earth's atmosphere is as intimately a part of us as is our breathing of it. Our first inhale at birth initiated our singularity as an organism and our last breath will end it. We are connected part and parcel to the watering cycles of earth and sky.

The path of evolution for species began through primordial openings founded in liquid H2O. Water is the magical elixir in which nearly all early organisms took their life form. More than 50% of the planet is covered by water. Fluidity made possible by water comprises close to 99% of plants, and is contained as 70% of mammalian bodies, around 50% of reptiles and a little less in birds. Some water moisture is necessary for life to live, every life. I also find it interesting that freshwater comprises less than 3 percent of the earth's total water yet is habitat to almost half of all species of fish.

The liquid medium of water is where the evolution of life began. How would you describe water to someone who has never known it, except as thirst? Describe water to an alien? A light compound that is… wet, liquid, fluid, transformative, translucent, buoyant, slippery, free, abundant, adaptive, absorbent, inclusive, seeping, pushy, embracing, tasteless, benign, opportunistic, changeable, transcendent, reflective, ephemeral, shining, supportive, clear, clean, dependent, cohesive, flowing, glistening, sweet, swirling, thunderous, heavy, rapid, pooling, receptive, loose, dainty, and so on. I appreciate this affirmative description:

Falling as a drop, water oscillates about the form of a sphere. A sphere is a totality, a whole, and water will always attempt to form an organic whole by joining what is divided and uniting it in circulation.

~ Theodor Schwenk

Consider the balance and spring of water surface tension. It is almost imperceptible, but it's there, so take the time to recognize her attractive elasticity. I refer to water as "her" in the feminine because water has characteristics that can be ascribed akin to primarily female complements within the Yin Yang dualism of many species.

Water is the equivalent of Yin essence in her misty shrouds which cling to mountains and slowly drift in undulating wisps downward and conforming to canyons and valleys with cool grace -- seeking, enveloping, caressing, unifying, nurturing. We can imagine her graces in the quiet of a peaceful pool with gentle flowing currents, lapping along embankments, swirling, flushing, racing, rushing and falling from a rocky cliff ledge into a long dark abyss. But other forces such as gravity and wind may carry her as Yang essence - in the energetic crashing of waterfalls and waves against shorelines, in the whirling whitewater and the rush of flood flashes. She may be a force to break boulders, uproot trees, cutting furrows in multiple directions, denuding and destroying all in her path. She is transformative and transforming when juxtaposed with solidity. In her gentleness, water slowly seeks in seeping and is propelled as fairylike crystalized droplets airborne on updrafts to dance as sunlit rainbow hues like fiery ether, only to vanish skyward.

Water holds not to anything, though it can be held, directed, absorbed, frozen, deflected, dispersed, surrounded, circulated, evaporated, condensed and dropped. Its bonds form, bend, break and reform though it changes not. It carves, twists and turns what might try to contain it; it changes not, yet absorbs to cause others to change. Creatures skip and skim it, slip and slide on it, lick and swirl in it, skitter and spin it, ripple and merge with it. Organisms dive and dip in it, twist and flip through it, paddle and jet on it, while others drift and pulsate or pump endlessly without rest. Its inherent nature of fluidity allows life and land to move in particular rhythms…

As water began to move I again heard the voices. Water furrows itself into shapes as it runs, immediately telling stories out loud, decoding messages from stillness into momentum.

~ Craig Childs, *The Secret Knowledge of Water*

Water epitomizes complete acceptance as she will always flow under, over, through and around us all. No matter what your perspective on how H2O came to be, life is possible because our planet is blessed with water.

In current scientific thought, Earth's first volcanoes began erupting steam and water vapor about 4.5 billion years ago; the vapor and gases condensed over hundreds of millions of years and slowly filled low-lying areas to form the first oceans. The present state of water took hundreds of millions of years to purify from the toxic elements of early earth and to oxygenate into the watery elixir it is today - ideal for copious biological life.

Buoyancy

Our own buoyancy in water can feel light or heavy relative to our movements, fitness and level of activity, as well as our size and composition, flexibility and comfort level. For almost everyone, exercising in water can improve overall health. It is easy on joints and by self-regulating the water resistance makes exercise more manageable while remaining buoyant in cooling temperatures. Water is about 800 times denser than air. Although we are a species adapted to live from air, we are receptive to motion in water, given our buoyancy and affinity to it during the first months of our lives.

In an aquatic workout, explore movements by changing angles of attack directionally, range of the motions and the reach in joints and limbs to modify variability in thrust and glide, speed, energy demand, buoyancy and water resistance. The motions available to you will alter control, speed, strength, balance and stability of movements in water. Each new patterning in motions and speed will affect all other parameters. For example, the use of breath and selected muscle sets for strokes coupled with speed variations, momentum or sweep angle in the sequences can reduce or increase the energy requirements and muscle strength needed with the use of inertia, thrust efficiency and glide dynamics. Awareness of these external forces and characteristics will help determine a particular continuum necessary to flow in an open and/or tight patterning depending on the form you emulate, even in a weightless drift.

It's a lot to keep in mind but time enough to consider how the first single cell microbes began moving suspended in their viscous environment.

Single-Cell Movements

Scientists constantly discover new unicellular microbes and struggle to classify them into species; currently the count for bacteria is over a trillion. New computing technologies such as AI, Crisper and other technology facilitate the work, but it is still a daunting task. Single cell microbes were the sum total of life on earth for nearly 2.5 billion years before the first multicellular organisms appeared. Yet another major milestone in single cell microbial evolution was the development of ability to store energy from feeding and to regulate that stored energy from activity centers within a cell nucleus. A cell's nucleus is essentially a control center for regulating microbial respiration, growth and metabolism from energy storage and the regulation of its production and dispensation. It was a milestone that changed the scope of genetic possibilities. Anaerobic archaea and primordial bacteria played a huge role in the mineralization of the early ocean through fermentation, metal reduction and in metabolizing sulfur and sulfates. (Woese, C., 1998) Around 3.5 billion years ago, bacteria began to form chloroplasts and through the process of photosynthesis were able to directly harness the energy of the sun for energetic needs. Photosynthesizing microbes produce oxygen as a by-product which on primordial earth caused another dramatic change in lifeforms with the oxygenation of the biosphere.

The first microbes did little but suspend, mat together, replicate and drift, absorbing and conserving energy until evolution made it possible to prompt an action. The first self-directed movements to consider in microbes derived from ability to sense through chemotaxis, sensing an external chemical difference. Microbial cell movement to reach or to flee from an exposure outside the cell began with simple shape-shifting - the first form of movement. This internal self-morphing by bacteria is still debated by scientists as to whether it should be considered self-directed movement. The morphing is called "cell migration" and is a primary motion in response to its environment. When a cell morphs the shape of its body directionally, the process is "streaming" wherein an internal plasmic reorganizing occurs inside the cell as its membranous shape shifts directionally. The exterior wall expands and stretches outwardly in one direction while contracting elsewhere in the cell structure.

There are many cells in our bodies that migrate by distending and deflating imperceptibly in this same way. The most obvious cell migration occurs when cells move together to heal a cut or wound from an abrasion on the skin. The same type of cell streaming is also common in vascular plants to move fluids in feeding new growth and is easily seen to happen under a microscope. Cell migration occurs with variety in organisms, from the most primitive to the most complex of multi-celled organisms, from bacteria and algae to animals. How slow can you go to flow in the first primordial movement?

Amoeba Float

~~~~Enter into water to a depth where you may float or cling and suspend ~~~~

~~ At least deep enough to hold and stabilize you minimally ~~

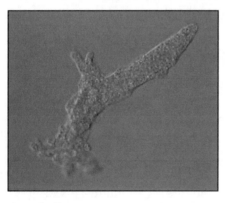

Amoebas are protozoans classified as eukaryotes which are single celled organisms with a nucleus. Their motility mostly occurs from changing shape, by morphing and pushing outward while contracting elsewhere internally, much like an earthworm will burrow through loamy soil.
Microbial life has guided many adaptations which allow organisms to detect, reach, surround, and attract food sources or to retreat in order to avoid an area of toxicity.

Amoeba Proteus

To emulate a single cell, visualize it on a cellular level in slight, slow micro-movements. Enter into water to a depth where you may float, cling and suspend.

Try it: Float at the surface easefully in a depth you can feel comfortable. If in deeper water, move only enough to stay afloat, using breath to suspend you and feel the spaciousness around you. Visualize your whole body as singular, a globular form adrift in a liquid medium. Let your breath lightly rock you and find where balancing can relax, then bring your attention outward to the physical edges of your body. Visualize initiating micro-movement from your interior and inhale directionally, streaming outwardly, out on one side while contracting inwardly on the other. Experiment with opening the space between the vertebral discs in the low back, in joints from shoulders to chin with each slow expansive inhale. Close your eyes and imagine your nose, toes, fingertips and other body parts swelling to appropriate more space. Take time to use mental visualizations of movements to morph into different shapes. Remain centered in physical awareness with slow movement in lungs along the spine to open ribs, chest and back. Explore, expand and contract intimately as a single, bacterial form.

Allow stabilizing tendons and ligaments to ease up; and tension to dissipate and relax all the way into the bone. You are a limp liquid form in a liquid medium.

Keep arms and legs softening but imagine thickening your membranous skin. Since much of your body is fluid and your blood has almost equal salinity as salt water, is it possible to sense floating in seawater as an extension of your fluidity?

The presence of water depends on a very delicate balance between the size of a planet and its distance from the sun. If a planet is too small, it doesn't have the gravitational attraction to hold an atmosphere and will lose gases, including water vapor, out into space. It would then be airless and sterile like the moon. A life-giving planet must be at the right distance from the sun so that it receives enough heat to melt ice, but not too close to boil water.

If you are a collective group and floating in water that is sufficiently warm, consider linking together to drift together as a bacterial mat. A few participants can anchor the group by clinging to the side of the pool, or if sufficiently buoyant (perhaps in warm sea water) lightly link to one another as you float and allow the natural rhythm in the water, current and waves to move you as a "collective" organism. Become as one. Explore the weightlessness of collective buoyancy.

Water surrounds yet isolates within its inclusive space. In water temperatures close to body temperature, the boundaries all but disappear. Regardless of the temperature differential, movements in water compel us to attune to its buoyant support.

Consider how single celled organisms are hydrophilic, meaning that they have an affinity for water. Microbial membrane walls attract water and when water molecules adhere to surfaces, they attract more water pulling layers of water molecules around them. How thick the hydrophilic layers are will depend on the density of the charged surface of a cell. Receptive and permeable, primordial tiny amoebas can detect and recognize different molecular configurations in surroundings and determine just how hydrophilic they are.

Self-Directed Movement

Single cell microbial lifeforms direct movement in many ways. They push and pull, spin and twitch, skitter, scuttle, corkscrew, whip and kick through aqueous environments. Some use a complex slingshot method to propel forward and others even slide by first laying down slime on which to slither. (Jabr, F., 2013) Their microscopic size relative to water molecules that suspend them confers a thick, heavily viscous fluid environment around which any motion at all not only requires the mechanics to move but the ready energy to move. For us, it is comparable to attempting to move in thick, heavy syrup with every movement labored, almost like having the drag of quicksand. Yet microbial evolution provided the various apparatus for a microbe to push against the thickly viscous environment. Motion was initially facilitated and enhanced with the development of tiny hairs on the surface membrane of microbe cells, filament threads called cilia. Another was a sticky pili substance for attaching and "flinging" microbes. Lastly but not least, microbes grew longer extensions, sort of motive appendages to self-direct movements or to attach to a substrate. The motile extensions were filaments, tail-like flagellum that could spin, whip, and undulate.

Cilia

Cilia are microscopic threads that thrash in a circular fashion to help an organism to move by pushing the surrounding fluid around it. Both nucleated and non-nucleated bacterial microbes are often covered with cilia, tiny hair-like filaments that sprout on the surface membrane.

The cilium aids in the capture and absorption of organic matter floating by; and they can also help to move food toward the groove of the "mouth" in some

Paramecium

species such as paramecium. Cilia developed as a microorganism adaptation to direct movement outside the cell and improve hydrodynamic motility. The fuzzy cylindrical filaments act as hairs to sweep the highly viscous fluid past the organism. Microscopes and fossils tell us that cilia motion spirals directionally in order to propel fluid past the cell surface. The evolution of cilia was one of the first most ancient means of locomotion in cell evolution.

The filaments beat in a circular whipping action with a wide sweeping motion to push fluid on by. As they whip around, the thrust stroke extends the hairs and is followed by a flexing recovery stroke to bend backwards along the surface of the cell body. In the sweep, the cilia drag the surrounding liquid along broadside on the power stroke. It is an effective way for a microbe to slowly move through thick, viscous fluid. Although ingenious, it only works where the symmetry of stroke is offset directionally. (Mackin,K.E., 1958) (Vogel, 1996) (Guirao, B., 2007)

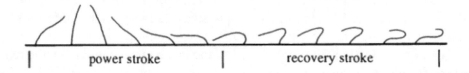

| power stroke | recovery stroke |

Vogel, 1996

Cilia take different functional forms - some function as sensory organelles and grow as long spiked antenna(s), or as a stiff barb for piercing, or as a fuzz working as filtering mechanism or to push debris along, or they can be purely motile to transport the microbe. Their sensory-related adaptations relate to chemical sensing, signalling, and growth control, but most frequently couple as motion drivers.

The motile cilium on cells in complex bodies such as mammals works as intracellular filters to sweep away and clean out phlegm, particulates and dust debris from the throat and lungs. Cilia also line female fallopian tubes in placental animals, including us, where the cilia help move the ovum (egg) into the uterus. Cilium in the fluid sac of the inner ear is a part of hearing in ears; and in animal brains, cilium facilitates the transport of fluids. Hair and fur also evolved from cilia to protect, insulate and cushion bodies.

Cilia in organisms have been modified as adaptations for many different uses: sensing chemical changes, to drive microbial movements, signalling, piercing, clinging, attaching, filtering, feeding and is instrumental as part of a sensory organelle for growth control.

Ciliate Sweeps

Try It: First, it's beneficial to loosen and warm up with body bends, try spirals before getting in water. Spirals massage and stimulate circulation to organs and spine.

In water deep enough to easily sweep your upper body around above the surface; use one or preferably both arms to start the sweeping motion going. As you twirl, use legs to stabilize and ground you in the motion with knees bending sideways too; fold slightly in and out lengthening as you spin. Try it at different water levels, perhaps with an arm tucked close to your body, the other arm extended to lead the sweeps, and then try it with both arms outwardly spinning, then reverse direction. In shallow water, try it kneeling, sitting, with or without one or both arms. Play with the movement.

    Try It: Stand on knees in chest high water with thighs together and lower legs bent back for stability, ground down with feet flexed, toes curled under.
    Press arms in at your sides and imagine your body as a rounded form. Keeping abdominals firm, rotate around with control, from the thighs up to shoulders sweep the upper body around with a slight lateral twist. Change direction. Then in a slightly more demanding movement bring feet together below and move to sweep from the hips and core. If standing in deeper water, you will have to be mindful of wave action and inertia. Keep the rotational circling small adding arm motion into larger circles slowly to allow for momentum. This is challenging.
    Modify for better stability with a hand on the rim of the pool.

Flagellum

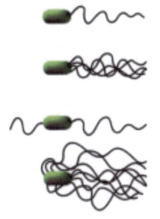

Types of Flagella

A flagellum is a squiggly tail on a microbe. Bacteria can have a single, non-motile flagellum for moving, probing, sensing or attaching the organism. In attaching with flagellum pseudopodia, some bacteria hinge to lever in swing movements but most non-motile flagella are sensory.

The primary use of motile flagellum is locomotive. At least half of known bacteria on earth have motile flagella to get around. The flagella filaments can be numerous and take different configurations on a single-cell microbe. The motile flagellum beats or squiggles either in a helical or undulatory pattern. Both actions create a waveform from the base to tip or tip to base to produce momentum from spiral motion.

    There can be a pair of flagella which move together in a push/pull propulsive action or move in a symmetrical outward/inward stroke (i.e. a breast stroke), or in helical strokes to glide as in blue-green algae - a very primordial algae microbe. Some have multiple flagella that appear as a tangle of haphazard movements: lengthening and contracting, whipping. Both flagella and cilia filaments are cylindrical, which as small whipping and undulating hair-like strands apparently works more efficiently in moving through the viscosity of water fluidity relative to their tiny size, than as flattened filaments. With the exception of non motile flagella and cilia, microbial filaments are all about the same in diameter also.

In single cell microbes, nothing in particular distinguishes flagella filaments from cilia filaments structurally or in how they dynamically are driven. The differences occur only in their function, length and number of filaments. Locomotion mechanically operates through motile proteins which convert chemical energy into muscle-like maneuvers along the tiny filaments. The only difference is that microbial flagella generate force to propel microbes to swim through fluid, whereas cilia sweep around mechanically to transport fluid past the organism.

With variable locomotion, most bacteria use motile flagella to beat it over to a food source or to move away from obstacles and when not so directed, they often tumble aimlessly through the water spinning (Tsuji, T. et al., 2010).

Mermaid Kicks n Tumble Too

Try It: To undulate along the full length of your body in the shallows, near the surface; begin standing and initiate the motion with your head - chin to shoulders, shoulders to hip with legs together, move the undulation from hip to thighs and bend knees to whip it down to feet and toes. Imagine how much slower your undulations would be if water was as viscous as syrup. Next, if the water depth allows, move as a mermaid to swim - feet together lead the kick, knees bend off to one side or forward, lengthen them and bend upper body, repeatedly to propel or twist around as the kick thrusts spiral. Pause and suspend to slow inertia, let your body fall and when feet touch, spin and tumble around laterally keeping limbs in together only using feet and arms to turn and stabilize you relative to the surface. Tumble along the spinal axis. This is how E. coli bacteria move, flagella propulsion followed by tumbling.

Tumbling is not easy as we are so heavy and large compared to the size of microbes. At the molecular level, size makes a big difference. Since we are comparably larger, the size of surrounding water molecules does not effectively support our mass except with buoyancy and feels like thin fluidity. Our "tail" thrusts would be much more effective if we were smaller, but not too tiny; if we were the size of a microbe, water would feel very thick and viscous. Our swim movements with every stroke and kick would require enormous effort as in heavy molasses. (Jabr, F., 2013)

How fast can tiny flagella move a microbe? Without viscosity, bacteria can traverse a strand of hair in a second. To consider how fast something is - depends on how rapidly it can traverse the length of its own body. If it moved across the width of a hair then the bacterium would travel 100 to 200 times its length. Relatively, they swim 20 times faster than fish. If the distance was equivalent to human sprinting, it would break the sound barrier

Modified: Try undulating in a non-swim version and stay standing in water or practice on shore. With legs together or comfortably apart, knees slightly bent, arms held loosely at your sides, exhale and draw the abdominals in, slowly bend the low back to one side, curl in the chest, twist and bring the arms slightly forward and circle them slightly around you. Allow your neck and head to follow with the motion. Move and straighten inhaling as you lift the chest, then raise arms outward in the opposite direction, and this time around, arch forward and off to the side. Begin again on an exhale to regain standing balance, arms in. Repeat.

During WWII, shipwrecked survivors from Allied ships sunk in the Pacific from wartime battles struggled to survive the ocean. Adrift, some servicemen together formed floating pods. Whether by instinct or logic or comfort, the sailors adopted an age old design of oceanic life. They waited and drifted as connected units, in effect, as organisms. Occasionally tiger sharks picked off a few individuals, but the cohesive action helped defensively support the seamen as an organic whole and reduced the likelihood of a feeding frenzy.

The earliest multicellular fossils found from primordial oceans were, unsurprisingly, typically cylindrical, such as *Lantianella laevis, Spriggina* and *Cloudina*. In a fluid environment, circular swirling motions may have influenced the rounded, circular forms of early life. The ancient organisms attached to oceanic substrates using a pseudopod or "false foot", much like the giant kelp fronds today take hold with rooting structures that are intended for grasping rather than to absorb nutrients.

One such early multicellular organism was called *Charnia,* it fanned from an attached stalk to spiral and sway along the seafloor during the Ediacaran around 685 million years ago. The open and flat fronds filtered and absorbed nutrients on wide surface areas to create some of the earliest known underwater landscapes after a long and extreme glaciation period that scientists refer to as White Earth.

Charnia Twist

Frond-like Charnia, segmented Spriggina, and the funnel-shaped Cloudinid represent some of the earliest known organisms fossilized on earth some 685 million years ago. The earliest imprints of the fossils indicate they were sessile animals that had possible ability to reattach and relocate. Whether concentric, tubular or frond-shaped, these early organisms moved around with ocean currents to rotate, spiral and undulate in motion. Today, six-foot sea pens attach similarly by growing a "foot" onto a microbial mat or seafloor.

Try It: Standing with heels together in shoulder deep water, ground down with feet angled outward, keep legs together and angle elbows out from your sides, hands flat against hip bones and make stiff circular sweeps. Begin the motion at ankles and knees, as you bend, twist slightly upward through the core, sway gently side to side. If necessary raise your arms loosely outward from sides to assist in heavier currents.

Freeform spinning: As you continue to twist side to side, come up onto the metatarsal, tippy-toe. Detach your feet from the ground and push upward, keeping feet and legs together. Rotate and spin straight with arms in. Spiral freely around in the water guided by arm-assisted motions to keep spinning. Keep the head aligned with the spine above the water surface. It's easy and fun at about a 15 degree angle to the water surface. Use arm control to change twist, speed and spin direction. Repeat in the opposite direction.

Many microbes propel by spinning their body or an appendage. Rotating on an axis is fun but exercise care; do not overtax the neck.

Two billion years was a long enough time for the only form of life on earth, microbes to evolve partnerships and associations to work collectively and extend their longevity, life cycles, synergies and relationships. Multicellular organisms evolved as an extension of those microbial passages to adapt, assimilate, build and assume molecular and biological functions. According to scientists, nucleated cells in general are rented, shared and occupied by symbiotic bacteria. (Lewis,T., 1974) An example, the storage "powerhouse" that energizes living cells is a tenant occupier in the cell nucleus, the mitochondria. It functions like a battery inside a flashlight. The entire field of collaboration in microbial evolution may not have initially begun with the formation of a nucleus in a cell, who knows, but the nucleated cell was a huge breakthrough for multicellular organisms. Much of cell assimilation, collaboration, cooperation and communication interchange evolved in microbes occurring in microbial colonies. These associations and networkings later evolved into specialized cell functions and paved the way for the specified differentiations of cells to take on different roles that make up multicellular organisms. But first...

Collective Queens

Before multicellular lifeforms, there was collective microbial life found largely matted together in biofilm colonies. The clustering of single cell organisms conferred many advantages on the inhabitants. In fact, most bacteria and archaea on earth today exist in biofilms - nearly 80%, the only exceptions exist chiefly in oceans; (Flemming, H.C., Wuertz, S., 2019) One of the earliest assemblies were the chloroplasts mentioned earlier. These microbial masses have had signaling mechanisms for at least 700 million years. How so? Many species of bacterial symbionts live clustered on and alongside each other using a complicated symbiotic system of linkages and molecular coding systems to direct the associations using collaboration, accommodation, exchange and bartering Receptivity and biological configurations recognize molecular differences which regulate and support a complex system of chemical signalling. (Lewis, T.,1974). Cell signalling in biofilms evolved with considerable complexity to guide sense, regulate and protect microbial life.

Recently, a group of scientists decided to test how we might define what constitutes a "body" using the baseline of single cell organisms matted as a biofilm. They took a single-cell algae species and reproduced the species over a thousand generations (their lifespan is quite short). Then an algae-eating predator was introduced into the biofilm. It was a large voracious single cell microbe that engulfs algae cells to feed. The scientists found that in less than two hundred more generations, the algae collectively had responded to the predator by reproducing in large clumps of hundreds of algae cells too large to be eaten by the predator. Over many more generations, the algae clumps slowly reduced in the number of cells to a clump of only eight algal cells. Eight turned out to be the optimum number too large to be eaten by the predator but small enough for each algal organism to attain adequate exposure to light to optimize growth. Surprisingly, when the predator was removed, the algae continued to reproduce as bodies of eight. It could be surmised that collectively, the defensive behavior brought about a new algal "body".

There are other colonized bodies that are even more interwoven in the degree of constructive mutualism. Consider the Portuguese Man-O-War, a jellie which is made up of thousands of individual zooids, all happily living together lethally. Then there are slime molds wherein the nucleated cells live freely, but when food is in short supply they combine together to form multi-celled reproductive structures that includes them all in a single contiguous streaming membrane to incorporate all of their individual nuclei. The singular individuals essentially become multi celled, complete with built-in commensal signalling and sharing food and resources. There are other incorporations in microbiota that form symbiotic, commensal, and other resourcing network mechanisms and systems in microbial life, many of which we know were around as early as the Ediacaran era.

According to fossil records, single nucleated cells began to develop multicellular organisms around 700 million years ago. All living organic creatures are animated by immeasurable amount of collaboration in each cell in a multi-celled body. From conception, each cell in an organism differentiates to take on just the right role for its' function whether it be to form the structural scaffolding of the body, or the supply and storage of energy within a body, or to facilitate its motility, to regulate the internal and external senses and networking systems, and forming neural systems or to regulate when cells divide and when they die; whatever it takes to complete a physical biological body with functions to detect, capture, digest and eliminate and reproduce. The differentiation of cells starts at conception and has for millions upon millions of years. All the living cells in a body have evolved to take on all the many roles through joining forces and incorporating efforts, dividing the labor, regulating, simplifying and adapting to create complete living systems. The earth's minerals and chemicals are incorporated in every organism simply because cells are resourced together to create life.

Grande Dame of the Seas

> *"... from jellyfish to human beings, connective tissue is the primary organ of structure, gluing cells into discrete colonies, defining their shapes, forming them into functional units and suspending them together in the correct relationships within the organism."*
> ~ **Deane Juhan from Job's Body**

One of the longest living multicellular animals on earth is also one of the most movement-efficient species on earth - the jellyfish. The oldest fossil record of the jellied ancestors pegs them at half a billion years on earth with some fossilized relatives living in primordial seas some 635 million years ago. Jellies (jellyfish is a misnomer, no fish there) are extremely adaptable, elegantly attuned to the extremes in water temperatures and chemical conditioning, and often surviving against all odds through some of the worst events in earth's violent history.

All lifeforms on earth organize locomotion dependent on the environment through which they move. Simple in design, jellies have a single layer gelatinous body that is basically a spherical muscle. As drifters, they have no front or back, no left or right, and no head. However, they sense, signal and differentiate relative to orientation. Jellyfish may appear to drift, but they actually have spatial sensing and exert control over directionality. The membranous jellies' locomotion is a flexing flutter of its bell-shaped body. The concave perimeter flexes and contracts in subtle motions adjusting angle of attack and orientation in an upward or downward direction.

Jellie movements efficiently conserve energy because the fluttering motion is minimal beyond water current depths and ripple effect.

Today, as the planet warms, many species of jellies have been found to be reliable indicators of temperature and chemical changes occurring in the oceans. With increasing acidification worldwide, some species have been found to have a mitigating influence on the oceanic chemical fluctuations; a larger number of jellie species overpopulate due to the warming trend. Having survived five extinction events on the planet, it is little wonder that the gelatinous creatures are capable of dealing with the oceanic chemistry change and higher thermal temperatures. While many fish and shellfish species continue to suffer, jellyfish populations are booming.

Jellyfish Flutter

Jellyfish are adaptable in many oxygenated water environments and are found in every part of earth's oceans, at all depths. As one of the most ancient multicellular species on earth, their basic body structure forms a hydrostatic muscle umbrella which functions much like the trunk of an elephant or human tongue. Jellies may have been a first multi-celled form with muscle structure. The muscle fibers widely circle their bell shape to form a mesh which pulses from the perimeter for swimming motion.

Try it: Float face-up in the water with your back rounded and limbs cupped outward like a half bubble, your head can be semi-submerged and relaxed. In this posture, you may easily gauge how to maintain the posture with your buoyancy and surface tension. You are upside down as a jellie with arms and knees spread just beneath the water surface, bent inward like an edge of a skirt. Gently flex lower limbs (mainly ankles and wrists) in and out simultaneously and evenly with your breathing in and out. The addition of a noodle or other floats under the armpits will help to keep the head supported and relaxed and provide a rimming. By simultaneously fluttering hands, feet and lower limbs, play with directionality and spin with changes to the angle and movement synchronicity. Floating with legs and knees opened at the water surface and circling hands and feet, make 360 degree turns in one direction, then the other. There's a good amount of range in motion.

In this semi-floating open knee posture, limbs shape an inverted bell dome and help to stabilize buoyancy at the surface. After circling in one area, travel down a pool lane or out into deeper water It is a good workout for abdominals, wrists and ankles. Imagine your body spread across to fill in the space around peripheral limbs. The movements of jellyfish are not pronounced and work slowly; emulate the subtleties of their effortlessness. Use diaphragmatic breath in buoyancy and explore lung capacity differentials of movements.

Precambrian and Cambrian Explosion

Around 2.7 billion years ago, oxygen producing microbial photosynthesis evolved on the earth. Cyanobacteria created algal mats that played a pivotal role in oxygenation of the primordial seas and atmosphere. Oxygen as a by-product from algae and other organisms set the stage for multicellular life to explode. The oldest known animal fossils preserved in ocean sediments appeared in the Ediacaran, with the advent of the Precambrian period 550 million years ago. Along with *Charnia* and other seabed organisms, *Dickinsonia*, an oval organism with a distinctive fractal pattern scuttled along the seafloor moving around the occasional *Cloudinia*. The funnel-shaped chalky calcium carbonate exterior housed a soft body. It is considered by some evolutionary biologists as a possible candidate for the first animal organism with reef-building attributes. It grew on microbial mats and in rock crevices, cementing to other Cloudinia organisms to form clumped towers. A mere ten million years later - around 540 million years ago ocean oxygenation ushered in an explosion of multicellular creatures marking the beginning of the Cambrian Period. (Wood, R.A. 2019)

Pre-Cambrian seas enriched with oxygenation in the sunlit shallows were rife with reef-building animals and corals. The shallow water corals profit from a symbiotic relationship between algae and coral reefs. Reefs are built from photosynthesizing algae that deposit calcium carbonate and cycle nutrients while the hardened reefs provide protected sheltering and the compounds needed for algae to photosynthesize. The calcification process also resulted in a plethora of soft-bodied molluscs with calcified external exoskeletons made of chitin and shell that fed on algae and each other. Reefs appeared first along with sedentary creatures like sponges and urchins that required less oxygen than locomotive organisms. But soon, oxygenated, nutrient-rich sea beds were filled with an overabundance of invertebrates, many with some degree of mineralized exoskeletons - all pushing, shoving and tumbling over one another in cascades of numerous and unique species. The locomotive motions in the multitude of multi-celled sea creatures were often strange and bizarre as they moved in a jumble of spirals, rolls, tumbles in undulating, twisting, whipping, spinning, crawling, jetting, flopping, thrusting, twitching, and pumping bumps in motion.

Fossils and fossilized imprints of Cambrian soft-bodied lifeforms with the carbonate exoskeletons such as echinoderms, arthropods, fungi, molluscs, and other invertebrates are enshrined in earth's geology; each prehistoric layer marking periodic organisms in deposits. The coastal seafloors are littered chitin and shelled creatures later were pushed upward to form many limestone outcroppings as the white cliffs of Dover attest. There were ocean crawlers, ambushers, drifters, predators and seekers that preyed and fed on bystanders and passersby. They are the predecessors of today's starfish, crab, lobster, sea urchins, and arachnids that eventually evolved into land insects.

540 million years ago, Cambrian aquatic creatures took body plan designs to meteoric heights. Many species were to become the precursor species to the next explosive period in evolution: bony fish and other vertebrates during the Ordovician Era. However, evolutionary advancements carried the typical drawbacks. Developing hardened stable and protective surfaces and exteriors in the form of shell and bone as a defensive protection on the seabed and reefs came with a cost of adding an uptick in energy requirements and a loss in flexibility, speed and fluidity, plus much of the ability to shape-shift.

Chitin and Seawater Shells

Before organisms formed hardened exteriors, multicellular organisms evolved largely by reconfiguring their soft body shapes to move and conform in a fluid environment. Evolutionary advancement meant adapting within the parameters of that liquid environment or acquiring behavioral attributes to compete and survive.

Given the molecular weight and structure of water, fluid organisms were adept in shape-shifting and their locomotive designs with protrusive modifications used to move, grab, attach, and spring. With the oceans developing more and more oxygen and other chemicals from photosynthesis, more creative avenues in evolutionary possibility continued to open new niches. Using the minerals in seawater new species evolved the ability to absorb and secrete calcium carbonate to grow hardened exoskeletal exteriors in the form of chitin and shell. The oxygenated water was also an energy resource which many organisms evolved systems to utilize and internally store to fuel energy needs and develop faster locomotion.

In the primordial oceans during the Cambrian, many strange and wonderful shapes of arthropods, mollusc, starfish, urchin, and other shrimp-like creatures roamed the seas. Optimized and successful, the hardened exoskeletons of their shells and chitin, a thin polysaccharide material, testify to the abundance of the inhabitants immortalized in numerous global limestone fields. Chitin is the second most abundant natural polymer in the world, second only to collagen. Chitin hardens urchin and starfish, forms many of the parts in crustaceans, arthropods and even hardens the beaks of octopuses. From the Cambrian era, chitin has sustained sea organisms as a light, pliable and surprisingly strong structural exoskeleton material, and also later adopted in land-based insects. It also is the material used in the cell walls of fungi and yeast. Not only is it found on the surfaces of cells but internal and external chambers and , in struts and wing feathers to maximize structural flexibility and stability where it is required. Our toe and fingernails are made of the same protein as chitin and our guts can carry enzymes known as chitinases to break down chitin. Lifeforms have shaped carbonate shells and chitin into mineralized exoskeletons for over half a billion years, but when ocean acidification is high, the process cannot be sustained as acid eats away the carbonates.

The nautilus is a mollusc cephalopod that evolved a chambered shell to house its flagellate muscle and arms into a remarkable pump to propel it through ocean waters.

Nautilus Pump

The nautilus is one of earth's longest surviving cephalopods. This strong, muscled creature absorbs salt into its blood, which helps it to regulate the different pressures in its shelled chambers to move into various depths. Nautiluses require little energy while feeding on zooplankton, tiny fish and crustaceans they catch in their tentacles. They can subsist feeding only once in a month. Often living at depths with little or no light, their pinhole vision eyes retain only primitive acuity. Prized for their shells, the rate they are being taken from the oceans is now threatening the nautilus with extinction.

Nautilus

The nautilus travels vast distances by the thrust locomotion of its muscle action. Essentially, the nautilus jets water from contracting a muscle called a hyponome, which is known to have evolved from the foot of a molluscan ancestor. We use our peripheral limbs to generate a similar thrust action as backward jetting propulsion from a flexion/contraction action.

Try it: Ideally this is practiced in open water at least chest high or deeper. The idea is to power the nautilus hyponome muscle action with arms, legs and spinal movements. Begin floating upright. Bend at your mid-section and pull in the abdominals while you bring hands and feet together in front of you near the surface. The movements are rapid to build thrust in jetting backwards. As toes come together at the surface, begin by first spreading legs and arms out wide keeping them near the surface and then drop legs down and behind at a 45 degree angle while opening arms back wide. This will arch the back and thrust your chest forward as limbs extend behind you. Then, quickly thrust your core forward to bring arms inward and legs upward simultaneously to jet your back and thrust concave backward. The momentum in the limb movements will propel you backwards as you push hard bringing limbs together and forward of your core. Repeat; build the movement by opening out; jet by folding inward limbs coming forward. Synchronizing limb motions apart and together, the submerged jack-knife motion uses water friction as though flexing a hyponome to thrust backward.

Legs and arms open to ready the action, power builds on the spring extension in the chest and flexion follows the momentum through in the pump action to jet backward. Once you get the thrusting motion running strongly, you'll feel the thrust in jetting. The bending of limbs back behind you energizes arms and legs, tightens in the gluteus maximus, hips and thighs and effectively widening and contracting vertebrae in the back.

Try It: If you enjoy wave action in the ocean, you may be fortunate enough to align the above extension/flexion movement of *Nautilus Pump* swimming in the ocean. As the gentler ocean waves come ashore, face them in the water chest-high or a little higher; begin floating limbs together and forward of you at the leading edge of an incoming wave. As the wave energy crests, open legs and arms and let it help pull on the limbs as you extend to open you as it rolls to crest. At the moment the wave begins to pass, flex inwardly and bring arms then legs forward as the wave pulls away, and your core thrusts back along with it. The momentum adds impetus to the "pump action" motions in quite an extraordinary way.

Soft-bodied molluscs and derivative and non-derivative soft-bodied species predate the arrival of bony fish and amphibians. The cephalopods, including octopus, cuttlefish and squid evolved around 450 million years ago came from mollusc ancestors. Arthropods are thought to have descended also. While nautilus is one of the most primordial of living cephalopods, the species as a whole branched into many exquisite, highly adaptable and intelligent species. They are said to have some of the most creative abilities in the repertoire of animal behaviours, both defensive and offensive.

Of all the ocean soft-body creatures, the octopus has maximized its ability to contract its soft body. Here's how you can emulate a movement in one of the more familiar species of cephalopod widely spread throughout oceans - the brainy octopus.

Octopus Dash

Giant Pacific Octopus

Octopuses have relatively short lifespans, ranging from six months to five years. Males only live for a few months after mating, and females die shortly after the egg incubation period of a little over a month. Octopuses have a systemic (3-part) heart and a highly complex brain with only a part of it located in the head. They employ a wide range of defensive/offensive strategies: camouflage and distraction, luring or detaching a twitching arm, and escaping with the release of ink. They are known to use mimicry to attract prey and to deter action in disguise as a predator's predator.

This first swim stroke in PyM is a modified version of an octopus's jetting motion. The lateral side stroke is optimized as a thrust and glide. Although an octopus uses eight arms and maybe its siphon to expel water, we have only four limbs; however buoyancy helps in the glide. Standing in at least 4 feet of water, squat to where your head is just above the water to begin. Visualize an octopus as it jets away. Octopuses arms fan out slightly and pull together to rapidly propel it away in a sudden burst and glide.

Try It: Kick off to the side from the pool wall or the floor for starting momentum, glide laterally, head just above the water surface. As your thrust slows, extend your lower arm beneath out to reach forward and pull downward to initiate the asymmetrical limb thrusts; the upper arm concurrently reaches with the lower with less extension, both push downward. Simultaneously bend knees and kick laterally- one leg slightly ahead of the other to match the above arm stroke. Thrust and streamline limbs to continue the inertia of gliding as an octopus (above) for a slightly off-beat four-limbed stroke forward. Your limbs pull upward again in the recovery stroke circling closely in and reaching to power the stroke. Keeping your head partially underwater will reduce drag. This sidestroke adaptation differs from a conventional sidestroke.

Be sure to repeat the strokes and move in both directions to balance the lateral strength and stretch. The spine stabilizes with an easy curve and actually little lateral movement. The movement is mainly in limbs - gathering to reach, thrusting forward and extending to glide. Try it underwater by pushing off from the substrate and pulsing upward in jets. It is a fun stroke and effective as a lateral strength exercise. Turn easily at pool corners; it requires a simple adjustment in the stroke length and the angle of attack, takes a little practice.

Visualize yourself as an octopus - a versatile, creative, intelligent, adaptable invertebrate loosely comfortable in water. The ease of this side stroke is especially enjoyable in a lake or pond as it allows swimming while also observing the shoreline, embankment and coastal curves. Enjoy the views.

Bones, Jaws, Teeth and Fins

Trilobites were tiny arthropods about the size of a fingernail that first appeared around 521 million years ago. They were flat, nondescript, segmented mud-dwellers and they had a hardened exoskeleton with millipede-like legs that allowed the animal to swim away if threatened. Trilobites spread widely throughout the world and survived as a species for almost 300 million years through several mass extinction events. As recently as 250 million years ago, the marine superbugs grew up to 8 inches in diameter, some with bizarre pointy appendages with which they crawled, burrowed and swam (by flexing their hind quarters) in mainly shallow benthic environments.

The ubiquitous trilobites were early harbingers of chordate structures, a central hardened or bony structure. The bilateral design of *Pikaia gracilens*, a wormlike species, had a hardened notochord and is considered the first of its type with a prototype of a spine. Notochords were supported by striated muscle fibers and a primitive nerve system to implement the motor control firing action in their locomotor swim movements. Bi-lateral body plans and notochords arose during the Cambrian period; discovered in the Burgess Shale in Canada, (Adler, J., 2013) and an earlier one in China. *Pikaia* marks the advent of vertebrate movement on earth. They were flat animals

Pikaia fossil

with a small mouth and a leaf-shaped tail which powered locomotion in a series of undulating S-shaped zigzag curves, similar to eel movements.

Species bilateral in design with notochord scaffolding and endoskeletal structures led to rapid ramification in the evolution in highly successful oceanic vertebrates, namely fish. The first structural strides were formative in the evolution of skeletal and systemic complexity in vertebrate life. Spines carry many advantages for stability with movement flexibility, providing protection for a central nervous system, bi-lateral balance in symmetry, new ranges of possible motion for locomotion and various other nerve and motor characteristics.

Chordate species pre-date modifications towards organizing a "head" in organisms to house and protect those anatomical systems of food sensing and feeding. The housing of the head facilitated centralizing sensing features in closer proximity to where feeding occurs, around the mouth. Hardened if not armoured, bony heads in fish became a successful evolutionary blueprint in most oceanic vertebrates as centralized sensory and nerve feedback centers. All the centralizing in the head predates the later swelling of nerve cords in flexible necks and brain centers of land animals.

Pikaia Pulse

Try It: Let's begin by undulating along the full length of our bodies as the early chordates did and eels do today. Keeping legs together as a single unit, point your toes and kick to initiate the undulating from the base of your legs as a mermaid tail in quick rhythm. The semi-flat oval of our body form can produce a two-dimensional wave action which will either tend to push or pull the body through the water depending on applied force from the curved thrusts and where the action initiates. Start in a horizontal position on your back with legs together near the surface. Tilt your head back and down under the water to roll from arching your back into curving your core down to your knees to finish the undulation off at your toes. Try the movement both face up and face down - it is easier facedown generally, as we have more flexion than extension. You may modify with support on hands in shallower water, dip head down first and ripple bodily down to your toes. It takes strength to undulate in water continuously but is possible with some quick repetitive motions. Having momentum helps, especially after just after diving in - you can easily maintain momentum by undulating through the water. You may wish to experiment further with a noodle float for better balance; undulating without thrusting with our arms is very inefficient aquatically. Again, if we were smaller in size, the water would feel thicker, more viscous with better support. On the other hand, you may better come to understand why almost all fish swim with lateral strokes.

Fossilized bone structures of fish and other vertebrate species of the Lower Cambrian and Ordovician eras reveal that the earliest fish were a group of small, jawless creatures with gills used for feeding, not respiration. Later, fish gills mutated for use in respiration some 480 million years ago when they began to diversify into fish with more complex heads that had bony jaw structures, protective plates, scales and fins. There is some speculation that the changes in self-protective armor in marine animals from exterior bony plates and scales led to jaws and teeth in both predatory and non-predatory fish and set in motion faster locomotion and more evasive tactics. All these factors helped to accelerate the evolution of fishes. The Lower Cambrian was when fast-swimming predators and higher resolution eyes began to appear. (Lacalli, T., 2012)

The Continuum of Fish

Fossilized bone structures in some chordate species appeared towards the end of the Lower Cambrian, over 485 million years ago. The evolution of fish is thought, although debated, to have occurred late in the Cambrian and the Ordovician period. While land masses during the Ordovician continued to be heavily barraged by asteroid collisions, the oceans thrived with new species. (Schmitz, B., 2016) The seas were rich in oxygen-

Placoderm

ation and had an abundant diversity of planktonic life, a ready food source. The earliest fish recorded at around 535 years ago, were a group of small, jawless creatures with primitive hearts and gills used for feeding, not for respiration. Gills adapted for underwater respiratory exchange as fish species diversification occurred, mutating into an oxygen transfer system.

One fairly common fossil species of early fish were placoderms that first appeared 420 million years ago, during the Silurian period. It was an early species known to have a bony head and body. These finned species had flanged flanked pectoral fins which helped them to skirt along the ocean sea floor. As far as is known, early pectoral fins preceded the other diversifications in fish fins - dorsal, pectoral, ventral, adipose, pelvic, tail and caudal fins. Fin diversification is a means to enhance locomotive speeds and has been a competitive factor in fish evolution. The first fish with jaws also appeared during the Silurian and in different classes of predatory fish. Many fish during this evolved bony plate armour and hardened scales for protection against predation. Speed and other defensive, offensive and evasive tactics have been raising the stakes in the survival of fish leading to attributes gained in both predator and prey species.

Post-Ordovician and by the advent of the Devonian period the seas were characterized by fast-swimming predators, many with a higher resolution in vision, faster reflexes, new camouflaging techniques and innovative behaviors. Fish diversification peaked during the Devonian Era, around 400 million years ago and is referred to as the Age of Fish. Altogether fish comprise a large chordate phylum with over 34,000 species. (Lacalli, T., 2012)

In celebration of their extraordinary success, the first aquatic vertebrates evolved two-chambered hearts, bony heads to protect sensory centers, streamlined endoskeletal spines and tail/fin configurations geared for their swim capabilities. Each species had respiratory systems geared for their lifestyle at varied oceanic depths and optimized for their particular ocean niche.

Crafty adaptations included various types of protective armory, schooling maneuvers, camouflage, concealment and distraction techniques or use distracting foils such as mimicry, lures, poison, shock and ink. And during the millions of years of marine animal evolution, wily defenses have only slowed some deadly and crafty pursuers. Speed in most aquatic fish bodies are gained by enhancements that either maximize thrust or reduce drag factors.

The late scientist and biomechanics pioneer Steven Vogel (1940 - 2015) studied and analyzed the many types of propulsive mechanics of different species over the course of his career. He analyzed numerous aspects of aquatic locomotion and the material surfaces that facilitate a species' movement - cilia, scales, skin, flagella, fins, paddles, flippers, flukes and wings, as well as other fluid dynamic pump mechanisms such as jets, lungs, valves and tubes, and the various osmotic and evaporative designs also. He consistently maintained that function in nature always determined the design that was optimized in each species whether it was in the propulsive or pump action, physical shape or surface characteristics. He found that locomotive actions were well-matched to resistance loads especially if the species were aquatic. His research contributed to our knowledge that most fish swim in a burst-and-coast fashion to conserve energy. Strong thrust action can be energetically conserved more easily in a fairly rigid body glide so that thrust is combined with drag. The fastest fish utilize lateral movements from tail structures initiated at a precise distance behind the main body for the strongest bursts in power and speed. The zig-zag motion a fishtail produces generates pure thrust in the side-to-side oscillations. (Vogel, 1993)

Evolution however optimizes advancements slowly. Each new form or behaviour expressed in a species - at one time or another evolved apropos to the environmental demands placed on a species with regards to the community at large. From microbes to animals - the wide spectrum of steps in a species' locomotive progression through the ages that mutate also genetically places demands on bone structures, complexity of nerve and muscle systems, stabilizing tissues, on the characteristics of respiration, and the chemical and energetic transfer components in species biology to create the movements a species is capable of.

The initial ray-like pectoral fins in fish died out at the end of the Devonian Period as far as we know. However, the present-day rays (stingrays, manta rays, skates, guitarfish, and numbfish) that currently grace the oceans reappeared in "convergent evolution", hundreds of millions of years later. It is described thus when similar features suddenly reoccur unrelatedly at different periods and/or at different epochs in earth history.

Stingray

Cowtail Stingray

Stingray species have adapted to living in various depths, temperatures and salinity levels. This basal species, a Cowtail stingray, is found in both freshwater and saltwater. Their flat ray bodies and fused pectoral fins skirt the substrate. They maximize glide motion while minimizing the energy their motions require. Some species are known to interact with humans, but care should always be taken to shuffle feet as most species' reflex is to pierce skin with a sharp and often poison tipped stinger if trod on.

This requires holding your breath underwater to emulate this beautiful creature:

Try It: Push off and dive down to the floor or seabed underwater to glide along the surface beneath. Pull in abdominals and bend elbows outward with hands alongside your head. Lightly skim fingertips along the plane of the floor as you glide along and imagine your body as wide and flat as a stingray and manta ray. If there's enough momentum in the glide, try a subtle flapping of elbows, and moving directionally just inches above the seafloor. Rays, skates and mantas use vertical undulations motions along the leading edge of wide pectoral fins and flap for thrust. We use ground effect and inertia, although a gentle lateral undulating may add to the motion.

Jaws and Teeth

The earliest jaw structures appeared in the Silurian era, 430 million years ago and are thought to have evolved initially as an opening through which to pump seawater to increase respiratory advantage. Yet there were obvious advantages to heads with jaws for feeding and even more so, with teeth. Teeth ensure a better grip on  prey and to threaten defensive action and offensive maneuvers with a bite. The hardening of jaws and teeth amounted to widening an animal's choice and exploitation of food resources aided by mandibles to pry, crack shells, grind chitin exteriors, and break fish spines and bone.

The fish that tend to epitomize a human vision of dangerous apex predators in the seas are fast with sleek streamlined bodies, possessing a good sense of smell, precision reflexes, and of course, massive jaws with rows of sharp teeth. None other is more manifest than in oceangoing sharks. Great white sharks, for example are older than trees but even the extant species today do not hold a candle to their primordial predecessors!

Shark

Sharks appeared around 445 million years ago and are an enduring primordial genus of fish. They have diversified into over 470 species and include the largest fish known, the whale shark. Their characteristic dorsal fin is large because it extends continuously into the base of the spine. The internal spine stabilizes quick movements while adding strength with efficiency especially in bursts of speed. Sharks need to constantly swim in order to breathe and to maintain buoyancy; generally they cannot sleep very long without sinking.

Hammerhead Shark

Try It: Given our human weight and form, we engage the lateral strength and twist of the spine in side-to-side leg kicks from a face-up position. Floating in water deep enough to swim in, lengthen out straight legs together, tuck your core in slightly and turn hips to one side, legs angled sideways and kick off; then twist over to the other side, hip up, and kick. Keep your legs together when kicking laterally as a shark's tail moves from side to side. Alternating in the side-to-side twist -- use your arms at the end of each kick to assist balancing the propulsive action through the twist turns. Your arms can be closed in at your sides during the power kick and glide; but will play as fins to stabilize lateral movements. Initiate kicks by bending your knees and generate backward thrust. You'll get the sense of just how much to flex and stiffen your upper body for sustained locomotion. Relax your upper body when twisting side to side; it also helps to keep shoulders and head partially submerged and aligned together. The twist kicks will drive the momentum, you can regulate speed and direction by lengthening or shortening the length of your tuck and kick. This movement strengthens the stabilizing lateral muscles of your core body, lubricates the low back and spine and can evoke a mermaid-like feeling as a single, tail-powered stroke. With a little practice, the single side-to-side kicks can become quite comfortable, and a surprisingly fast way to move through water.

What we eat makes a difference. Oceana reported that in 2018 alone, over 73,000,000 sharks were killed globally –most were cruelly tossed back into the sea after cutting their fins for shark fin soup. The oceans' sharks are being overfished and require global regulatory management and oversight for survival. Research shows that sharks are essential to maintain the health of oceanic ecosystems; all other fish species will suffer if we fail to protect them.

The PyM aquatic movements of the marine animals that follow below also include some familiar ocean mammals. The progression that ensues is based on aquatic movements rather than on evolutionary chronology which obviously must be set aside here with inclusion of mammals. PyM continues from the Devonian age in the next chapter with the arrival and evolution of species on coastal landforms.

Dolphin Kick

Combining leg kicks with the paddle motions of the upper body together delivers a homologous limb-together motion of *Butterfly* stroke. Porpoises and dolphins power their thrusts through water with the up/down motion of muscular tails. A similar motion can be emulated with legs-together as dolphin tail movements in the semi-submerged stroke. If you've ever practiced the conventional *Butterfly* stroke, you'll know the required stamina and physical strength it demands to power the rotational thrust movements of the shoulder girdle. My preference is my father's face-up version below.

Try It: Push off facing down in the water and kick legs together; bring your arms up, circling them back, out and around forward as butterfly wings through the water. As arms raise up - your head dips beneath the surface and lifts on the upstroke and ripples down the spine in an extension/flexion undulating motion. It is a classic homologous (forelimbs/hindlimbs) stroke moving limbs apart and together simultaneously. Check out the butterfly swim stroke on YouTube or Wikipedia. Feel free to experiment with your own expressions of dolphin movements. My father's easier version was an upside down Butterfly backstroke coupled with single leg kicks.

Try It: Facing upwards on your back, kick your legs steadily and couple the movement by circling arms together, moving them up, outward, around and back over your head. Reaching back and kicking, cleave through the water with cupped hands down and around and back in front. The stroke opens and extends the back and chest in the back-reaching motion. Submerging your head lessens drag and helps to pace your inhales and exhales with each powered thrust up and submerged recovery stroke. It's a fun and more easy-going alternative.

Whale Spin

Orcas shown here are technically dolphins but both dolphins and whales are known to have well-developed pod communications that allow them to work in teams. Some species collectively make columns of bubbles to force schools of fish to densely gather near the surface. In coordinated behavior, the pod will then rise from below to feast on the fish at the surface. Whales are known to pass on hunting and evasive techniques to younger members in a pod, even - how to safely remove a snared fish from a hook. Given how social they are, how can we doubt that they experience joy in their leaps and spins?

Orcas

It's easier to spin above the surface of water than when submerged given the friction of water. Some momentum is required both to leap and spin but first try a *Whale Spin* from the water.

Try It: Raise one arm straight above your head to initiate the spin and use your other arm plus the legs to kick and begin the twist around using your body as a spindle. Keep legs together as you twist with your toes pointed. It should come naturally as to how the second arm will adjust in downwardly circling to balance your spinning. Use the actions of the arms to speed up or slow down your spin speed and angle and then add the raised arm. Optimally you should be circling at around at about a 15- to 25-degree angle from the surface. If you do so, your feet will form the center point in the motion circling the spins. Enjoy spinning several times in one direction, then turn and raise the other arm to spin in the other direction (as you spiraled in *Charnia*). Then, try a small leap to see how you might jump from the surface. To better feel a leap - spiral up through the water by pushing off from the sea or pool floor and break through the surface in a spinning leap. Try it also continuing from a surface dive from under the water, push off the substrate spinning as you leap from the water surface. As you break the surface, lean back as a whale to land backwards. Many mammals of the seas may breach for the pure joy of it -- though some have speculated that it might be to clear unwanted parasites from the skin. There may be more anthropomorphic reasons to wonder, but what I experience is sheer delight.

In the 1800s, the whaling industry hunted sperm whales to less than 10% of their former population, threatening extinction. Until just recently, humans had never attempted to study the renowned sea mammals. Sperm whale brain size is 6 to 7 times larger than human brains. The brainy mammals have had millions of years to refine their global communications. They could easily pulverize a human with their 15-foot flukes but are known to shy away from divers with bubbling tanks, although they are known to engage with free divers. Free divers are now making new research possible as they can dive for long periods on one breath, to near sperm whale sea depths.

Kraits and sea snakes are slick, sinuous serpentine ocean-evolved species. They may have been among the first to defensively evolve amniotic behavior to safeguard their offspring by laying eggs on land. Moving on land however, is very different than swimming in the seas. Sea snake tails also modified into a more flattened version for the push onto the land.

Sea Snake

Sea krait tails are flattened to propel thrust in paddling. They feed on small fish and eels in corals which they catch and paralyze with a neurotoxin ten times stronger than rattlesnake venom. Preyed upon by sharks and other fish, they are known to deter predators by mimicking the tail movements of their venomous heads.
On land, sea kraits move only at about a fifth of their speed in water Sea kraits spend much of their time on land resting and digesting, and for reproduction by laying their eggs on the land

Sea kraits are similar to the water snakes that can be observed along flowing spring-fed creeks, streams and rivers of the Sierra Nevada mountain range. Unlike eels, wary water snakes view the embankment as they swim along with their heads a few inches above the surface of the water. It affords the snake an awareness of both opportunities and dangers as it passes in the currents.

Try It: The position of shoulders and head are angled above the surface, facing sideways to swim direction. Thrust action is propelled in the legs that kick together in a laterally-oriented undulating kick. The motion can only assume a snake-like body as both arms help to power and balance the serpentine movement. Lean off to one side and reach your lower arm ahead to the side and push off to begin the stroke. As your arm pulls back in under your body, side lateral muscles stabilize the sideways motion as you kick. Use the arm atop (closest to the surface) to synchronize with the lower arm movements in a similar powering motion with a slight delay. Reach and pull in thrusts. As arms simultaneously stroke downwards to the centerline of your body, try a legs together stroke, but a steady kicking will maintain steady forward motion to pull from your core. Remember to balance the strokes and lateral stretch from both sides. Circle a pool or explore an embankment equally and view the surroundings from opposite directions. This is especially enjoyable along the banks of rivers and inlets with moderate current.

These next exercises simply make for good aquatic workouts! In continuing a chronology in the evolution of movement -- fins that modify into limbs. So, Jump into amphibians…

Frog Kick

Frog hind limbs are connected laterally to the pelvic girdle. It emphasizes a stable bilateral body plan indicative in frog species. Limbs are neurologically wired independently for movement with well- evolved amphibious nerve and joint systems and highly functionally versatile centerline fulcrums in their body plans. Environmentally sensitive, most aquatic species breathe through their skin. Although the genus adapted to a wide range of habitats; their numbers have greatly diminished with pollution, disease, roadways and the inability to migrate.

Pond frog

Try It: Try frog kicks standing as squats in water at levels mid-thigh or lower. Rotate your legs to open out and gently rise up to bounce on legs up and down, feet turned outward. Try it also leaning on a rock, table or chair, or perhaps in shallower shorelines in scampering hops. In deeper waters, frogs will move through water in bursts of kicks and glides. With knees bent outward, flex your feet and kick out, moving arms in a circular motion. Make sure abdominals are pulled in and arms open at your chest in a circular motion.

As a four-limbed water stroke, enhance the action by adding short fins and hand paddles. With use of the upper limbs, the movement differs only slightly from the standard breast stroke as the head is kept above water; feel free to dip your head in the recovery stroke. The emphasis in ***Frog Kick*** is to synchronize the push-kick of the legs with arm motions to introduce limbs in the homologous reach-and-pull together motion.

Otter Float

Otter

Sea otters are diurnal animals; most of their day is spent foraging and grooming. They forage in kelp beds and rivers as much as five hours a day as their metabolism requires them to eat at least 20% of their body weight every day. Floating on their backs, otters break and pry open mollusk shells and urchins atop their bellies with a favored rock which they store in underarm pouches. Pacific Coast otters wrap themselves in mats of kelp (attached to sea beds) to prevent them from drifting away in the sway of currents while they rest and feed.

Try It: Lie back and float on the water's surface and fill the upper portion of the lungs to find the right measure of buoyancy. Keep a slight curl in the low back as you float with feet lifted. Use the diaphragm to consciously breathe down into the low belly. Having found your floating equilibrium, relax your arms comfortably. The human body is more than 70% water, attune to the water and flow of your breathing by using your diaphragm as a buoyancy interface as an otter. Play with this, try a side roll and circle back up your floating position or another favorite, the barrel roll.

Otter Barrel Roll

Otters are playful, quick and flexible and they give us many fun movements to emulate, one is the barrel roll. If you have access to noodle floats, the buoyancy support will allow for all sorts of otter movements.

Try It: Beginning at the (pool) edge with a kick to power a barrel roll. Hold on to an edge in water deep enough to roll backwards. Draw your knees up close to your chest and kick the wall or rock face to create momentum to dive back into an underwater backflip. Arch back and dive down below the water surface (no need to hold your nose as momentum will not allow water in). Hold your breath and like an otter, keep arms in at your sides initially, then use them to complete the roll as needed. To slow your curved ascent, open your arms outward and let your buoyancy glide you back to the water surface. Try twisting as you descend, like otters do, angling into a twist downward, and maybe push off from the ground to accelerate to the surface.

Dog Paddle

If you have ever been repeatedly "rescued" by your loyal, loving pet while swimming, you'll recognize this most instinctive movement. No matter what the breed, dogs all swim the same way -- as do many other four-limbed, furry mammalian species, including sloths and monkeys. The typical dog paddle uses all four legs in cycling motions. It looks instinctive, but it's actually the result of some degree of complexity. It occurs in creatures where the motions in the limbs are balanced or almost so, equalized in the spine spatially and across the shoulder and pelvic girdle. Dog Paddle uses subtle contralateral motions to help balance and keep the animal afloat in water while keeping head motions somewhat independent.

Try It: Push off in water at least four feet deep and swim facedown, move adjacent arms and legs in an easy reach-and-push forward motion in a crawl. Opposite arms and legs move in a continuous synchronicity, asymmetrically contralateral in their reach/pull back motion. Keep your hands slightly cupped and elbows comfortably beneath your sides as you paddle. Wrists and ankles strengthen in the flex and extend strokes. It is perfect as a beginner stroke from a graduated shore with the possibility of standing up. An infants' first swim is often quite instinctual to dog paddle.

Beaver Glide

Beavers are sociable, , family-centric animals and industrious home builders in meadows and wooded areas where water flows consistently. Equipped with powerful front incisor teeth, they can fell local trees and cut branches to build breakwater dams and dens in flooded and river flow areas. Beaver dams often moderate flow fluctuation extremes and flooding downstream, and reduce embankment erosion. Their dams also catch much water debris and filter streams often facilitating the breakdown of toxins through the silt retention. Beaver dams typically increase biodiversity by creating pools and habitats for frogs, ducks, snakes, turtles, fish and insects. They are the world's largest living rodents and deserve our admiration for their eco-industrious efforts, conserving fresh water to the benefit of many species.

Beaver release

Beaver tails deliver a sudden burst of power when needed; but typically, it is their strong legs and large webbed hind feet that give beavers' thrust power and direct their underwater movements. When beavers swim, they kick with hind legs to maneuver their rounded bodies directionally while their flattened, broad tails act as a rudder for steering control. Their broad tails also slap the surface water in warning and it serves yet another purpose - to store fat during the long winter months. Beavers have a keen sense of hearing and smell in the wetlands.

Try It: If you have short fins to assist you as you swim and glide, it is better with their use. Dive down and swim underwater, then paddle kick into a long glide along the very bottom of the pool or pond as beavers do before surfacing through an underwater opening in a beaver lodge. Again, with momentum, no need to hold your nose, just hold your breath. Be sure to fold your limbs in together to streamline your glide along the underwater substrate.

You can add momentum as needed with a swift kick off the ground.

Running Rabbit

The hare's ability to out-race predators is a primary defense reflected in their agility and physical proportions. Rabbits are built with longer muscular hind legs in comparison to forelimbs. While the reach in the forelimbs is extensive, a running rabbit reaches its hindlimbs to full length to drive the quick, meandering maneuvers to make evasive twists and abrupt turns. Rabbits can quickly attain their optimal stride lengths solely by running on the front toes of their paws when sprinting.

Common Hare

An aqueous environment makes this exercise more accessible as a workout than on land – working without impact but with all the intensity. And, it's more fun in water. *Running Rabbit* is pure synchronous action of push and pull in the limbs moving together. You may have emulated it as a child as leapfrog or bunny hop over friends.

Try It: In deeper water, at least at shoulder height, "jump" with bent knees outside the arms and simultaneously push down between the legs. Keep both arms parallel between knees to generate more "lift" in the knee pumps. Keep your head above the waterline to stabilize pump action of the arms pushing down and legs pulling up. Legs briefly come together as you straighten upright in the recovery stroke. Bring your arms back up towards the chest to ready the "hop" again. Create a rhythm; you can always modulate the speed as you wish. Emulating a rabbit running is a nice cardio-strengthening workout in the arms, chest, back, abdominals, legs and buttocks; a great exercise similar to sculling. *Running Rabbit* can be timed to incoming waves in deeper water, or at a slower pace in shallows where use off the ground will create more bounce in the knee lifts. In the former, simply open your chest more forward on the way back up when pushing down with bent legs; arms will move slightly more outward on the upstroke to maintain balance better. Always cup hands in the downward push-pump action.

Once familiar with creature movements in emulations, it's easy and fun to combine the different species' moves by choreographing them together into an aqua aerobics series. Here are some favorite combinations:

Try It: Begin with legs straight, feet together, and toes at the surface -- as you would in *Nautilus*. As in *Nautilus,* move to open your arms and legs wide and push back, opening out in extension. Then, as you fold limbs together in front, reach one arm out straight above your head at the water surface and transition into a *Whale Spin* with one arm raised above your head and spin. As you come out of the 360 degree spin legs together, flex into the semi-upright jack-knife posture with limbs moving together close to the surface to repeat the beginning of *Nautilus*. At the end of each thrust, alternate the spin directions to the right and left by alternating a leading arm to initiate a spin. Try this and other combinations ~ *Octopus* to *Shark*, then *Otter Barrel Roll* down into *Beaver*. Let the imagery flow in your body!

On the Shallow Edge

The following movements use water resistance to strengthen so enjoy the liquid pushback without impact. Feel free to add your own impressions.

Bird Wing Shenanigans

Using arms as wing foils underwater provides gentle resistance necessary for effective bird wing movements to strengthen shoulders and arms.

Try It: Begin in water chest height. Face out towards the deeper water and come onto the balls of your feet, on tiptoe. If in a pool, practice this on the slope of the pool if possible. With arms outstretched, lean to fall forward slightly. Avoid toppling over using arms to rotate from the shoulder around and down and straighten up while rotating arms up, back, around and down to make figure 8 movements, like bird wings do in flight. Bend elbows slightly as your circle arms back. It will take a little practice to learn to control the pace and balance required to "fly" meshing effort, resistance, inertia and buoyancy in water. You may wish to try it initially with elbows bent and hands tucked in under your armpits. As you lean forward and come back, imagine the leading edge of bird wings dipping, rising up and sweeping back. Or try hovering in shorter strokes, chest opened as a bird often does before landing. Play with this as you've seen different birds flap and fly; how your hands lead angle motions is subtle. The down and back sweeping movement is a "leading-edge" flap, evolved in dinosaur pterodactyls flying during the Triassic era. Check out how penguins swim in the next chapter. Our scapula is comparatively small to the design mechanism in bird flight wings but can emulate them to strengthen in this cardio exercise.

Serpent Sway

The serpent's side-to-side movement in water strengthens lateral muscles and the connective fascia of the core. In this exercise, you can easily regulate just how much water resistance you wish to apply by regulating the speed through water.

Try It: Water should be at least waist deep. Facing the pool perimeter, hold on to the lip of a pool rim or other surface in open water, separate hands at shoulder distance or wider to brace and support the side-to-side swing movements. From the rim, lengthen your body line just below the surface, with legs together and pull straight over to one side of the pool rim. When parallel to the side of the wall or embankment, press into hands again to push off from the side using lateral muscles to swing legs, keeping them straight together to the back around behind you, and continue moving to the other side of the wall. Feet flexed to push off the side. It's a continuous swinging side to side barely below the surface, moving in a 180-degree semi-circle. On reaching the sides, flex your toes and bend knees slightly on impact to gently kick off with a bounce to initiate and guide the push/pull to the other side. Keep legs together at all times, and maybe add a little twist midway as you swing back and pull over to the other side. It's a workout for core lateral muscles, arm strength and spine as a side to side push-and-pull. Modify by gripping onto a pool ladder or low diving board to swing and sway laterally side to side, like a serpent down all the way down to toes.

Boat Rock

Try It: Work your way to the water's edge where you can access shallower water. If you're on a shore, lie down and accommodate to the wave rhythm. If the waves are gentle enough, breathe in as the waves flow to you and exhale out as they pass by. Then move your limbs gently up and down to match the wave motion; relax as each wave recedes. Depending on how you may wish to work out - lift legs beyond the surface with the motion, bending knees and crunching in abdominals in any way you feel is right for you, either to exercise or simply to blend movements with the rhythmic wave frequency. As a boat - pull in your abdominals and lift your arms and legs up 90 degrees in a "V" shape above the surface in the traditional *Boat Pose (Paripura Navasana)*. As the waves pass by, let the waves rock you as a boat swaying, side to side and around. This is a dynamic version of the classical asana to better challenge the isotonic posture in water and will quickly tone your core, hips, abdomen, psoas and leg muscles.

Sitting, another wave motion to work the abdominals begins by extending your legs straight out at the water surface, toes out. Slowly open and close your legs straight at the surface of the water, arms extended out ahead. Another is as a side curl motion by bringing knees inward to your chest on each gentle wave, twisting with the wave motion, and then lengthening out to one side as it retreats. With each wave crossover, change side extensions. There are many exercises to choose from that gently strengthen muscles and lubricate joints with the assistance of wave action and surface tension. Be creative, each thoughtful rendering will help you engage the nature of water.

There are many other ways to enhance your perspective of evolution as a reciprocal experience in the external world. In the aquatic environment; explore what creatures may come to mind based on swim in different water levels and speeds: if you only have 18 inches of depth in a moving freshwater stream, try amphibian and insect movements. Experiment with differences in buoyancy or current, play with it in rolls in tumbles, floating and drifting. Always challenge yourself with movements of as many creatures from the perspective of their evolution under the particular aquatic conditions. The chemical and situational settings will alter the effects of motions that are available to you – in control, speed, strength required, balance, inertia and your stability in a body of water.

The Distance of Our Fallibility

In a strictly genetic sense, all organisms on earth are of one family, descended from a common ancestor, the living cell. The commonalities are numerous for all multicellular life forms especially at the molecular level. Protocells were made of a polymer matrix; a gelatinous hydro membrane exterior that humbly carried the beginnings of all life by moving in a bioelectric magic of seawater. Tiny primordial bacteria, archaea and protists – were a drift of microbial life through generation after generation for billions of years, absorbing and exchanging chemically for energy in order to self-replicate and mutate. From such beginnings the evolutionary steps just multiplied as the living cells evolved to store and use energy, sense and promulgate moving actions in the form of streaming, cilium, flagellum, grappling hooks, tunnels and footholds to morph, move and attach. Eventually the building blocks of life evolved DNA with data strands thousands of times longer than the cells themselves along with the data processing needed for autonomous self-regulating systems. Microbial organisms worked together into phalanges using cooperative and complex signaling; evolutionary interactions leading to cell differentiation and multicellular organisms with tails, shells, bones, flanges, fins, paddles, appendages, feet and limbs to move about, to compete and complement one another. With each process of tagging, manipulating, mutating and modifying; and with each new adaptive species, they changed the world around them. With successive advances and interactions the multiplying species on species enriched biosphere dynamics into living systems and within those systems, created new systems… through the eons of time. And here we hominins, billions of years later, with all the complexity our cells were built at their complete disposal, with all the past receptor and regulatory processes of identifying, attaching chemical tags, silencing or activating proteins either to build scaffolding for or to wall off accessibility to DNA, processing layer upon layer, in constant play in us -- they are our bodies, the scaffolder cells and the amazing life perpetrators on which we rely for daily living, but think nothing of.

We are the result of all those evolutionary steps taken by many earlier species and we are as much them as they are us. There are billions of cells working together in, for and through each multicellular body, including ours, in an untold magnitude of associative relationships as ancient as they are fundamental. Thus far, our species existence has been largely unfettered by biological compromises; but our freedom to ignore the continuum of microbial species under our very noses and exercise aberrant, destructive behaviours among all other species cannot last. There is much to discover in cell complexity, differentiation procedures, symbiotic cooperation and networking, signalling transference and many other billion-year-old processes that create living systems. There is much to untangle in the mysteries of life bound within molecular parameters. Currently there is a choice, either to learn how to understand and best preserve primordial and extant species based on their numerous roles in living systems or not. One way or the other, life will surely respond.

References

Alder, J. (2002), *Offering from the Conscious Body: the Discipline of Authentic Movement,* Rochester, NY: Inner Traditions.

Bengtson, S., 2002, Origins and Early Evolution of Predation. The Paleontological Society Paters, 8, 289-318.

Black, R.; Blosser, M. A Self-Assembled Aggregate Composed of a Fatty Acid Membrane and the Building Blocks of Biological Polymers Provides a First Step in the Emergence of Protocells. Life 2016, 6, 33

Boisvert, C. The pelvic fin and girdle of *Panderichthys* and the origin of tetrapod locomotion. *Nature* 438, 1145–1147 (2005). https://doi.org/10.1038/nature04119
Boraas, M.E., Seale, D.B., Boxhorn, J. (1998) Phagotrophy by a flagellate selects for colonial prey: A possible origin of multicellularity, Evolutionary Ecology 12:153-164.

Childs, C., 2000. *The Secret Knowledge of Water.* Sasquatch Books: Seattle, WA.

Fish, FE; Lauder, GV (2006). Annual Review of Fluid Mechanics. 38 (1): 193–224.

Gatesy, J., 1997, More DNA support for a Cetacea/Hippopotamidae clade: the blood clotting gene gamma-fibrinogen 14 (5): 537–543. Doi: 10.1093/oxfordjournals.molbev.a025790.

Gillis, J.A., Dahn, R.D., Shubin, N.H. (2009). "Shared developmental mechanisms pattern the vertebrate gill arch and paired fin skeletons". *Proceedings of the National Academy of Sciences.* 106

Guirao, 2007. Propriétés physiques des cellules ciliées, PhD thesis l' Université Pierre et Marie Curie -Paris VI.

Hanczyc, M.M., Fujikawa, S.M., Szostak, J.W., (2003) Experimental Models of Primitive Cellular Compartments: Encapsulation, Growth, and Division. Science, 302, 618–622.

Hanczyc, M.M.; Mansy, S.S.; Szostak, J.W. Mineral Surface Directed Membrane Assembly. Orig. Life Evol. Biospheres 2007, 37, 67–82.

Jabr, F., 2013, The Science of the Great Molasses Flood. Scientific American Magazine, August, 2013, 90-95.

Juhan, D. (2015). *Job's body*. Barrytown/Station Hill Press, Inc.

Lacalli, T., 2012, The Middle Cambrian fossil Pikaia and the evolution of chordate swimming, EvoDevo 3, 12.

Lewis, T., 1974, *The Lives of a Cell*, Bantam Books.

Lopez, A., Fiore, M., 2019, Investigating Prebiotic Protocells for a Comprehensive Understanding of the Origins of Life: A Prebiotic Systems Chemistry Perspective, Life, MDPI.

Machin K.E.,1958. Wave propagation along flagella. J. Exp. Biol. 35, 796–806.

McCartney, J., 1978. The Philosophy and Practice of Yoga. L.N. Fowler & Co.: Romford, U.K.

Alexey V. Melkikh, Oksana I. Chesnokova. (2012) Origin of the Directed Movement of Protocells in the Early Stages of the Evolution of Life. Origins of Life and Evolution of Biospheres 42:317-331.

Margulis, L., 1998, *Symbiotic Planet,* Basic Books: Perseus Books, New York, NY, USA.

Murillo-Sánchez, S.; Beaufils, D.; González Mañas, J.M.; Pascal, R.; Ruiz-Mirazo, K. Fatty acids' double role in the prebiotic formation of a hydrophobic dipeptide.

Pollack, G. H. (2001). *Cells, gels and the engines of life: a new, unifying approach to cell function* (p. 305). Seattle, WA: Ebner & Sons.

Schwenk, T. (1965). Sensitive Chaos: The creation of flowing forms in water and air. Rudolf Steiner Press.

Purcell, E. (1977). Life at low Reynolds number. *American Journal of Physics, 45* (1)

Shaevitz JW, Lee JY, Fletcher DA. Spiroplasma swim by a processive change in body helicity. Cell. 2005 Sep 23;122(6):941-5. doi: 10.1016/j.cell.2005.07.004. PMID: 16179261.

Schmitz, B., Yin, Q-Z., Sanborn, M. E., Tassinari, M., Caplan, C. E., Huss, G. R., 2016. A new type of solar-system material recovered from Ordovician marine limestone. *Nature Communications.*

Shubin, N.,2009, Wings, legs and fins: How do new organs arise in evolution, University of Chicago.

Tsuji T, Suzuki M, Takiguchi N, Ohtake H (2010) Biomimetic control based on a model of chemotaxis in Escherichia coli. Artificial Life 16N (2):155–178

"Primordial Fish Had Rudimentary Fingers" ScienceDaily, 23 September 2008.

Vogel, S., 1994. Life in Moving Fluids: The Physical Biology of Flow, Princeton University Press, NJ.

Wood, R.A., 2019 The Rise of Animals, Scientific American Magazine, June 2019, 26-31.

CHAPTER 4

Land Dynamics - Etrahnai

Animal physiology is largely influenced by how movement efficiently evolves to meet the physical and competitive dynamics in the world. Forged by environmental conditions and genetic change, locomotive abilities often will optimize a species' particular function in an environment. Growing into a 300-pound male gorilla? The benefits of evolution can modify a gorilla body selectively, in just the right ways through inheritance and chance to take on new roles with each roll of the genetic dice, and will likely be tailored just so to environmental parameters that supports species movements. Gorillas don't just appear suddenly; new species come from mutations and adaptations that appear in the preceding generations. When fish began fin-floundering in the mud shallows, their limbs and joints adapted to form joints and into limbs better suited to the land; and a path for the structural fundamentals of four-limbed body plans emerged on earth.

Beginning in this Earth series, **Primordial yogic Movement** launches into the skeletal formation of our ancestral species within the context of a geo-historical past in order to gain a better understanding of who we are as a hominin species. As always, we look to the physical body first and foremost, as it contains the secrets to evolutionary conditions that connect us with our ancestors. This is what *Etrahnai* and the following land movements will examine: how furry, quadrupedal mammals evolved from the fishy species that ventured ashore with almost impossible mandates of adapting to the atmospheric gases and volatile land environments. The way to break ground, so to speak, on the topic is to consider the substrate - the very root of our being, that prompted the first primeval baby steps that impelled the pioneering creatures on their merry and terrifying way.

We have a clear picture of how it all began... In the earth's first turbulent years in her formation, the emerging seas were volatile and inhospitable to biological life. Solar stardust had coalesced into a spinning mass surrounded by swirling gases from the massive explosion of the "Big Bang." The planet became denser as it spun around a metal core and super-heating the surface of bubbling molten rock. Semi-vaporous liquids settled into what is known as Hadrian's Plain - a steaming, seething inferno on a violent, vulcanized mantle. Land were mere rocky masses of burnt and burning crags that endured a maelstrom from spewing lava fields and explosive, churning noxious liquids while pummeled by asteroid bombardments. The billion-year-old planetary process constantly recycled and recombined itself, stirring metal and mineral amalgamations through the violent fury pounding the planet's mineral substrate into a nascent terra firma. Minerals coalesced from the settling of stardust elements under conditions that flipped wildly in the planet's early developments of superheated periods to glacial freezes from pole to pole. Land constantly shifted in contraction and expansion to form a myriad of composite geological landscapes.

Emergent caustic seas and a volatile mantle shaped by climatic rhythms, not only from lenghty ice ages and periods of overheating from volcanic field activity but by periods of drought, evaporation and condensation and other refining and settling processes that pushed for organic, biological changes. The early seas had so much available free energy that during planetary cycles, that eventually the first populations of primordial self-replicating cell life emerged. Movement had always been there at the outset. Kinetic energy from the H_2O and the CO_2, with the chemical exchanges of protons and electrons self-organized and created true dynamics from flux – made the elixirs of primordial earth. Dancing seawater and the humming songs of potentiates. Sea life slowly helped form more hospitable seas, facilitated clearing the atmosphere through photosynthesis and oxygenation and created conditions more conducive to the emergence of complex life. Hundreds of millions of years later primordial life mutated again strategies to use oceanic minerals for structural advantage developing chitin, shell and bone. Every vertebrate on earth, each with its own unique design, shares an oceanic connection to all others by virtue of their bones.

Over four and a half billion years and our *Homo* species evolved from the verdant planet earth we recognize today. From the shores of early seas to the vast inland stretches, the earth formed countless ecosystems that have sustained a plethora of biological possibilities. The planet continues to self-cleanse the land and oceans through cyclical winds and tides and the evaporative and precipitating recycling of water vapors through clouds and rain. The oceans feed and refresh the land and the land enriches the oceans with its nutrients. The living seas act as a carbon sink to exhale oxygen back into the atmosphere in a slow, but immensely re-fortifying and sustaining life-giving process.

Land means different things to different people, does it not? Some have a very real emotional attachment to the land simply as a result of being in daily touch with it. Some feel strongly about the land due to the significance of historical attachments that date back generations. Some use the land as a means to an end and no more. Others may often feel abused by it and question its changeable or static nature as a personal affront. Some care for the land out of a sense of duty, while others do so out of love or a sense of nurturing.

All too many of us accept it with general disregard – we may objectify, ignore, reshape and work against many of its life-giving aspects.

There are many perspectives and approaches to land in general, and not just from an individual, collective or cultural viewpoint. Comparatively, all hominin associations and attitudes to the land have changed dramatically since the time our species first walked on the earth. One early ancestral *Homo* species, *Homo Erectus,* lived a million years ago and must have felt more closely bound to the land than the vast majority of humans sense today. Most are neither required nor are compelled to have the same degree of contact with the land as did the earlier hominins that walked the earth. *Terra firma* constantly challenged them, whether by exposure to the variable weather or inopportune bouts of drought and starvation, they were driven by the necessity of finding food. And each venture in search of food posed a danger of "eat or be eaten". Their nomadic livelihoods on land meant daily contact with lethal microbial life, from bacterial, viral to diseases ranging from pneumonia and poxes, gangrene and rotting teeth, infestations of head lice and intestinal parasites, all with seasonal pestilence. Early man lived with manners of extremes from which today, we are protected. Hominins descended from arboreal ancestors to become grounded as a fully upright bipedal species, living off plants and hunting animals that shared the landscapes. It was the land that shaped hominin posture and movements, forming the way we breathe, walk, sense, manipulate, socialize and feel physically. As our family species' birthplace and crucible of growth and evolution, it should be honoured.

Primordial Soup to Swamp

It is easy to see that just as the songs of the sirens enticed lost and lonely sailors in Homer's tale of *Odysseus* to risk shipwreck, the lure of *terra firma* might have beckoned many water-bound creatures of the great oceans. They held a promise of stability and protection in the calm safety of warmer waters. Although highly oxygenated seas thrived with a plethora of life, they were also abundant with predators both monstrously large and viciously small. One of the many reasons for the arrival of oceanic species moving onto land during the Ordovician was a constant threat of predation. Many species seeking safety found protection in the rocky coves, mangrove and grassland estuaries and other sheltering shallows of the coastal land masses. Perhaps even more tempting was the prospect of abundant plant life and insect species along the lush shorelines, rich inlets and swamps. There were however, many obstacles to surmount in venturing deeper onto the land itself. Adapting to the new firm frontier required some physical adaptations. Of the many problems associated with terrestrial life, a few of the biggest were from an inherent dependency on the chemical nature of seawater. Fish had gill respiration and the lipid chemical nature of water minimized dehydration, a huge leap to overcome on the atmospheric land. Structurally, aquatic species moved their weight with buoyancy whereas terrestrial organisms required more rigid weight-bearing skeletal factors. The water-dependent physiological systems of fish would not last long in a thin, energy-depleting atmosphere. How were they to effectively supply the oxygen-chemical exchange for their energetic needs? Plus the movement of fins to bear body weight without buoyancy, it was daunting. Any pioneering species could not withstand exposure to the sun's cell-destroying ultraviolet rays for long and easily suffered from fatal dehydration. Rainwater gave no relief as it was largely mineral depleted. Moreover, coastal areas frequently experienced weather extremes with fires, floods and landslides. Danger was ever present on the terrestrial biosphere, yet it was populated by all sorts of flying insects, microorganisms, bacteria, fungi and plants that were also rapidly evolving defensively and offensively, adapting with strategies in the new environment. In short, moving onto land was dangerous, hostile and energetically draining. The challenges of land were almost as daunting as forging life from the primordial soup.

    No matter how creative or strange a species' life, physical success is determined by factors of how well the form functions over time. All methodologies and apparatus that once benefited a creature's locomotion were first crafted and chronicled in and by the aquatic environment. Within each evolved body plan laid a success story of system mechanics, buoyancy adaptations, structural compensations, chemical balancing and more; factors which at one time or another, were well matched to a fluid environment. There's no doubt that moving onto a new frontier of land would pose new biological, locomotive, aerodynamic, systemic, chemical, mechanical, structural and physical evolutionary challenges.

    However, there was likely no better place for evolutionary changes to occur than in the calm shallows along coastal lands, places where the oceans met the land. They were then and are still some of the most productive areas of life on earth. With abundant inlets, estuaries, swamps, beaches, tide pools, mudflats, lagoons, deltas and sheltered bays - harbor life had real advantages. The interplay of land and water provides a fluid stability to encourage growth in areas where nutrients and minerals concentrate from land runoff. It is where the energy of numerous food chains abundantly and actively are exchanged and resourced among a vast number of species. Places where inherent contrast and competition is played out daily to challenge every species' evolutionary mutability, and where abundance and opportunity exist as juxtaposed in a rapid overflow of exchange. Juxtapose coastlines with oceanic life and you find the "urban" centers of life and evolution. There's no purer contrast, no better definition to compare yin and yang, than where fluidity and solidity meet in flux – where water meets the land.

Thus far the evolution of movement has focused on invertebrates -- the soft membranous, mollusc, and muscled organisms that evolved mechanisms of propulsion through sweep, thrust, glide, spin, spring, pump action and buoyancy. During the Paleozoic Era of the mid-Ordovician, plants appeared on land around 470 million years ago. (Wellman, C. H., & Gray, J., 2000) Invertebrate arthropods followed the heels of the burgeoning flora onto the rich shorelines initiating a new era in terrestrial insects and arthropods during the Silurian period 423 million years ago. All along the primordial coastlines, many a gate to evolutionary expression once again was cracked to open a flood of novel dynamics of creature appearing in new habitats. In tidal pools and bays, in sheltered and temperate substrates, rich with nutrient runoff from the land and freed from the extremes of tides and wave actions, they ventured ashore. Species of serpentine and fishy creatures came from the depths, undulating and moving fins to gain higher ground were among the first explorers. Life in the oceans remained abundant, so much so that the Devonian period 380 million years ago is considered the Age of Fish - given the explosive number of new species that filled the oceans, and ancestors of fish today.

Fish to Amphibians

The new frontier was on land. Evolutionary biologists think that amphibious tetrapods evolved from fish and among the pioneering species were fish whose lateral fins lobed downward. Indeed, it's logical to speculate that opposing lobed-fins could brace more effectively against the solid substrates for movement cross ground. Opposing appendages not only would provide more balance and stability against unpredictable shoreline wave action, but may have influenced limbs as a jointed. By the late Devonian era, some fish were already equipped with primitive breathing lungs and some were found to also have joints and even jointed digits in webbed appendages, a characteristic of early amphibious tetrapods. The fish-like amphibians gulped air at the water surface and swam in protected coastal areas.

Recently, fossilized skeletal remains from 375 million years ago of a rare but recognized transitional fish-to-tetrapod species, *Tiktaalik*, was discovered. It had four opposed, fin-like appendages with simple rotating wrist bones and ray bones indicative of primitive webbed bony flanges, pre-fingered. The digit-like flanges were clearly weight-bearing, because the shoulder and humerus were muscular with an expanded scapula (shoulder girdling) for weight-bearing locomotion. There is some evidence the creature also had chest ribbing indicative of possible primitive lung formation, in addition to having gills. *Tiktaalik* had the beginnings of a primitive shoulder structure distinguishable from the head with a possibility of slight head movements. (Shubin,N., 2016)

There were other species evolving on land. A stem tetrapod named *Acanthostega* was among the first vertebrate animals to have recognizable limbs rather than fins. It appeared in the late Devonian era, about 365 million years ago. Although it had distinct digit-like bones in its webbed "hands," it did not have wrists and could not bear much weight across shoulders. (Clack, J.A., 2009) It is likely that its locomotive movements were paddling in water and holding onto aquatic plants. (Boisvert, C., 2005) Despite these few developments evident in limbs, scientists note that the early amphibian species remained primarily in shallow, aqueous environments for 60 million years before venturing onto the land for any extended period of time. The water-bound tetrapods were slow to evolve onto land, unlike arthropod species – the scorpion and crab-like predecessors of centipedes, millipedes, dragonflies, spiders, roaches and other insects walked, flew and slithered on land for at least 420 million years. Arthropod adaptations onto terrestrial life may have been comparatively easy given the hardened outer exoskeletal chitin and lighter bodies.

With a nod to the first land creatures whose ancestors roamed the oceans for 500 million years and whose subspecies are found both in tide pools on land; we begin the series with the ubiquitous Sea Star.

Starfish/Sea Star

Sea Star

Sea stars have five or more arms covered with many tubular sucker "feet" and a simple mouth centered on the underside. Their chitin exoskeleton forms various structures made from hardened calcium carbonate as dots called ossicles. The ossicles connect together, supported by collagen fibers. This enables the sea star exterior flexibility as needed or it can induce stiffening of the arms. Sea Stars are thought to have descended from earlier bilateral organisms. In walking; they use preferential leading arms to coordinate their direction and balance through sensory and motor control.

Typically, Sea Stars move flat across the seafloor on tubular feet with alacrity and often fall from the ill-defined subterranean terrains. On such occasions, they often find themselves upside down or askew with the need to reorient in an "upright, feet down" stance. Our emulations engage the stretch required in the movement.

Try It: Lay face down, with chitin-straightened limbs splayed outward. Imagine you have five flexible uniform arms spread out across the ocean floor but are flipped over upside down. Take a "leading" arm (right or left) and raise it up reaching out beyond the line of your head. Your lateral side lifts, lower the adjacent arm down and inwardly in the opposite direction to the rising arm. The third "arm" below the leading arm also rotates from the hip socket backwards to roll out pushing and turning the centerline core over to flip upward. Do not forget to disengage your sucker feet! Drop the middle "arm" down and tuck it in assisting in the rollover. As the center of the rotation is tucked under and gravity pulls you upright, slowly pull out arms and stretch them facing up, ready to try it with another leading arm. Remember the moves are with limbs straight and stiff. The slow motions stretch and open the joints and vertebrae in coordinating extension of limbs. Savor the slow-motion micro movements in Sea Star.

The third period of the Paleozoic Period on earth, 443 to 361 Mya, was a time of abundant, biodiverse oceanic life. On land, plant life was gaining a foothold to modify the landscapes. Initially life on the land was sparse yet tenacity and time brought a greening of the land and many different forms of life began to diversify during the Carboniferous period, 358.9 million years ago.

Four-limbed Tetrapods

Before the Carboniferous, during the Devonian era around 390 million years ago, shoreline animals ushered in the enduring class of tetrapods. Their remains reveal limb and lung adaptations that formed the foundation of true amphibians, the first four-limbed animals to walk the earth. The emergent species swam and scuttled in ponds, creeks, swamps, shallows, mudflats, and other areas where the land met the sea. As their appendages evolved more useful as limbs, paddling became more efficient and in some, bony finger digits and limb structures adapted to control weight while moving and feeding. Amphibian respiration evolving from gills to lungs utilized the locomotive movements to facilitate breathing. Some of the early adaptations initiated amphibious attributes that are still present in living species today. One such extant species is an amphibious fish called the mudskipper, which propels itself forward in a wiggle hop using their sturdy oppositional lobed fins along with a simultaneous side flick to lift its tail. Amphibians are defined by their reproductive preference for damp or aqueous environments. We tend to be more familiar with the amphibious descendants of frog, newt, toad, and salamanders; another species group includes the caecilians that live beneath ground in South and Central America.

Amphibians are defined by their preference for moist muddy, benthic environments. Amphibious limbs in the early species evolved and adapted  through numerous tryouts and limb designs. (Green, Sessions, S.K., 2019) Ankle structures initially varied widely with some fossils revealing ankles with many bones initially fanning outwardly but then later settled into a simpler joint with just two supporting bones which is now common in most amphibians, and by extension, reptiles and mammals. Some amphibians initially had eight digits on each limb, but the number declined to seven, six, and finally five jointed fingers - now the number of digits commonly found in most tetrapods. Early in amphibious development, eyes in hardened skulls faced out to the sides as they do in fish, but they slowly repositioned towards the front of the heads. This allowed for binocular vision, better suited to view overhanging vegetation along shoreline embankments. Not surprisingly, heads also became less rounded. In fact, we can witness the same shift in eye repositioning in real time by watching the growth development of tadpoles, the eyes migrate from the sides of the head in a swimming tadpole to a frontal position of adult frogs which then provides for more depth perception on land.

As amphibian limbs evolved, intersecting limbs on vertebral spines grew more robust; initially in the forelimbs from new shoulder structures and shortly after, in fortifying hind limbs with stronger pelvic structures. (Molinar, J. L. et. al.,2018) The amphibious pectoral girdle also modified as the limb-to-limb locomotive efforts on land pulled forelimbs back coordinating with pushes from the hindlimbs. In some amphibians, the pelvis fused to the spine to increase the strength and stability required for push-and-pull locomotion. Fused spines have come and gone many times over in evolution and there are still many vertebrates with fused pelvic girdles, including in some mammals. They most likely occur in pelvic structures where the sacrum requires a strong fulcrum for vertebral actions; for balance and pivot from a stabilized base. Vertebral fusing initially evolved in some aquatic species such as fish, so it was not unusual to also appear in semi-aquatic animals as a convergent evolutionary adaptation. In general, the parameters in the weight-bearing motions often will determine what succeeds in a structural design.

The first four PyM postures in the ***Etrahnai*** series are resting stretches you can do to emulate some of the first four-limbed body plans of ancient amphibian tinkering. They are primordial descendants you'll also be familiar with**.** The postures are designed to give you a sense of body structure; and with added imagination, they can inform how physiology has influenced what their descendants do today, go ashore to rest from the fluidity. Remember that moving from a liquid environment onto hard substrates with gravitational pull required much for a species to adapt; even now they are some of the slowest species on earth.

In the aquatic series, a primordial cephalopod was mentioned, the nautilus. Our first posture in ***Etrahnai*** is another ancient shelled creature of the sea. Sea turtles spend little time on land and look rather awkward moving on land. But they have proven themselves resilient having survived a few extinction events. Turtles predominantly swim with forelimb flipper thrusts in a homologous flapping motion to *"fly"* in the seawater.

Sea Turtle

Hard-shelled sea turtles appeared on land at least 120 million years ago. There are 7 remaining seagoing species that today travel the oceans. Six are now threatened with extinction due to human impacts both in the sea and on land. Today sea turtles can suffer from "floater syndrome" when their buoyancy becomes uncontrollable from ingested plastics that trap air and gas internally. Without the ability to release enough air to dive down for foraging food, the sea turtle starve. Other drivers of extinction include loss of nesting habitats on empty beaches and wide net fishing practices.

Try It: Lay face downward on a cushioned surface. Bend knees in and tuck legs in along your sides, widen the knees slightly outside the armpits and keep the lower legs and elbows close in - wrapped alongside outer hips to form the outer edge of a carapace (turtle shell). Relax by rolling a pillow under the abdominals to round over and lift the waist and back, lower down the chest and sternum by folding forward face down. If available to you, place your forehead down or on another pillow to breathe without pressure on the nose bridge. Your back and folded arms should round to form a broad turtle shell with the support of the pillow beneath you, retreat inwardly. Angle feet back out slightly, as a sea turtle back flippers angle outward. With arms bent, form wrists and hands as the fore flippers by fanning hands just outside the carapace edge of knees and calves. Ease and relax down, as a turtle in quiet repose. This restful flexed posture is best on a bed, mat or other soft surface. Emulation in *Sea Turtle* form is an effective method to calm nerves quickly. Blood, synovial and other fluid flows are slightly constricted at key points in the posture and result in a gentle compression at the hips, knees, and elbows. When compressed, nerves suspend much of their firing. Relax your neck in a comfortable, supported position. This is especially calming in the nerve passages through the neck and may induce a sleepy, soothing state. Another resting posture for you to try is *Resting Frog* below.

Taoist texts tell the story of how turtles mastered longevity: A family escaped to the mountains during a time of war and were forced to hide in a cave. A sudden landslide blocked the cave entrance and no amount of digging could liberate them. As the food supply dwindled, they noticed a turtle in the cave they had previously assumed was a rock. They observed that the turtle remained in its shell and rarely moved, emerging only to take a few sips of water. Imitating the turtle's closed posture and moving very little, the family survived for weeks conserving their energy until the entrance blockage was removed and they were freed.

Resting Frog

Frogs have spread worldwide as a genus group with numerous amphibious species. They are masters of camouflage with many exotic defenses. Most species will hibernate in low temperatures or drought for long periods if the need arises. They were among the first four-limbed vertebrates to establish life on land, appearing 265 million years ago. Today frog numbers have diminished with many becoming extinct. Destruction of habitats and migratory routes, pollution (their permeable skins make them especially sensitive and susceptible) and diseases have all taken a toll.

Try It: This posture has a little more stretch than *Turtle*, just as frogs are more flexible than turtles. Again, a soft surface is best as this is also a folding posture. Begin lying supine and gently bend legs to your chest, opening the knees out as wide as is comfortable to stretch, keeping calves tucked in with your thighs. Ease your legs down flat, knees wide. Resting frogs have their feet forward - so with heels tucked in below hips, rotate your feet out at the ankle and place them in a forward position (this may take some repetitive practice to relax connective tissues in the ankles and feet). If you have the flexibility, flex and spread your toes apart with the big toe pointing forward and down to maximize the stretch in the inner side of the ankles. It may become easier with practice. Ankle ligaments and tendons stabilize and ground us in balance and movement; be gentle and ease them into stretching incrementally over time. Frogs have beautiful rotational bone structures in their hips, knees and ankles. Tuck a pillow under ribs and fold bending down, with elbows at the top of knees and forearms facing forward, fingers spread like a frog. Reposition a pillow beneath to support your brow and have space to breathe, relax in the stretch. Ribbit!

Golden Toad - Extinct in 1989, South America

In the stationary postures above, the legs rotate from the hip sockets, compress the knees in lateral rotation and stretch the ligaments in the legs. This is how joints are positioned on four-limbed tetrapods. The evolution of limbed movement in tetrapod joints on land is very much peripheral-based with outward rotating femoral heads. As you can see in the Golden Toad photo above, its limb appendages are positioned laterally at the sides of their bodies. The first bony vertebrates on earth had limbs joined at the spine with outward rotating joints which later differed greatly from the evolution of quadrupeds and bipeds. Revisiting the outwardly rotated lateral limb posture is beneficial - it invigorates cells, flushing joints with fresh synovial and other connective tissue fluids by compress and release stretch which helps to maintain joint flexibility – ultimately to protect against joint injury.

Anguilla/Eel

The reproductive life cycle of eels is as astonishing as the lifecycle of butterflies and frogs. It is a metamorphic process which begins in a larval stage deep in the ocean that develops tiny transparent elvers. The glass elvers migrate into estuaries and streams, where they slowly develop skin pigmentation. They then spend adulthood in freshwater creeks and rivers. Afterwards eels go through yet another physical change to return to spawn in the ocean depths. Wild eels are now also "threatened" due to fishing and farming techniques which have polluted and blocked access to historical habitats.

The following eel posture both contracts and opens vertebral discs laterally in the spine. Don't worry - spinal columns are built to move that way. It improves flexibility also in the fascia and lateral support spinal muscles. Keeping strength and flexibility in our well-articulated vertebrae is essential to maintain core structural health. A*nguilla* not only invigorates the spine but helps flush the cerebral-spinal fluid which feeds the brain.

Try It: Begin on the floor supine and propped up on elbows in a Sphinx position. Bend your left knee out to the side and perpendicular to the core or raised higher, press the pelvis as flat as possible; before you lay down, thread the left arm across your chest beneath you and parallel to the clavicle (across the upper chest). Place your arm straight to its full length crossed under the chest and out over to the right, palm facing down, gently lower your weight down. Relax to stretch the right shoulder and arm joint and the opened pelvis and rotation in the right femur socket, be sure to keep both hips down flat. This is a resting stretch. The simultaneous action of pressing the arm down and rotating the same-side leg outward pins the left side equilaterally down into a convex lateral bow, to open and extend the right-side vertebrae while adding lateral compression to the left. You may need to gently encourage flattening downward by using your other arm to brace against the right side from rising up. Rest your head down to the side, relax and ease into this weight induced stretch. You should feel the pull on the connective tissues of the shoulder and an opening along spinal vertebrae laterally on the right down to the lumbar. In effect, it causes a lateral "C" curve in the spinal column and further down into a kind of "S" curve by lengthening the right leg and pressing the hip down. Relax and enjoy. Release slowly, then move back to sphinx and reposition to begin again opening on the other side. While resting two minutes or more in the posture, think of the vast distances that eels cover in migrating from the depths of some of the deepest trenches in the ocean to the rivers and streams on land and then back again to complete the lifecycle.

The next exercise explores the lateral spinal curve inherent in a fish body. I like to visualize a flounder with both eyes atop a flattened head.

Flapping Fish

Try It: A cushioned floor or other soft surface will help in this posture. Lie facedown; turn your head to the left. Slowly bend your left knee out to the side as high as possible while remaining flat on the ground. Leave your other leg straight in line with the spine to maximize an open pelvis in the posture. Bend your left elbow and try to touch the top edge of your bent left knee. Your left hand continues the curve of a fish from your shinbone-to-elbow to your head with the touch of your chin or forehead. Touch sensation will help you visualize the outer left-side curve of a flat fish. Be sure to gently flatten your hips down. This will open the right side of ribs in a little concave curving in the left spine just like the rounded shape of a fish on its side. Keep the right arm in close to the right side of your body to follow the fish curve down to the end of the extended leg. Now that you have taken the form of a fish in the shaped outline, experiment with the "flapping" the fish.

Try It: Hold the posture and micro-move short lifts in the fishtail (extended leg) with upward pulses. Keeping the fish outline intact, flap as a fish does, by lift both the upper body and head and the legs simultaneously. Feel your fish head (as outlined by your bent arm, head and neck) and tail flap like a fish out of water. Release from the posture and repeat changing sides. ***Flapping Fish*** will challenge more than you may think in this exercise.

The Rise of Reptiles

The swamp fern and cycad forests of the late Devonian era along the coastal semi-terrestrial regions were some of the earliest terrestrial flora that the amphibious tetrapods inherited on land. The new world had experienced a relatively rapid oxygenation of the atmosphere and plants grew in crowded clusters while giant insects crawled, slithered, marched, hopped and flew about. For the first time in earth history, the world was alive with sounds of whizzing, buzzing, crunching and skittering of insects; and close on their heels, the rustling, munching of tetrapods. Atmospheric oxygen levels continued to rise during the Carboniferous, the period 360 to nearly 300 million years ago, reaching a mind-boggling level at 35% level in atmospheric oxygen. Compare that to nearly 21% level today! As a result, insects grew to gigantic proportions -- debris crunching millipedes grew over six feet long and dragonflies flew on wingspans nearly three feet across. The high oxygenation likely also assisted adaptations in amphibian evolution towards lung development and larynxes to supply the oxygen needed to support longer periods out of the water. Tetrapod blood chemistry changed in their organs to utilize the available oxygen and conferred much needed energy for terrestrial locomotion. Yet even with the increased efficiency in movements and the extended excursion periods out of water – it took time for tetrapods to transition from their amphibious lifestyle. Then, as today, amphibian species must return to water to reproduce or they would not be what they are today, amphibians.

The evolution of amniotic (egg-laying) reproduction likely provided the decisive push for tetrapod species to shift to a life on land and evolve reptilian species. At the start of the Carboniferous Era, 360 million years ago, tetrapods favouring retreating onto land to reproduce may have led the branching into new species. The amniotic tetrapods formed a new class of creatures land-based and reproductively specific as land-based and distinctly, reptilian. As the landscape changed, more and more ecological niches harboured possibilities for the new flora and fauna on land, including herbivores and carnivores. Survival odds increased dramatically for both offspring and adults with the ability to release and hide eggs, nourished in the self-contained amniotic fluid. Reproduction of offspring could grow much like a seed outside the mother in a nutrient-rich fluid encased in a hardened carbonate shell and ushered in a long reign of successful reptilian species.

Tetrapods - whether serpent or snake, amphibian or reptile, with few exceptions, all the species moved primarily in lateral motions, either belly-dragging or high-stepping. They moved slowly through the dense vegetation, often in wide variables of terrain - swamps, mudflats, estuaries, sandy beaches and jungle.

A primordial posture to stimulate lateral stretching in limbs follows in ***Crocodile Sprawl*** which not only works on connective tissues but refreshes the movement of fluids in the pelvis and femoral joints through rotation.

Crocodile Sprawl

Crocodiles are an ancient reptilian species, appearing over 250 million years ago. Crocodile strength and cold-blooded aggression have placed them as one of nature's top predators. They are fierce carnivores with fearsome jaws and a powerful bite force. Their ambush speed is formidable, historically, some species ran on two legs, and today, crocodiles have been clocked at 11 mph. In water, they tuck in their hind legs and feet and swim swiftly with the lateral force of their tails. They can survive long periods without food, an attribute of a slow metabolism crucial to a wait-and-lunge ambush strategy.

Enhance this moving posture as a transition out of *Turtle* or *Resting Frog*. With a pillow rolled beneath your stomach, open knees as wide as you can manage, then lower your legs down with heels in together and feet out to the sides. This will rotate legs outward at the hip socket. Or try the following:

Try It: Come to your elbows and knees facing down. It's nice to place a pillow just below the ribs to lean down into. Open knees out and gently slide them downwards. Lean forward to inch down in increments, the upward shift will push you forward so make sure you have enough room ahead for a slow descend down. With knees opening out and femurs rotating outwardly from the hip sockets, lower down to lie atop the pillow. Keep angling the knees, feet and thighs rotated out and continue to slowly straighten knees into a laterally oriented upside down "V" shape. As the legs come down flat, press into the hips to assist in widening the pelvis. Keep knees and feet angled outward, pressing on the inside of the feet. In this posture, slowly inch your legs back together, heels together, feet out, to continue stretching inner ankles. If you have a pillow beneath you, leave it under your belly for the extra lift in the inner legs and relax to round down in low back and sacrum. This nerve-calming aspect of compressing joints and fascia (connective tissue) laterally in hips, knees, and ankles will help to flush and invigorate the joints to compress and stretch connective tissues in the slow controlled downward lengthening of the legs.

As you slowly draw your legs together, bring heels as closely together as the outward hip rotation permits. The traditional yoga Crocodile pose, *Makarasana*, adds in lifting up on your elbows to bring curvature to the low spine (as in Sphinx). Try also if you like but remember: keep abdominals in, hips and belly grounded and shoulder blades together and down, neck elongated. *Crocodile* outwardly rotating legs from the hip sockets revisits how primordial limbs in tetrapods were formed, and will refresh those rarely used postures. See *Salamander* below – for movement in early tetrapods.

Imitating the early amphibian in resting *Crocodile* appropriately has our bellies on the ground with limbs laterally rotated. Characteristic of all amphibians and reptiles, the shoulder and pelvic girdled structures of tetrapods support a horizontally oriented spine for side-to-side lateral locomotion. Early tetrapods, as well as nearly all extant (those existing today) amphibians (i.e. chameleons, salamanders, frogs and turtles), have humerus and femur thigh bones in almost horizontal joint sockets. As a result, tetrapod spines are on the same plane where their girdled limbs attach and rotate. By practicing this outwardly rotational posture - the joints of the hips, knees and feet can be flushed and ready as relaxed; but if you were predatory - a crocodile waits to ambush. Crocodiles rest, hunt and wait on their bellies; but when the opportunity to strike arises, only a brief rustling in the grass or bush will indicate an attack. (Bennett, A.F., 1994)

The above initial resting positions gently work on circulation and joint health in ligaments and tendons. Initially, you may feel tight in the postures because of age or strengthening workouts which typically result in shortened connective tissues. Until you attain more open flexibility, adding pillows will increase comfort.

Homologous Movement

The first fish vertebrates on land moved in a predominantly homologous fashion to pull their bellies on shore. Their finned appendages evolved into more efficient limbs in a reach, pull and push forward locomotion. This homologous motion required coordination of fore appendages pulling upward together with rear appendages. We see this action still in amphibious frogs. They spring forward on hind limbs while simultaneously reaching out ahead with both forelimbs then pulling back in together to repeat the homologous action. The limbs-together motion is seen in mammals such as rabbits hop forward in a homologous reach and jump motion and sea life, in turtles and penguins who swim by simultaneously flapping forelimbs with hind limbs acting as rudders. Locomotive techniques has more variety and variability in animal swimming, crawling and jumping movements, ranging from hops to a scrambled ambling in which each limb works independently. The homologous pull and push up movements indicative of primordial creatures were transitional as it is quite inefficient and slow as a locomotive method on land.

From the above ***Crocodile*** resting posture, explore homologous motions (limbs pull/push together) using small micro movements of your shoulders. It is a movement easily observed in lizards - if you've ever watched lizards sunning themselves on rocks; you've likely seen them move in ***Lizard***

Pump below. This movement is good for maintaining flexibility in the low back and helps to prevent age-related rounding in flexion.

Lizard Pump

Try It: Lying face down from *Crocodile* in a sphinx posture, upper body lifted up onto both elbows beneath the shoulders, keep your neck long, shoulder blades down and chest open and supported. Your low back will curve upward in extension; try to release any tension in the sacral and lumbar muscles of the back. This up-down pumping action occurs only in the shoulder girdle. Push into the elbows and move your shoulder blades down along the centerline of your back to lift across the shoulder girdle. Then relax back down in a slight shrug of the upper thoracic spine (between shoulder blades), repeat in a rhythmic up-and-down motion – opening shoulder blades apart, rounding, and then bringing them together as you lift. The motion occurs where muscles and ligaments connect at the crossbeam of the clavicle and the shoulders join at the arm sockets. The action alternately widens and contracts the upper chest and the connective ligaments at the base of the scapula. The small amount of movement available allows you to push down the shoulders down to open the chest gently compressing the vertebrae of the low back in pulses. A short but sweet action, *Lizard Pump* increases circulation in the connective tissues deep within the shoulder girdle itself. Be sure to always release any tension in the curved low back when pressing shoulder blades downward. Practice of this exercise can work to counteract poor posture to correct long hours sitting at a desk. As you pump, gently squeeze your lower ribs together and gently contract the lower abdominals, belly relaxed. If you find your legs moving from the *Crocodile* position into a more comfortable straightened position, allow for it. Focus on the upper body and shoulders lift and release – as a lizard. I suggest 108 lifts, at least.

Optional is to follow **Lizard Pump** is to shoulder stalk like a cat. The rotational lift and drop in the shoulder motion ensures that each shoulder blade reaches its lowest point down the back. It also lubricates the lumbar cartilage side to side.

Add an Arm Stretch: After the *Lizard Pump* repetitions, from Sphinx position stretch elbows forward overhead until you come down flat. Elbows bent, forearms are bent and folded back behind you. Increase the triceps stretch by turning your head first to the right bringing the left hand down the centerline along the back. Place your right hand atop the left and gently push down to stretch the underside of the upper arm. Hold and repeat for a left arm stretch.

***

Homologous movement involves spinal extension as the chest pushes upward to initiate forward movement. Imagine you are a fish wallowing in a shallow pool, movement is initiated when "fins" grip and thrust upwards to lift body weight. But then, as an emergent fish on land, how do you coordinate hind-to-fore limbs together? Is it more energy efficient than wiggle dragging? This homologous coordination of the limbs affects a basic aspect in vertebrates to modify body plans into cross-sectional girdling at shoulders and the pelvis. The spine flexes to bring hindlimbs forward – pulling in and up, the chest extends to bring forelimbs in position to push up again. Homologous land motions also parallel the very first movements infants make in their first movements. The newborn infant first lifts her head, and then braces on upper limbs to discover forward motion with a head lift and push. Soon after, the infant can coordinate the motion with hind limbs. The first homologous motions directly connect us to the early heritage of movement evolution on land.

Frog Squats

Frog Squats will generate warmth in the body quickly to build strength in the hips, lower legs and thighs. It also tones muscles in ankles and feet. The squats are especially fun at the water's edge or by an embankment, where frogs like to swim and reproduce, and locations apropos to PyM enhances our ability to imagine and emulate other species.

Try It: Keeping the back straight, simply turn feet and knees outward as you slowly bend down and up to raise and lower hips in squats, up and down. Imagine yourself as a springy frog. If you place palms on the floor just inside legs on each descent keep your back upright. You can also modify thesquats by using a chair back, ledge, wall or other support. If your knees are weak, modify by shortening the bend in your knees to where it is still comfortable or, by lifting up onto the balls of your feet - practice raising and lowering heels while leaning over a chair. Up down motions will also strengthen the muscles in the arch of your feet and work the Achilles tendons and lower legs. Energetically, spring up like a frog and land on both feet as you come down. Repeat only as long as it is a reasonable challenge. *Frog* Squats are much easier on ligaments, joints and tendons when performed in deeper water or in shallower, use a pool step for additional balance support if needed for stability.

The ancient predecessor of frogs and toads appeared in the Devonian, 370 million years ago. *Icthyostega* discovered in Greenland is the earliest Fossil remains known of four-legged "fish" amphibians. The lissamphibian species (frogs, toads, newts, salamanders) pioneered the prototypes for complex shoulder and pelvic girdling around 265 to 295 million years ago. The formative years in limb evolution also brought about the development of a central nervous system in quadrupedal coordination with a protected nerve system centered within a bony vertebral column and hardened skull. We can credit the evolution of these sensitive creatures their amazing structural and neural complexities that grace us also.

With very few exceptions, amphibians are deliberately slow and few extant species are known to be pursuit predators, such as bullfrogs. Amphibian speeds often reside in a lightning speed tongue to catch insects; and from accumulating energy for a mounted spring contraction of ankle extensors which, in frogs, initiates their fast-moving leaps (Roberts and Marsh, 2003). Evolving in a gentler time of easily available energy (high oxygen levels), amphibian species are sensitive, delicate creatures now under constant threat of extinction in their historical habitats. Around the world, many frog species, chameleons and salamander species have historically migrated at certain times of the year when seasonal rains make way for them. Corporations, city planners and communities could do more to avert the destructive impact urban development has on amphibians. Concrete infrastructure in cities and towns can be sensitively designed. If we do not value an amphibian right to pass, move and migrate around buildings, under roads and away from sewers and storm drain systems by providing pathway diversions in the form of curbless ramps and tunnels – then their ability to migrate and survive will continue to be compromised. They will join the countless species impoverished by insensitive habitats and hominin lifestyles designed for one species only to ensure their permanent disappearance from our communities.

After all, you are the melody of the Universe, and the harmony is the song of the other creatures.-Jamie Sams & David Carson

Blue Whale

Blue whales are the largest animals on the earth; some males can be over 100 feet in length. Once found abundantly in every ocean, blue whales were nearly hunted to extinction due to high-power boats and explosive-tipped harpoons. These gentle baleen giants have fringed plates instead of teeth to filter a crustacean diet from the ocean. It is not surprising given their size that, blue whales have the loudest and lowest frequency vocalizations made by any animal on earth. They have had protected status in international waters since 1967.

Try It: This will both strengthen the vertebral backbone and improve tone and flexibility of the supporting lateral tissues and muscles of the spine. Lie face down with arms at your sides and engage abdominals. Lift with muscles from the hip bones up to and including the lower ribs suspended off the floor. Broaden your clavicle, press arms in and roll your shoulder blades back in the chest lift with shoulders and arms tucked in (elbows level with hips). Continue to lengthen the back and neck in the upward lift. The more you extend contracting lower back muscles with lift, the more the chest opens. Remember to keep the belly of a whale in firmly. With the upper body lifted slightly raise one leg fluke, then the other. Also try rotating feet turned out to form tail flukes, then pressing both legs up together move your "tail" up and down slowly as a whale's horizontal flat tail.

Homologous Asanas (traditional yoga)

The yoga asana tradition from the East is full of animal morphological names that emulate primordial forms and movements. The ones I have listed below fit within the "homologous" category of extension and flexion. They are here for you to try, some of which bear the names of other species. Their animal names help to visualize their shapes and motion.

Locust (Salabasana), Fish (Matsyasana) Boat Pose (Paripurna Navasana), Garland Pose (Malasana), Plough (Halasana), Supine Cobbler (Supta Baddhakonasana), Camel (Ustrasana), Tortoise (Koormasana), Bridge (Setu Bandhasana), and last but not least is one of my favorites, *Crow (Kakasana).* And those found in Sun Salutations: *Swan Dive, Forward fold (Uttanasana), Down Dog (Adho Mukha Svanasana), Up Dog (Urdha Mukha Savanasana), Chataranga, Chair or Fierce Pose (Utkatasana).*

Homolateral Movement

It had to happen... in animals dragging their long bodies ashore, wiggling and hopping; there came a time when the amphibians adopted lateral movements for increased efficiency. It was a likely easy departure from homologous movement given the central vertebral design and past lateral swim motions of fish ancestors. Once shoulder and pelvic girdles evolved sufficient weight support, homolateral movements effectively became the signature gait of all four-limbed tetrapods on land. Spinal columns stabilized locomotion with femurs angled laterally in the hip socketed joints in keeping the characteristic low, slow sprawling body plans. Their humerus was also positioned parallel to the ground and the tibia and fibula angled inwardly at the posterior. While many amphibians, such as newts and salamanders, still drag their bellies, many terrestrial species transitioned to evolve a more raised posture. As reptilian speciation spread on land, many had thicker, more robust girdling structures for bearing more weight and adding lift when needed in a run. Femurs then were angled more forward beneath the pelvis to position and bear more weight, adding push strength in hind limbs with more range of motion.

The amphibian to a reptilian transition as fully independent of aquatic environments also resulted in limbs with better rotational ability and wider, limb-independent movements. Some species evolved more vertebral and cervical length, quickened reflexes and robust musculature and even bony armour. While many amphibious species evolved to breathe through their skin, typically they also have elementary lung apparatus for respiration. The early terrestrial tetrapods evolved primitive lung sacs to utilize available oxygen with lung compression assistance from their lateral swim movements. The motion conferred respiratory advantages with the lateral wiggle movement translating into lung expansion and compression. Amphibians originated the sprawling gait over 360 million years ago. Today extant amphibians, reptiles and monotremes (primitive egg-laying mammals) engage in a sprawling sway of homolateral walking. It is a common gait also seen in many invertebrate insects, even those with numerous legs. The gait is grounded in the associative development of primordial limbs and lungs in tetrapods and is derivative in all other four-limbed walking gaits.

Exercises in this series emphasize lateral limb movements with bellies grounded.

Salamander Sprawl

Amphibians were the prevailing land vertebrates on the earth for nearly 70 million years. During the Permian period, salamanders branched away from the amphibian order to form a distinct family of amphibians. Red salamanders retain many of the primitive genetic characteristics in their DNA and breathe through the skin. They are often thought of as a type of reptilian lizard, but they are no more related to lizards than they are to mammals.

Red Salamander

The sprawling gait of tetrapods moves the spine laterally, side to side, and rotating the shoulders shifts the spine gently.

Try It: Come into the Sphinx position with the belly and hips grounded, come up on your elbows. Make sure that the shoulder blades are pulled back and downward and abdominals are firm. Legs are together and extended long with the tops of feet flat down. Rotate the shoulders in a rolling motion adjacently to each other pushing one scapula down, followed by the other. It does not matter which direction you roll the shoulders, forward or back. Focus on lifting and widening across the chest as the shoulder blades rotate back and down. The motion will cause sideways movements in the spinal posture and a gentle lateral motion in the low back where the spine is grounded. For more of an amphibian motion, add a simultaneous lift of the hip on the same side pulling upward as the scapula pulls downward in this homolateral gait. For locomotive action in an amphibious sprawling gait, also try the following lateral stretches along the spine below, preferably on a soft surface.

Try It: Lay face down and bring arms close in at the sides, rotate thighs out and spread knees open, feet flexed outward, heels together. Lift the head and upper body but keep the pelvis well grounded. To move forward, lift the upper body up slightly off the ground onto wide elbows bent outward, then reach forward with the right arm. As you pull back with the right arm, bring the right knee out to the side and upward. Bend inward laterally to compress the ribs on the right as elbow-to-knee comes together. As you push the right thigh down and back, begin to reach up with the left elbow forward and raise the left knee as the left arm pulls. The hips will naturally shift over to the right as you open and move the left thigh forward to crunch the left side laterally. Once you get these homolateral motions going, try to widen the range and quicken limb movements, using the quadriceps with elbows bent will keep the motions ideally close to the ground. This is a limb-together lateral swaying motion that moves hips strongly in side to side crunches. The spine curves in lateral motion dramatically. Watch a salamander, newt or chameleon move to better emulate the movements and the homolateral sprawling gait may become more accessible.

Modify this as a passive spinal stretch in the following – only on a soft surface.

Try It: Lie straight face down with legs extended. You will need to lift up momentarily to bring your right knee under the chest to the sternum and, if available to you - outside and below the right armpit on the right side. Flex your right foot slightly under you if necessary to protect from overstretching knee tendons. Lower the chest down and raise the left arm bending at the left elbow and reach it forward just to the left side of your head. Slowly bring the right arm around to settle it down and in next to the bent right hip. The posture opens the left side and laterally compresses on the right. With hips flat, stretch forward with the left arm and lengthen to open ribs. Feel free to bend your left elbow and arrange it above your head. Relax. As the ancient primordial movements are revisited to revitalize the spine, stay awhile to stretch. Repeat on the other side. This will open, compress and flush shoulders, vertebral column and their connective tissues.

Like frogs, salamanders have been greatly declining in their numbers. More than half of the world's salamander species are now listed as threatened (IUCN data). Habitat loss and diminishment of food sources, the use of fertilizers and herbicides, water diversion projects and road construction contribute heavily, as do the more frequent periods of drought from global warming. With salamander populations becoming more and more fragmented into smaller and smaller pockets, there is a loss of genetic variance in many species. Many of the salamander species have only recently been driven to extinction - such as the Yunnan Lake Newt; and many more are close to extinction - such as the Giant Salamanders of Japan and China. It is time to honour them by taking appropriate steps to ensure their survival.

***

Generally we tend to insufficiently challenge the vertebral column laterally, primarily due to the species' favoring forward motions and actions. Yet lateral motions help keep the low back vertebral structure healthy and fit as we age. Stretch, twists and moving side to side can keep the low back vertebrae joints, cartilage and connective tissues more "juiced up" from lateral motions. We also need to maintain the cerebrospinal fluid (CSF) which is encased along the spine, bathed in its own reservoir of fluids. The CSF reservoir is a protected area that transports nutrient fluids to feed the brain what it requires. Into adulthood, the body adds fluids to the cerebral spinal reservoir as we grow. That essentially stops upon completion of childhood growth. On reaching full body growth at around 24 years of age, our bodies' no longer add fluids to the CSF reservoir. From then on; it is only through stretch and movement that the cerebrospinal fluid can be assisted in its flow along the spinal column. Motion is the only lotion for the CSF.

Amphibians with sprawling gaits are typically slower and have a more sluggish metabolism than reptiles. Scientists confirm that homolateral locomotion is more suited for short bursts and is not easily sustained for long durations. (Vogel, S., 2013). As you may have found from experimenting with the sprawling movements above, it is a gait that is mechanically precise but energetically expensive. Amphibian speed and stamina is limited by smaller lung capacity more closely associated with that of fish whose respiration is driven by muscles in the head. Lung respiration in amphibian species is a process of inhaling through mouths, or gills, and exhaling by compressing throat muscles. There is also another reason for the deficit in stamina. Primitive tetrapod lungs have no diaphragmatic muscles to move oxygen so diffusion into the bloodstream is comparatively slower than in other species such as birds and mammals.

Under optimal conditions evolution has tended towards more efficiency rather than less in species. When tetrapods evolved movement-assisted respiration, it was a step in successive anatomic adaptation to diaphragmatic respiration. Evolving on land, tetrapod breathing shifted from contraction in the throat (from earlier gill respiration) to the contract/expansion muscle action of the torso. (Cieri et al., 2020) Reptilian species with movement-assisted respiration walked freely with bellies lifted off the ground and had characteristically longer, stronger ribcages to protect the lungs and the tissues that worked them with each lateral step taken. Their rib movements alternating compression and expansion from lateral convex/concave motions which helped to force air into and out of the lungs.

Lumbering Lizards

During the late Carboniferous Era, 315 million years ago, reptile species began to emerge as the major land vertebrate on the earth. Paleontological records indicate that the dinosaurs appeared during the Permian period, around 250 million years ago. Dinosaur and crocodile species ramified many new species and spanning nearly 200 million years. They often out-competed one another in attaining tremendous sizes and ferocity, speed and defensive and offensive characteristics. To attain prominence in the competitive need for speed, a species with greater clearance off the ground could claim distinct advantages. While sprawling locomotion might have sufficed for herbivores, many meat-eating and predatory reptiles relied on ambush strategy and speed. The evolutionary adaptations vying for stealth and higher speeds largely relied on fitness but gained ground with improved visibility and minimizing tangling encumbrances in the dense undergrowth also played a role.

As often occurs with a size increase in limbs, reptile limb length improved undergrowth clearance and visibility leading to the "high walk" of dinosaurs. The raised body plans resulted in changes to the patella (knee) and ankle joints, and the femur angle in shoulder and pelvic girdling. Today, the reptiles that have a "high walk" carriage are monitor lizards and the Komodo dragons of the Galapagos Islands. Adding lift in the gait with raised frontal postures meant firmer containment of organs and a stronger abdominal wall and extension in the ribcage. The evolutionary progression towards more limb ground clearance also increased demand on the lungs and brought further modifications in thoracic and subsidiary muscles leading to diaphragmatic respiration.

Komodo Dragon

Komodo dragons are the largest lizards in the world. An adult Komodo dragon can weigh around 150 lb. (70 kg) averaging eight feet in length, although males can grow to more than ten feet. They detect their food the primordial way, with tongues to taste sense the air. Like crocodile cousins, they are ambush carnivores and consume carrion whole. Their numbers have greatly diminished in recent years, and Komodo dragons are listed as a vulnerable species. Juveniles take 3 to 5 years to mature and presently, there are fewerl than 350 breeding females in existence today. Adult dragons live up to 50 years.

There are many ways to move homolateral, facing up or down, in water or on a roller – Do it often!

Try It: Crouching and moving in homolateral movements will require a little strength to move from an elevated position with elbows and hips outwardly rotated. Begin on hands and knees or on the balls of feet with knees deeply bent near the ground. Start to move to a lateral sway of a dragon by moving to one side laterally as you bend around towards the hip to look behind, one side then the other. Reach forward with the right hand and as you pull back, bring the right foot or knee forward. Then reach out with the left hand, then, bend to the left as the left foot or knee moves forward. Repeat bending side to side curving in laterally and stretching open on the opposite in a dinosaur high walk. Experiment with it on knees opened and lower the midline of the body to a more horizontal level with bent elbows also outward. Repeat the lateral back and forth swaying in the gait. You'll get a sense of how the low lateral sprawl of tetrapods evolved into a homolateral high-walk of dinosaurs. The gait strengthens biceps and works hips, ankles and feet. Have fun as a Komodo dragon, stop to twist deeply around with a sideways leer and try to "taste" with the tongue. Try a standing **Komodo Dragon** - think of a string marionette prancing, limbs and joints open laterally, moving simultaneously in a kind of loose side-to-side trot. With music, it can be a workout.

A toast to tetrapods for the success of a four-limb structure!

Homolateral Asanas (traditional yoga)

Homolateral movement stretches one side and contracts the other along the spine, hip and shoulder. Surprisingly, only a small share of asana postures can be considered directly homolateral. They are as follows:
Standing Side Stretch (*Ardha Channdrasana I*), Tree (*Vrksasana*), Triangle (*Trikonasana*) and Revolved Triangle (*Parivrrta Trikonasana*), Side Angle (*Parshvakonasana*), and to a lesser extent – Warrior II (*Virabhadrasana* II) and Half Moon Pose (*Ardha Chandrasana*).

Bipedalism and Birds

The greening of the land may well have enticed animals to venture inland into interior ecosystems 275 to 250 million years ago during an eco-evolutionary lush period on earth. It was a time of drama and growth as the ground beneath was in constant rumble and tumble from the tectonic plate movements and volcanic eruptions. Fast forward another 50 million years and reptiles were well established and formed many new groups on land and in the seas. It was a time when the first conifer tree species began to appear alongside abundant cycads, ginkgos and fern; and dense jungles filled the landscapes. Reptilian amniotic species had proliferated, adapting as the world around them evolved with some species quickly increasing to immense sizes, taller in height and with greater density in number. During the Permian Era, some lizard reptiles had modified spines like sails on their backs roaming the Pangean continent; some grew more than 14 feet in length. The heavy-boned sails on their backs are thought to have gained the reptile exposure to soak up the sun's warmth under the dense canopy. Reptilian senses modified, such as smell and vision and improved competitive advantage for some foraging species. For predators and prey alike, leg adaptations enabled greater speed through the forest undergrowth. Some species evolved more upright with sagittal limbs in which the hind legs were positioned beneath their bodies, such as in the *Inostrancevia*, a very impressive reptile predator with 6-inch teeth. But it was still early in the era of reptiles, and not yet the advent of the dinosaur age, before birds and even the high-walking crocodiles. The Permian era was a short-lived flourishing; it came to an abrupt end with a massive extinction event, 252 million years ago.

The extinction period lasted a rather short 600,000 years but effectively destroyed an estimated 90% of life in the oceans and 70% of terrestrial life on land and that is why it is often referred to as "The Great Dying" among scientists. The mass extinction was caused by enormous amounts of heat and ozone-depleting carbon dioxide from colossal volcanic eruptions in a vast, continent-splitting area two million square miles centered in Siberia. (P. Brannen, 2019). The catastrophe poisoned the entire biosphere and depleted atmospheric and oceanic oxygen severely; the seas acidified and suffocated life, the land was scorched and smothered in ash and toxic gasses. The Permian extinction almost annihilated all plant and insect life and it took over ten million years to regain the conditions for restoring vibrant life on the planet.

And then, twenty million years after the Great Dying, something beautiful happened. It started raining. And it rained, and it rained. And it kept raining.
~ Peter Brannen, T*he Ends of the World*

The few plucky species that survived radiated into many new species groups, including the dinosaurs and mammals of the Mesozoic Era. One of these, the *Archosauria* group (the "ruling reptiles") of ancestral dinosaurs split into two major clades, one of which was *Ornithosuchia*, the dinosaur lineage to the bird-like species such as the unique pterosaurs, *marasuchas*, *icarosaurus*, and *scleromochlus*. Evolutionary changes in the mesotarsal ankle of dinosaurs permitted an upright stance in these bipedal ancestors of birds. With gaits more parasagittal positioned beneath the body, their stride lengths evolved much faster running gaits. These first bipedal dinosaurs appeared with hind limbs that moved parallel to the vertebral column directly under the core; they had strong ankles and the ability to run distances more vertically upright. The new bipedal body plan ramified into many dinosaur lineages and species that proliferated through the Jurassic and Cretaceous eras spanning 150 million years.

The other major clade of archosaur ancestors was the fierce "high-walking crocodiles" of the Triassic who also had bipedal capability, if only temporary by raising up their 3-meter bodies in short sprint bursts, typically to attack.

An upright bipedal carriage in dinosaurs meant that forelimbs were free to move and evolve quite distinctly from the hindlimbs. Unfettered, forelimbs included modifications to slash, grasp and hold prey, gather and handle food, and evolve wings for flight. In other bipedal species, the non-locomotive forelimbs evolved exclusively for swimming, digging, feeding and combat. The first avian reptiles capable of aerial locomotion were pterosaurs. Their tough, featherless skin stretched like canvas across long, relatively thin bones of wings that spanned upwards of 30 feet across. Yet their locomotion across the ground resulted in an awkward sprawling gait as their anatomy and large claws were more inclined for climbing and clinging to trees.

By the close of the Jurassic Era 145 - 150 million years ago, the earliest known bird fossils date from 150 million years ago with the Archaeopteryx. They had the lightweight feathered wings of modern-day birds. Feathers on dinosaurs initially had appeared much earlier, in the Triassic. And there is much evidence from recent discoveries that support that feathers evolved for insulation from the elements and not initially, for flight. The downy feathers kept many dinosaur species warmer and were later co-opted to enhance flight. As dinosaur forelimbs evolved their locomotive wing and, later, flipper designs – forelimb functions were further relegated to the hindlimbs. Today birds multitask their two hind legs in versatile ways: walking, jumping, hopping, climbing, running, paddling, steering, perching, scratching; and also for grabbing, holding, eating and carrying prey evolved all those functions at different speeds, in different ways in different species.

Birds are the *only* animals besides long-extinct pterosaurs and species of bats to have gained advantage with the surprising leap into the ethereal biosphere: the air. The vast majority of bird bone structures are light in weight, even often hollow, and yet remarkably strong in ways that grounded species can only imagine. Thin hollow bones and virtually weightless cartilaginous feathers are designed to shed water, fine-tune the bird's flight maneuvers, and to insulate and protect. The only real weight often resides in the chitin-hardened beak and, in some species, high impact skull bone.

Birds exceed all other species on the earth in travelling long migratory distances. In stamina, speed and agility, they surpass many other animals in their ability to go distances and in the duration of flight, and also in sprint speeds.

The fastest bird today is the peregrine falcon which has been clocked at 240 mph; and the fastest running bipedal animal on land is the flightless ostrich which has been clocked at 43 mph. Although the fastest bipedal mammal comes close to the ostrich speed - within seconds, the red kangaroo.

The Whimsy of Common Ancestry

The morphology of reptiles and mammals are non-consequential, yet share many similarities of the basics in their skeletal form. Four-limb bird and mammal morphology have the same two bones in the leg and arm anatomy although birds typically walk on their toes rather than the entire foot. However, limbs differ in the number of joints and are substantive in locomotion with bird leg bones jointed to bend back behind the centerline of their bodies, in contrast to the forward-reaching knee joints in mammals. The similar skeletal scaffolding derives from the shared common ancestry of the first land pioneers, the tetrapods. Although you could say, going even further back to fish species as the humerus, radius, ulna and tibia are also found in fossilized lobe-finned fish. Function determines form in evolution. Obviously biological structures are very different between birds, frogs, canines, humans, and whales. All these complex multicellular species primarily use the power of thrust in locomotion, but have evolved very different methods.

Whale tails flatten horizontally and power locomotion in up and down motions while fish tails and fins streamline to the slip of fish in moving laterally. Amphibians and reptiles move in homolateral side to side motions, and birds flap their wings up and down in a forward rotational motion through air, while water birds flap their wings and flippers differently by back sweeping for thrust underwater.

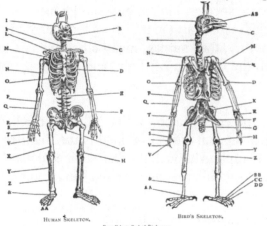

Birds, reptiles and mammals may all share basic structures, but their forms evolved quite differently for a variety of purposes. They have filled niches that have often re-emerged and converged long after having disappeared from extinction events.

As you can see above in the 1555 sketch by Pierre Belon (above) from his study of comparative anatomy, human and bird forms are functionally different. An interesting factoid is that even as the total numbers of bones in a bird's body are less than in mammals and reptiles, birds exceed the others in their neck vertebrae and have a stronger, fused collarbone. The extra vertebra, of course, adds more flexible neck movements with twist and turn for grooming feathers and viewing what's behind. While most two and four-legged animals have parts of the pelvis fused for added stability in running and walking, birds are the only vertebrate animals known to have a fused collarbone in girdling neck, breast and wings.

Penguins appeared during the Jurassic Period, 66 million years ago. Their wings are thought to have evolved independently in a reverse form of convergent evolution in reverting wings to swim from their previous use in flight. Their wings sweep back to "fly" underwater on very strong shoulder plates in up and down strokes. Penguin athletic musculature and their aerobic capacity make them one of the speediest and most maneuverable of the oceanic predators.

Penguin Neck Roll

Emperor Penguin

During their winter breeding period, Emperor Penguins remain upright with very little movement for up to 4 months to incubate the eggs, oversee and nurture their chicks. They huddle together and slowly shuffle positions relative to one another to insure that penguins on the perimeter get a turn within the warmer, protective group center. Penguins are agile underwater and profile efficiently with little drag. Their tuxedo appearance is shaded to camouflage against predation. If seen from below an orca or leopard seal may strain to distinguish a white-belly penguin from ice floes and the reflective surface above. Their dark plumage coats further disguises them when viewed by predators from above.

Well adapted to the extreme conditions of the Antarctic, Emperor penguins endure some of the worst storms and lowest temperatures on earth. They incubate their eggs between their feet and body in some of the most remote reaches on earth, shuffling very little *en masse* to warm and protect offspring together from the harsh weather. The only movement to the four months of being almost stationary is in their manner of neck rolling.

Try It: This motion can be performed just about anywhere, from any posture. So, if you are seated at your desk, in the car, standing, at an angle or even lying down – you can often release tension with this movement. First, lift your chin and angle your head straight back, then slowly turn your head to one side, hold, then continue to lower your chin toward your shoulder, rotating it down until it is centered on your chest. Bring your head slowly back up, and then on the other side – first, your head drops back and turns to the opposite side, hold momentarily, then bring it down towards the shoulder and around to the front, rotating your chin along the clavicle. Repeat -- back, side and down, up; alternating from shoulder to shoulder, stretching all along the periphery of lateral and back muscles in the neck stretch. Feel free to linger in any position along the neck to encourage relaxation where needed and ease the tension. Penguins know how to move what matters most, when they are able to move very little!

A friend of mine says *Penguin Roll* is what she does when she feels dizzy; it seems to help her regain a sense of balance. You may enhance the stretch further by placing a little added pressure with fingers placed on the head to better direct and add stretch while bending downward, to stretch the opposite neck muscles. Remember to drop and relax the opposite shoulder as you do so. Another way to enhance the neck roll movement is to add more twist:

Try It: Either in standing posture or seated, place your hands strategically to help brace against twisting the upper body – one hand back behind on a buttock or chair seat and the other hand at the opposite hip or braced outside the knee to begin. Start turning from the waist to twist around behind you. Hold the twist and begin your **Penguin Neck Roll** moving the head in the opposite direction of the twist. If twisting to the right and braced, roll your head up, around, and down to the left. As you do so, focus on the muscles at the base of the neck and twist a little further to stretch the tissues that run down the upper shoulders. Repeat, twisting to the left and roll - Play with it!. The posture and movement helps to open, relax and stimulate circulation at the base of the shoulders and neck to release tension.

Bird strutting is a distinctive characteristic of bird movement. This is clearly characterized by many birds as seen in the prideful waddle of Peking ducks, geese and swans and or in a deliberate, slow prance of a heron. Strutting about may be part of the show when birds are courting. The strut of course is more pronounced due to their back-bending knee joints and seems to further display the prominent breadth of the bird breast. As mentioned, they have a singular fused collarbone, a shape similar to fusing two ship keels. A bird's wide breast anchors the wings with strong musculature for all shapes of wing positions in flight. In bird evolution, the bipedal lengthening in legs enable them to forage upright, a stance that has also added prow in their breast whether the species had wings for flight or not.

Cormorant Stretch

Cormorants, like penguins, are an ancient species, versatile in their habitats and found in both freshwater and coastal regions. Cormorant species typically fly and swim underwater. Swimming for fish underwater down to depths of 150 feet, their wings are comparatively shorter to other birds. As a result in flight, cormorants expend more energy than aerial birds. However, cormorants do migrate long distances. They often engage in fly-and-glide to conserve energy just above the water surface using ground effect and wave action for sustained lift. Although cormorants are slower swimmers than penguins, their wings are also built lighter to fly, especially when dry.

Try It: Imagine the lift of the cormorant breast as she opens her wings, stretching to dry her plumage. Seated or preferably standing, begin to arch your back opening out slowly in extension, slide your arms down behind the thighs or onto a waist-high bar for support behind you. Tilt the head slightly back and keep the neck comfortably lifted and gently tilted only slightly - to open and lift the sternum, clavicle and throat. If your hands are stabilizing you from behind, stretch the chest forward to hold in an outward angle. Enjoy the stretch, with or without support. If you are sufficiently grounded and stable from the hind quarters, open the arms wide moving them up and down and rotate gently in small micro-movements, one direction and then the other. Keep the scapula down; neck long out to "wing tips". Breathe in and out deeply to open the diaphragm, thyroid, sternum and lungs.

All swimming birds use their wings in a flapping motion that produces a lift-based thrust, much like a propeller. (Clark and Bemis, 1979) Biomechanics researcher Steven Vogel found that underwater bird wing motion in flapping and hind limb paddling -- "both typically rely on a variance in the degree of lengthwise twist while reversing the direction of the strokes. Change of wing angle and rotation in order to direct and generate lift in net-forward thrust by aquatic birds is complex, but he attributes the movement to a far earlier precedent as is "found in the earliest stroke of sweeping cilia." (Vogel, 1994). Evolution efficiency is duplicitous, the aggregate flexibility in the aquatic waveforms affords them the greatest thrusts in speed and maneuvering ability with the least amount of energy expenditure underwater.

California Quail

It's almost a pun to say that birds are light on their feet since birds solely walk on their toes, or the metatarsus. We share a similar structure called the metatarsal, or the 'ball' of the hominin foot. Groundwork in the following *California Quail* posture is to flex and stretch the ankles, the metatarsal muscles in the arch of feet and the Achilles tendons. *Quail* is beneficial for bones, muscles, ligaments and the tendons of the feet, ankles and lower leg. It also can provide a better understanding of other species' foot structure.

Try It: Kneel on your knees and flex the toes of your feet to place your toes curled up beneath your feet on the floor, heels upward. Then, sit back onto your heels, toes curled under to experience a stretch across the metatarsal and the underside arches of your feet. If the muscles and connective tissues in your feet are not stretched regularly, they can shorten over time and this may be as far as you're able to do for them at this time. The first time you do this will likely be uncomfortable; it gets easier with practice. If you find that weight on flexed feet is too much, then ease into it by sitting on a block between legs as a prop to assist in the posture until you can withstand it more comfortably as the muscles in your feet relax, which they will over time. Use blocks higher if your knees cannot bend comfortably atop flexed feet. Begin with one minute in the posture, work up to two and perhaps a little more. This foot/leg stretch begins at the feet but does not end there:

Remember, lengthening keeps connective tissues strong and flexible – but move slowly to allow for accommodation. Finally, bend your body forward over bent knees to stretch the Achilles tendons.

Try It: With feet apart, bend your knees and come down to a squat on the balls of your feet. Lower your knees down low or on the ground, exhale and contract the lumbar spine (low back) and roll shoulders back to open the chest. Further enhance opening the chest by bringing your elbows close together behind your back and thrust your sternum up, keeping your shoulders down. Rest here and breathe into your upper ribs. A supportive block may be used if necessary. This pronounced posture benefits tissues and circulation in the feet, ankles, hip flexors, calves, low back, chest and shoulders. It is fun to play as a bird… Lift and hop forward, move your arms as though chicken wings; feel free to make bird sounds, or race about squatting. Don't be surprised if you topple!

Crane (below) is one of the ten animal movements in the Chinese Shaolin tradition. Historically the movements are referred to as "the Frolics" and practiced to strengthen the body in preparation for the rigors of meditation. The exact historical movements are not known in the original forms as they were passed down physically in training. However they are a part of classical martial arts in the Shaolin lineage.

Crane

This is a principally a balancing and strengthening pose. Imagine the light, graceful form and balance in the movement of cranes. Like many prehistoric shoreline birds, they are frequently seen standing with one leg tucked up beneath their bodies. Honour the grace inherent in these birds in ***Crane.***

Try It: Standing, bend the left knee out to the side and bring the left ankle up atop the right knee, foot flexed. If possible, continue sliding the left ankle up high to the top of the thigh. Stretch up tall on one leg with palms together at the sternum. With a slow exhale, begin to bend over forward, folding at the waist and bring the upper body down with a straight spine, pushing hips back to fold down over both the thighs. Relax your neck and keep the chest open, bring elbows back then straighten the arms and lower them forward and down, fingertips to the ground. Hold the posture with your head slightly raised, hips squatting low. Hold. Then rise up, straighten and repeat on the opposite - with the right knee bent on the upper thigh and fold forward. Try different foot positions on your thigh and proceed only as far as where knees are always comfortable.

How do you create interpretation of the joyful, aerial dances of *Crane* posture and movements?

One reason birds are so numerous today is largely due to the fact that all non-avian quadrupedal dinosaur species were wiped out during the Cretaceous Paleogene extinction 66 million years ago. A large asteroid struck in an area now known as the Yucatan peninsula region in northwest Mexico. The massive impact triggered earthquakes and massive volcanic eruptions all over the planet. Virtually all the dinosaurs were killed off. Some small avian species did survive the blasts, the tremors and the intense heat most probably by retreating deep inside cliffside nesting holes away from the blast impact. (Brannen, P., 2014) The bird lineages that survived have evolved into today's wide variety of avian species around the world. Today they are extensively distributed, numerous and widely variable. As migration became more accessible to humans, many of the flightless species remaining on remote islands were easy to catch by the wandering mariners and other mammalian invaders to effectively extinguish many flightless species. Birds have been on earth 66 million years and exhibit a wide variety of modifications in adapting to the many different environments. Consequently, they are found in virtually every land mass and ecosystem on earth.

Their evolutionary adaptations are inspiring to witness. How perfectly attuned birds of prey are when they hover almost stationary; adjusting angle and inclination with the changing wind shifts. Consider how a predatory bird sees the slightest motion from an astonishing altitude. We may only watch with awe how an osprey, bald eagle, skimmer, pelican, or shearwater can anticipate the fleet dash of a fish beneath the glittering surface with amazing precision to dive headlong for a capture.

At speeds faster than our eyes can track, there is effortless eloquence in the quick and exacting wing movements of hummingbirds. There is evolutionary elegance in an owl's soundless flight; in the bowerbird dance to entice a mate, in the turkey vulture's ability to soar at high altitudes and circle for hours on rising thermals, and in the social ingenuity of magpies. All these and more show a long history of sensory optimization that has evolved in birds.

The next three PyM emulations are included to practice and express the poise of soaring airborne birds.

Swan Dive

Among lake and shore birds, the swan is a proudly fierce and territorial avian species. They will often exhibit aggressive behaviours in defense of an area, a nest or mate. The aggression is exhibited by charging, chasing and biting. And with their wings spread wide in an attack, their otherwise graceful neck arches back, poised to strike. When at ease, however, swans are often seen opening their chest and wings to stretc, whichh has inspired the description of a "swan dive".

Try It: From the standing position, feet slightly apart and arms comfortably at your sides. On an inhale, slowly lift arms out and up as wings open to broadly stretch out over the head. Lift your chin and on an exhale, turn hands outward and arch the back to slowly begin to lower arms straight out and down, keeping them wide. Also keep the arms and chest open and wide at the sternum as you fold over, bending from the hips with a straight back. The chest leads as you fold down; remember to keep the torso and neck long. Exhale fully. Repeat in the reverse – turn palms together inward and on an inhale rise up with a flat back, arms straight opening out wide and back up. Visualize grace in your own *Swan Dive* - from the tips of your fingers to the opening in your sternum and in the arch of your back.

A legend in Norse mythology relates how the water of the sacred Well of Urd is so pure and holy that all things it touches turn white. One day, two swans happened to drink from the well and they and their future descendants thereafter were as white as snow. In eastern cultures, someone who attains a high degree of spirituality may be called "Great Swan" on account of his or her spiritual grace and ability to travel between spiritual worlds.

Soaring Bird

The following emulate the soaring ability in birds, from turkey vultures to swallows.

Try It: Begin standing, step one foot forward as a "standing leg" in this balancing posture. Open the arms out wide level with shoulders and parallel to the ground. Begin by tilting the upper body forward in a flat, stiff posture and simultaneously lift the back "flying" leg straightened in an upward direction aligning it with the upper body. Continue to lower downward, folding forward until your core is perpendicular to the ground. Balancing, soar with the back leg as a long tail of a bird; maintain this core body posture and move to a horizontal plane. Stay poised soaring as a bird on the standing leg, bent at the hips, body parallel to the ground. I like to spread my fingers as the wingtips of turkey vultures and to fine-tune the balancing of arms in lifting them slightly above chest. Fine-tune the 'flying' balance by adjusting alignment. Repeat with the other leg lifting. And feel free to use a wall for wingtip support; just knowing that a wall is there if needed - can be liberating. Play with this as if turning into the wind, dipping for a swoop or as in the following, diving.

Diving Bird Stance

Try It: From a soaring posture above - imagine as a bird preparing to begin a plunging dive for prey. Continuing from the previous posture arms out soaring, the chest broad, the "flying" leg is pointed behind and balanced like a tail. To dive, bring the arms straight in along your sides just as a predatory bird tucks in its wings to streamline for an aerodynamic descent. Arms held in and aligned with the body, elongate the neck and tuck the head in as you drive a slow, deliberate head first plunge leaning downward. Visualizing the plunge, lower both hands to the ground and slowly rise back up to standing. Repeat on the other side.

Try also the following traditional bird asanas which are predominantly balancing and strengthening postures and movements also.

Bird Asanas (Traditional yoga):

Eagle (Garudasana), Crow (Kakaasana) and Rooster (Kukkutasana), Partridge (Kapinjalasana)

Dances that imitate, emulate, honor, celebrate to embody birds can be found in many indigenous tribal traditions. They are often enjoyed as ritualized methods to acknowledge different avian species. You can find many traditional indigenous dances on the web as experiential examples to incorporate in defining your appreciation of birds on earth.

Anthropomorphism

Anthropomorphism is considered a mostly denigrating term for how we ascribe human attributes to describe and value other species. Much like language guides human thinking, comparative analysis of our species to other species is considered inherently biased as it cannot inclusively evaluate an animal's evolutionary and living context, much less individuality beyond the characteristics of a species' sociability. Nowadays most anthropomorphic descriptive references of animals are culturally devoid of the degrees of kinship to hominins, with the possible exception of pets. The animals that we grow up with may carry an intrinsic worth in human societies but any other species, domesticated or otherwise, are mostly viewed as inferior. Descriptive social, cognitive and physical abilities of other non-human species are all too often labeled as dumb and undesirable comparatively to a more intelligent or useful one; worth ascribed only to its use. Our references and discussions are all too often a matter of imposing a value according to a human standard, such as whether (or not) a species possesses consciousness. The main gap exists mainly due to our inability to communicate with other species. This may seem a facile thing to say, but to truly understand other species exchange is necessary.

Languages are uniquely human. That is not to say that other species do not communicate within their own species, they do. But the human ability of communicating is unique in that it allows for pools of gathered information that build specialized aggregates and repositories of information, allowing for selectivity to discuss complex and abstract issues among other humans. With such a linguistic history passing knowledge down through generations, language crafts and is crafted by culturally-based communicative pathways. Our verbal skill is only possible as we are the only primates who have voluntary control of the larynx for vocalizing quite a variety of distinct sounds in speech. (Kenneally, C., 2018) Unlike our ape ancestors, our larynx-enabled speech has resulted in less overt communication by adding layers of dimension and mannerist subtleties in communicating. By refining our linguistic iterations of speech, many substantive portions of body language and referencing along with gestures have been replaced with words. Other mammalian species communicate sounds more overtly, although we cannot know the communicative subtleties that exist in other species, such as whales. Yet our linguistic subtleties can easily be secretive, diplomatic, and deceptive when acculturated. Most other nonhuman species cannot fathom our chatter and witness us only through our actions with a possible result of widening our species-to-species gap. There are perhaps exceptions - those who coo to the birds or speak the special lingo of loving pet owners of course may be considered passably communicative. But in the absence of direct communication with other species there is much room to express our impressions of others.

While it is indeed difficult to appreciably comprehend and evaluate a nonhuman species' significance and its complexity relative to the natural world, the issue of anthropomorphism varies due to a species relative importance in an environment. All birds and mammals can learn, memorize, compare, anticipate, and plan from their observations. Other species have hierarchies, innate instincts, symbiotic and commensal relationships, defensive and offensive mechanisms through which they communicate intentions. Socially, many species exhibit care and empathy, and make choices on whether and whom to cooperate with both in their own groups and cross-species. Even while acknowledging the similarities or mysteries that are inherent across species in behaviours and expressions, there are many characteristics that are shared and similar. Yet even recognizing shared expressions may be considered too "anthropomorphic" for some. I would argue that by not acknowledging these similarities and shared traits, a sense of kinship and self-knowledge is lost at the cost of accuracy. That expense seems a shame for both species when shared connection cannot be reciprocated or expressed, only equivocated by us. Similar emotions are known to exist cross-species and referencing likenesses should not be missed from underestimating their value. How could we not have similarities having evolved simultaneously with others in our short history? Imitating and expressing a characteristic in PyM is first an acknowledgement of another species' merit which carries no intent to belie or belittle other merits they may also have. Emulating with the intention to honour another species experientially is an effort to assimilate with the species - their forms, behaviours, natures, and emotions with motions that make them unique in a shared and largely interwoven past. Charades relay creatively and meaningfully to allow us to witness and experience our connections and reciprocity. If anthropomorphism parses and prohibits expressions meant to shine a light on the evolutionary journey just because all the details cannot be acknowledged, then look more closely! Visualization and expression is a method to transcend limits of the human experience. It allows us to identify with new heights of creativity, vitality, biodiversity and perhaps eventually, attain new heights in the force of our being as a species, those already reached in other species.

References

Bakker, R.T., 1970. *Dinosaur Physiology And The Origin Of Mammals.* Department of Vertebrate Paleontology, Museum of Comparative Zoology, Harvard University, Cambridge, MA.

(Belon du Mans, P.) Arbel, B., 2017. The beginnings of comparative anatomy and Renaissance reflections on the human–animal divide. Renaissance Studies, Vol.31, Iss. 2, 201-222.

Bennett, A.F., 1994. Exercise performance of reptiles. In *Comparative Vertebrate Exercise Physiology: Phyletic Adaptations*. New York: Academic Press. pp. 113–138.

Boisvert, C. The pelvic fin and girdle of *Panderichthys* and the origin of tetrapod locomotion. *Nature* 438, 1145–1147 (2005).

Brannen, P., 2017. *The Ends of the World: Volcanic Apocalypses, Lethal Oceans And Our Quest To Understand Earth's Past Mass Extinctions.* Simon and Schuster.

Carrier, D. R. (1987). The evolution of locomotor stamina in tetrapods: circumventing a mechanical constraint. *Paleobiology*, 13 (3), 326-341.

Cieri, R.L., Hatch, S.T., Capano, J.G. , Brainerd, E.L. (2020) Locomotor rib kinematics in two species of lizards and a new hypothesis for the evolution of aspiration breathing in amniotes. *Scientific Reports* 10, 7739.

Clack, J. A. (2009). The fin to limb transition: new data, interpretations, and hypotheses from paleontology and developmental biology. *Annual Review of Earth and Planetary Sciences*, *37*, 163-179.

Clark, B.D., & Bemis, W. (1979). Kinematics of swimming of penguins at the Detroit Zoo. *Journal of Zoology, 188*(3), 411-428.

English, A. W. (2009). Limb movements and locomotor function in the California sea lion (*Zalophus californianus*). *Journal of Zoology*. 178 (3): 341–364.

Fraser, C. (2009). *Rewilding the world: Dispatches from the conservation revolution.* Macmillan.

Green, D.M., Sessions, S.K., 2019. Amphibian Cytogenetics and Evolution. Academic Press: San Diego, CA.

Habib, M.B. (2022) Dawn of the Din, *Scientific American Magazine*, January 2022, 42-47.

Modesto, S. P., Scott, D. M., & Reisz, R. R. (2009). Arthropod remains in the oral cavities of fossil reptiles support inference of early insectivory. *Biology Letters*, *5*(6), 838-840.

Mizuno, S., Macgregor, H.C., (1974). Chromosomes, DNA sequences, and evolution in salamanders of the genus *Plethodon*. *Chromosoma* 48, 239–296

Molnar, J. L., Diogo, R., Hutchinson, J.R., Pierce, S.E., (2018) *Evolution of Hindlimb Muscle Anatomy Across the Tetrapod Water-to-Land Transition, Including Comparisons With Forelimb Anatomy.* The Anatomical Record, Vol. 303, Iss. 2, p. 218-234

Roberts, T. J., & Marsh, R. L. (2003). Probing the limits to muscle-powered accelerations: lessons from jumping bullfrogs. *Journal of Experimental Biology*, *206*(15), 2567-2580.

Shubin, N. (2008). *Your inner fish: a journey into the 3.5-billion-year history of the human body*. Vintage.

Vogel, S. (1993). *Vital circuits: on pumps, pipes, and the workings of circulatory systems*. Oxford University Press, USA.

Vogel, S., (2013). *Comparative Biomechanics: Life's Physical World,* Princeton University Press.

Vogel, S. (2020). *Life in Moving Fluids: The Physical Biology of Flow-Revised and Expanded Second Edition*. Princeton University Press.

Wellman, C. H., & Gray, J. (2000). The microfossil record of early land plants. *Philosophical Transactions of the Royal Society of London. Series B: Biological Sciences*, *355*(1398), 717-732.

CHAPTER 5

Earth Series

Primordial Yogic Movement does not assume to be an exact chronology on how movement evolved on earth. It attempts to provide a generalized sketch to give us a sense of when animal morphologies and certain locomotive characteristics emerged based on research in paleontology, evolutionary zoology, biology, bryology and earth history and other sciences. An evolutionary progression must be interpretative for it to be also experiential. By choosing which particular organisms and animals in evolutionary chronology are sketched, the broad strokes of PyM impressionism paint an evolutionary history. The progression is science-based but generalized and should be considered a lay person's guide to the evolutionary timeline. Anthropologists, evolutionary biologists and paleontologists are the true detectives of history and employ a cadre of science-based tools, records and evidence from various fields to ascertain how species emerge, adapt, split and ramify into other species. While PyM taps into the research, the factors involving assignment of characteristics, movement, relationships and behaviours in species genetics is frankly mind-boggling. Paleo and evolutionary scientists will admit the scope to comprehend how a species might have led to another requires expertise from the many different research fields - given the compound complexities in cell biology, neurology, genetic and mutative change rates, ecosystems and species to species interactive shifts, geo-effects of historical climate swings, and more; even then the evidence gathered will be incomplete. Biodiversity and ecology will always have untold mysteries embedded in framing of evolutionary chronology with sections showing only that a particular characteristic has disappeared or reappeared. If historical evolution were only a history of descendant new species having mutated and adapted from earlier ancestral species, which we know can happen, then evolution itself would be simplified as linear. But it isn't, it is more like quantum physics with pop-ups. What is sketched in this book as an evolution of movement, with its inferences and general assumptions should be viewed as broad epochal strokes across earth's history.

PyM practice can provide a basic sense of evolutionary timeline and ancestry with the derivations and similarities that connect us as we focus on the future. One of the very first multicellular organisms on earth were sponges. The primordial structural protein of sponges is collagen, a protein that comprises a good part of the biological scaffolding of every living animal. Chitin and shell preceded the formation of all vertebral body plans -- Bone in! Amphibian ancestors evolved with four limbs spawning scores of quadrupedal species for hundreds of millions of years and led to furry mammals. Ya Fuzz! At different points in history, all evolutionary morphologies and their cellular modifications whether skeletal, muscle, organ or nerve structures were systems that, at one time or another, went through a period of do or die. To survive, all organisms are compelled to adapt to the changing environment. Animal locomotion on land began with inefficient flopping and physical struggle, body-dragging on inadequate limbs, shallow breathing and debilitating environmental conditions took generations adapting to the task.

While the amphibious mugwumps kept close ties to their aquatic environments, we'll never know whether it was diet, genetic modifications or just plain luck that made some tetrapods amniotic as reptilian species. We do know body plans were modified for stronger, faster, and more useful limbs, often with better defensive and offensive capabilities adapted to dig, climb, burrow, catch, and attack. Locomotion became more efficient in running through bush with body plans in upright postures on two legs only, leading some species to fly. Outer protective exteriors changed from soft, layered skin, to have scales and platelets, armour, fur and feathers. In some species, fins adapted into limbs then adapted into flippers in species returning to the sea. In short, the evolution of movement is sketched with the perspective of how physicality might have progressed given the milestones that have been discovered.

Somatic movement researcher, Linda Hartley studied the physical movements of infants and found that newborns typically follow the same progressive movement patterning in lifeforms. In the first days of life, human baby movements track a similar progression as did the advancement of fish to amphibians. Beginning with the homologous, push and pull movements of fins on land; within days of birth, an infant's first movements are to pull upward on forelimbs and to raise the head. Pushing up with forelimbs to help leverage raising the head is the start for a synchronized push forward on both forelimbs. When strong enough, the infant will then engage in push-pull movements using forelimbs to pull up with a move to push the hind limbs - just as primordial finned vertebrates did in their efforts to move on land. Clearly following the gains by other limbed organisms, the infant will progress to then experiment with homolateral movement just as amphibians did, dragging their bellies across the ground, in a lateral side-to-side coordinated baby crawl. Thereafter, as speed also increases with asymmetrical coordination, the lateral reach and pull forward will transition into contralateral movement, a true signature of climbing primates and other mammals. These movements are often accomplished as a rapid progression within weeks of a human infant's life, almost as fast as in newborn monkeys. As latent transitions formerly achieved in the evolution of amphibians and our stem mammalian predecessors, the early beginnings attest that it was only uphill to becoming bipedal. Why our tiny forms as infants inadvertently follow ancestral movement patterns as animals transitioned from oceanic beginnings to tree-dwelling primates begs the question, what can we learn from that? Getting to know our physiology in a historical context simply points to the fact that we evolved on earth in the same way all morphologies grow from cells. Every amphibian, reptilian and mammalian species has proceeded down the same path -- from cells differentiating according to an inherited plan. Each from a billion-year-old blueprint inherent in each cell with all the cell functions working together to form and provide the systems to store and regulate energy for access and agency, all previously made for the purpose of creating a vital life.

Cells work together within their context organized from a backdrop of alliances, cooperation and coordination with procedures that call them to form structures as body plans from a chemically-based, self-organizing, life-giving system of growing cells. Each cell may be seen as representing pathways of creation to form bone cells, cartilage, collagen and skin cells, coalescing into organs with different functions, lungs and blood that utilize oxygen, into a centralized system of nerves and hormones, with homeostatic mechanisms to regulate fluids to feed muscles, ligaments, tendons, bone and cartilage, not to mention the cells; all to shape and perpetuate a creative, complex life forms.

So, perhaps the right question should be: How could our early infant locomotive progressions be anything different? We owe our form, structure and emergence on this planet to primordial life that has come before. Preceding us it is simply another reason to find space in our hearts, a place for each ancestor as guests of honour. And with humbling gratitude, perhaps we may find new meaning and metaphors to cherish their amazing forms, movements and transitions. And, you never know… nourish a new vision through recognition of the astounding biological basis of our species.

Humble Beginnings and Rebounds

Early in the age of the dinosaurs, a new reptilian species split away from the family of reptilian species into what paleontologists consider the stem mammaliaformes that preceded mammals. They were still reptiles but had characteristics that set them apart. The earliest evidence of stem mammaliaformes dates from the mid-Permian period, around 270 million years ago. Fossil remains reveal structural body plans that differed with limbs more sagittal - positioned beneath the body, a departure from the lateral sprawling limbs indicative of most reptiles. The Permian bones show a gradual transitioning as mammalian forelimbs acquired more forward parasagittal positioning possibly from habitual digging, earlier than was true of the hindlimbs. (Frobisch, Reisz, 2009) There is debate that the repositioning of limbs may have been influenced by change in animal respiration.

Shortly following the debut of the stem mammaliform animals, the earth's third mass extinction occurred 252 million years ago, the Permian-Triassic, which destroyed 76% of all plant and animal species on the earth. The surviving species barely eked out existence on the hellish earth, enduring without regenerative plant life for tens of thousands of years. The planet went into a lengthy period of overheating and the continents began to shift. India moved towards Asia forming the great Himalayas and in the process released immense amounts of CO_2 into the atmosphere causing yet more planetary warming and intense acidification of the oceans. The cumulative effects has been coined "The Great Die Off" whereby more than 90% of ocean species were annihilated. (Brannen, P. 2017) On land, the numbers of stem mammalian burrowing species underground contracted with survivors moving northward to polar areas to escape the intensely hot temperatures. Of the stem mammaliaformes that had roamed the earth during the Permian, only a single family order survived. Within that family, three genus groups survived, one of which is thought to have given rise to the lineage of therapsid species from which mammals emerged.

Therapsids comprised a number of mammal-like reptile species. One of the species, cynodonts, appeared around 225 million years ago. The reptilian cynodonts had dog-like teeth (a mammalian marker), a robust jaw musculature and a widened face with cheekbones indicating that they were almost certainly carnivores. Cynodonts also had some body fur and are thought to have had an early version of endothermic regulation. Endothermy refers to an autonomous regulation control of internal temperature and is characteristic in mammals as opposed to a "cold-blooded" system of reptiles whose body temperature is regulated by external temperature. There are a few exceptions however, in some reptiles such as pythons, some mammal species have endothermic regulation during their reproductive season. There's also some evidence that cynodonts had movement-independent diaphragmatic respiration. Breathing independence with a diaphragm to work the lungs essentially freed mammals of the dual function of movement for breath-assistance while also taking a key biomechanical constraint away from the reptilian backbone. (K.E Jones et al, 2021)

Mammalian Ascension

It took almost 30 million years for vertebrate biodiversity to return in appreciable numbers and not until the Late Triassic did mammalian species increase in appreciable numbers. (Sadney, S., Benton, M.J., 2008) The burgeoning flourish however, was short-lived as the Late Triassic period ended with yet a fourth extinction around 210 million years ago. The mammalian species that managed to survive in that die-off (over 76% of species died) were furry, quadrupedal burrowing animals equipped with strong forelimbs for digging underground. While living as burrowers in subterranean lairs accounted largely for the mammals' survival, evolution also favored them with sharp senses, adaptive motor coordination and an elevated metabolism due to endothermic regulation; an important role in ensuring survival. Mammalian speciation ramified into new niches creating whole orders, family and genus species matching the plant ecology that followed post extinction. (Brusatte, S.L., Zhe-Xi Luo, 2016) They are the foundation of the mammalian family branches of the Jurassic era and the ancestors of mammals today. There were egg-laying monotremes and eutherians, the mammalian species that lead to marsupials, such as kangaroos, koalas and possums, and then later split to include all placental species. Between 174 and 164 million years ago, the numbers of mammalian species began to skyrocket. The many different mammal species were functionally unique with varying forelimb specializations for borrowing, walking, running, swimming and climbing. Some species had simpler shoulder girdles than their reptilian therapsid ancestors and dinosaur cousins which afforded them higher degrees of range and mobility to add versatility in their movements. Each adaptation honed their limb motions to suit living in a particular niche and at some point their quadrupedal morphologies modified further for climbing capacity in arboreal settings. A tiny four-inch (head to tail) creature from 165 million years ago in China may be one of the earliest climbing mammals to date. The bony fossil remains show some adaptations to arboreal life with climbing with (finger) digits adapted for grasping and possibly clinging. However, such a species apparently appeared only briefly. (Frobisch, J. and Reisz, R.R., 2009). Quadrupedal animals ramified and speciated dramatically continuing to multiply into new genus groups so that by the dawn of the Cretaceous period, 145 million years ago, the essential modern mammal was firmly established on earth, to distance the mammal lineage distinctly apart from their reptilian ancestors.

One defining characteristic of mammals is endothermic regulation, the warm-blooded animal metabolism system for regulating internal temperature control. Internal temperature control regulation has many advantages over exothermic regulation. It reduces a species exposure to extreme fluctuations from the external change in temperatures. It is obvious that reptiles are exothermic, a fact easily witnessed in the sluggishness of reptiles on cool mornings. Until the sun rises to warm their body temperature sufficiently they cannot move about with much speed. Internal regulation in mammals avoids this dependency on outside warmth. Internal temperature regulation makes metabolism more efficient with higher levels of energy activity, such as running, possible for longer periods without causing overheating in mammals. Most importantly however, endothermic regulation stability is significant for sustaining consistent internal temperatures for developing embryos, whether it is a marsupial or placental mammal; it is a bonus to the survival of offspring. Eutherians first evolved epipubic bones, a pair of bones that jut forward from the pelvis bone making it possible for the marsupials to carry young in a pouch. In marsupials and placental species, epipubic bones serve to strengthen the torso in support of the abdominals and the reproductive organs and also in conjunction with hindlimb musculature, to provide a stronger lift in belly positioning of quadrupeds.

 Over 164 million years ago, the mammalian lineages split into three main groups: the egg-laying monotremes, the pouched marsupials and the placentals. Monotremes, such as the present-day platypus, have had a long, yet less divergent evolutionary history. They retain the sprawled gaits of their reptile ancestors. The marsupial genus split fairly early from the monotreme lineage. And the third mammal group, the placentals, mammals that gestate their offspring internally, were the mammalian latecomers yet quickly have become the most diverse group of mammals on earth. Their diversification was fuelled by a major change in earth's flora. Around 130 million years ago, gymnosperm palms, ferns and cycads comprised prehistoric plant life. Gradually they were replaced by angiosperms, flowering plants that brought about radical changes in the many phyla of lifeforms on the planet. Trees and shrubs produced reproductive flowers and bore fruiting bodies and the attendant insects exploded into new species leading to pollination adaptations. Grasses replaced ferns and diversified, filling the fertile landscapes with seeds; and everywhere the earth flora heaped on new herbaceous species upon the omnivore species modifying the clade into new niches and creating whole new ecosystems. After millions of years of quite humble beginnings, mammalian species and their numbers continued to climb. By the dawn of the Cretaceous period, the modern mammal blueprint of today was founded in the ancestors of today's mice, badgers, shrews, opossum, raccoons, weasels, otters and beavers.

Mammal species however, were also to be tested and yet again the burrowing species underground again proved to have an edge on survival when a sizable asteroid hit the earth 66 million years ago. The impact is thought to have caused a massive volcanic chain reaction of eruptions on the other side of the planet resulting in yet another mass extinction. (Brannen, P., 2014) The asteroid impact effectively extinguished all dinosaur species except for the avian species. The few animal lineages able to survive the heat blasts, earthquakes, tsunamis and poisonous atmosphere from erupting volcanoes also struggled through hundreds of years living in a darkened, toxic biosphere. Of the three mammalian family groups to have survived, the marsupials were hardest hit with most of the genus groups snuffed out in the devastation.

Gradually, the earth's heat subsided and the atmosphere began to clear. Life awoke again and the planet began the process of rebalancing and renewal. Over millions of years, entirely new ecosystems re-emerged with wide grasslands, flowering plants, revived estuaries, and forests. Bird and mammalian clades catapulted into a myriad of new species as was typical in the other post-extinction times on the earth. Mammals again diversified into every available niche; with mammalian insectivores and worm eaters, plankton and flower eaters, grazers and stalkers, predators and burrowers, aerial gliders and climbers, clingers and swimmers, floaters and waders.

Although the majority of those mammalian ancestral species are now extinct, their morphologies are biological legacies that are carried in present-day kangaroo, capybara, armadillo, hippo, anteater, echidna, elephant, bear, beaver, lion, hyena, sloth, oxen, moose, wolf, cat, otter, and camel species, among others. Since the last re-greening of the planet, there have been long stretches thousands of years, when tigers, rhinos, camels, sloths, antelope, water buffalo, bison and elephants all roamed among one another together on earth. Well-grounded quadrupeds have walked the earth in abundantly large groupings for over 200 million years, far outnumbering their quadrupedal and bipedal dinosaur reptiles, in a mammalian age.

Monotremes were some of the first primordial mammals, appearing early in the historical record yet only very few of the curious creatures remain today. The first PyM posture in the land series is to emulate one of those extant species, the echidna that retains the ancient sprawling gait of the reptilian ancestors now so atypical in mammals. Like the first reptilian amniotes, monotremes are egg-laying and come from within the therapsid lineage that evolved during the late Jurassic-Triassic era, 210 million years ago. Therapsids split into many different species - fierce predators, arboreal herbivores and scratch-digging insectivores, one of the latter was echidna. Nowadays there are only four extant species of monotremes from this group -- the furry, elusive duck-billed platypus and three species of echidna, insectivores living primarily on ants. All echidna species have prickly protective coats of stiff spines and all four species roam the remote forests of New Guinea and Australia. As a group, they are the last of the monotreme species and the only egg-laying mammals on earth.

Echidna Stance

Echidnas have strong limbs turned inward with long claws for digging and scratching to unearth termites and ants. They walk in a sprawling gait due to limbs that are laterally jointed along the sides of their bodies as in high walking reptiles. Interestingly, their hind legs are a little more parasagittal- beneath the body than their forelimbs which are optimized for digging and uprooting forest debris as they forage. With a formidable barbed porcupine-like coat and a prominent shoulder girdle - they can easily hold their ground under threat.

Short-beaked Echidna

Play around with this posture on hands and knees or on deeply bent knees, feet and hands. Monotreme knees are not bent to the outside of the forelimbs but are slightly parasagittal, bent inward close to the underside of the body and with feet supinated. The shoulder girdle angle is aligned with the curve of their protective ribs, so imagining a flatter, broader chest elbows are lateral and forearms bend inward. Echidna finger digits are curved, widely spread and rotated in for digging.

Try It: Imagine how such a species might move and sense with a long snout to detect the smells of forest insects. First, test the forward weight in forearms and wrists by swaying back and forth contralaterally with weight heavily forward, head lifted. The slightly lifted rear stance tucks thighs in along ribs on supinate feet. Try walking in a homolateral, side-together sprawling walk. The monotreme gait reflects a crouched morphology inherited from the stem mammaliaformes.

Along with monotremes, an enormous number of marsupial species disappeared in the Cretaceous extinction. However, some marsupials survived the Cretaceous end and recovered enough to recolonize the vast emerging grasslands and forests of New Guinea, Australia and Tasmania. They include unique koalas, wallabies and kangaroos.

Formidable hind legs appear to propel kangaroos hopping like a rabbit. But recent research using slow motion video has revealed that their forward motion is impelled by its' large tail which pushes downward to briefly support leveraging the hind legs off ground. Assistance from the tail is unique to kangaroos and isn't found in any other biped with a tail.

Kangaroo are energetically suited to the drier climates of Australia; and although they may look somewhat ungainly, they are athletic, muscular, strong, and very fast. As mentioned, the red kangaroo may one day easily claim the title of the fastest *bipedal* animal on earth (they are not tri-pedal while running).

The Great Plains and Grassland Ungulates

Following the Cretaceous asteroid impact that expunged a majority of life on earth, it took a fair amount of time to re-establish biodiversity. Scientists put estimates at around 10 million years; but eventually, the long, slow greening process resulted in rich, flowering forests and vast grassland areas. Species followed the plant and insect momentum with numerous species building new ecosystems. Birds ramified and filled the skies and land mammal species exploded into the many rodent, canine, feline, and ungulate families, accompanied by giant sloths, mastodons and armadillos; and immense predators such as mire wolves, saber tooth tigers, massive lions and vicious terror birds. They all vied together in hunting *paraceratherium* (giant rhinos), *hyracodonts* (hippos), *eohippus* (horses), *heptodonts* (tapirs), *diacoddexis* (deer), and *edentate* (giant anteaters) and each other.

Eland

There were mammals that moved to hop, walk, climb, amble and cling. However, the most by far were the ungulate species that walked on the immense grasslands of the plains. Four-legged ungulates grazed in vast herds on rolling and expansive savannahs for millions of years. Today their descendants include such hoofed animals as camel, elk, water buffalo, oxen, caribou, rhinos, boars, zebras, giraffes, hippos, and antelope species. Zoologists also include cetaceans in this diverse mammal group as having descended from the hippo lineage. They split to fully return to the sea around 55 million years ago.

Many ungulate species are migratory such as reindeer, elk, moose, eland, elephant, impala, water buffalo, deer, caribou, gazelle and bison and, of course, whales. Those herding mammals walk and run on vast areas and are some of the fastest and most far ranging of all animal species on the planet.

All ungulates are quadrupedal with parasagittal limbs; their walking locomotion is in a similar fashion, limbs move predominantly in adjacent patterned movements independently coordinated and contralateral. Movement is initiated first by a forelimb and followed by the adjacent hind limb and opposite forelimb, followed by the adjacent hind limb. By design, both the shoulder and pelvic girdles in ungulates are nearly similar in weight-bearing support of the spine, girdling bone and muscle anatomy for easy, energetically minimaized movement. The near-constant grazing pattern of ungulates is a code of *protocol* in migratory herds. They roam in mass groups as a defensive type of "schooling" behaviour that has a consumptive element too as their migratory travels help assure an adequate supply of energy from grasses. Grasses as a food source have low energy yields and their habitual moving insures not only an adequate amount of intake but possibly better nutrition with a greater variety of plants encountered. Ungulate morphology is based on a lifestyle of mobility as grazers.

A favourite ungulate in PyM to mimic descended from an extinct Pleistocene creature, the woolly mammoth, the heavy-hooved elephant.

Trunk Sway

Elephants are in the family of Elephantidae, grouped in the order of Proboscides, nicely self-descriptive terms. Yes, they are elephantine and noticeable by a conspicuous proboscis. An elephant's trunk can grow to six to eight feet and contais more than 40,000 muscles but no bone; their lengthy nose can weigh up to 350 lb (150 kg). Elephants rank among some of the most social of mammals; they are widely known to show empathy and concern for individuals in their groups. Globally, as habitats continue to shrink, elephant populations have been impacted dramatically and reduced by more than 70% in the last century alone.

Photo by Johan Swanepoel

Try It: Begin standing and with a straight back, fold strongly to forward bend at the hips; keep legs straight as possible on the descent, balanced and stable. Settle the weight of the upper body and relax the lower back to hang down from the hips. Imagine your legs as forelimbs of an elephant standing upright. Firm abdominals in and keep easing any tension in the hamstrings and down the posterior of the legs. Relax tendons and ligaments down from the hips, hanging the head, neck, chest, arms and back. Imagine your upper body as the heavy trunk of an elephant, dangling. Where your arms comfortably extend and come to rest in this ragdoll posture, place fingertips - on the floor, ankles, tops of feet, lower leg, where they reach. Using fingertips gently bounce the upper body up and down and sway in pulses to gently pull on hamstrings and the low back. The motion will gently stretch the connective tissues running from the pelvic girdle down the back of the legs. You may feel some easing of resistant tension in the legs to the Achilles tendons. The bouncing, swaying side to side easily mimics the heavy movements of an elephant trunk. Play with the elephantine motions and relax the lumbar spine.

Ruminates have stomachs divided into compartments that slows the digestion of grasses and other plants due to the soaking and softening processes to detoxify the indigestible compounds and to pre-digest seeds and grains with regurgitation cycles.

In general, ungulates have long, ventrally directed ribs attached to their spines which protect and support a rather complex digestive system and reproductive organs. Especially in the larger species, stronger spinal backbones restrict axial flexibility and broad lateral movements due, at least in part, to its core role in body stabilization. Their rib cages have separate connective and muscular structures to support the anterior girdling of the spine as integral in the often necessary abrupt, forward sprints. (Padian, 2015) Additionally, the pectoral and coracoid muscles stabilize ungulate shoulder joints to connecting movements in a straight orientation forward. They also stabilize against rotatory motion in higher trotting and running gaits. In the lighter, swifter species such as antelope, the shoulder girdles are structurally less connected to ribs to allow for longer extension in their forelimb strides at higher speeds. Their pelvic structures and hindlimbs are also adducted in line with their undersides to maintain better balance in coordinating moving forelimb forward orientations. With little exception, herding species on vast stretches of the plains over the last 60 million years have evolved morphologies with quite similar highly balanced spines and very stable girdling in support of fore and hindlimbs.

Not all ungulate species are ruminates, though all are herbivores. Elephants, rhinos, goats and giraffes not only eat grasses but leaves, branches and a variety of fruit.

Ungulate Grazing

Try It: Lie face-down and come up to a Sphinx position onto elbows. This is more enjoyable if you place a block or pillow in front for support. This will help to stretch with support to relax the neck and shoulders. Press the elbows down and spread shoulder blades dropping the scapula down the back to spread the clavicle (collar bone). Draw in abdominals and drop your head down towards the mat, onto block or a pillow. Place the top of the forehead or top of the head to touch down for support, without slouching. It's good to stretch the cervical vertebrae at the base of the neck. Lightly lift and forward angle the head side-to-side gently to stretch all sides in the back of the neck, hold each angle to release neck tension and relax tendons. You'll also get a sense of support in the connecting structure of the shoulders. Move your head back up and stretch it right-to-left and left-to-right as a long-necked ungulate.

Another ungulate neck stretch is with the movement of dropping the head supported by the elbows in *Sphinx* and rolling the shoulders. Just be sure to alternately pull each shoulder blade down completely as you roll them back. Placing a pillow beneath the head and forehead will help to relax the neck and head even more while the shoulders gently extend one side and the other of the neck in the rolling, stalking motion.

Today, one of the most disheartening aspects of human cruelty to another species continues to be in the practice of making veal. Young calves taken from their mothers are restricted in pins scarcely larger than their bodies. It is forced upon young calves within months of finding their leggy balance on the ground at birth. Held in solitary confinement standing only to fatten and unable to move the bodies they were endowed with to roam. It is a brutal practice in the domestication of animals and we should question its cruelty especially in light of the violation in how the animal has evolved to live.

Ungulate herds walk slowly over vast tracts of land adding variety to diet and conserving energy consumption. When needed however, the efficiency of engaging faster gaits can also be sustained in their metabolic stamina at different speeds. (Carrier, 1987) Depending on a species' particular agility and vigor, the main propulsive force from hind limbs at high speeds reaches their maximum forward thrust and extension with quick adjustments and may assist in adjusting change to the forward direction. , In other words, certain gaits will optimize direction control adjustments to allow a herding animal swift, efficient control of inertia in maneuvering quick turns. Across the full spectrum of ungulate species, limb patterns in walking, trotting, and running (cantor) gaits are similar in many species with little discernable difference. The various gaits are determined more in timing and pace rather than from any difference in body plans. Horses, for example, have many different gaits: walking, trotting, cantering, and galloping based on speed. (Bertram, J.E.A.; Gutmann, A.,2009) Gaits are distinguishable by placement positioning and the timing of limb movements as speed increases in a quadruped. In running, an animal charges forward and the pattern of limbs making ground contact alters to produce the particular gait with forward motion.

Antelope Turns

One of the most graceful life and death dramas in motion is in the stealth and chase of a predator cat hunting the quick and agile antelope. Consider how a mountain lion, cheetah, or a lion's agility can be matched by an antelope's evasive actions in every twist and turn, every leap and burst of acceleration in the life or death drama. At maximum speeds, an antelope leaps in long strides and banks with lowered haunches to maneuver in quick, abrupt turns.

Try It: On hands (or elbows) and knees, sweep the right arm out and forward at an 30-45 degree angle keeping the core body low and level to the ground, shift far forward leaning right and bring the arm around to the side (without falling over) and back and forward onto hands and knees. Your left elbow and upper body will bend and stretch to maintain balance. Then move your left forelimb forward likewise circling to the left as low to the ground as possible. Imagine the movement quickened, going 40 mph in slow motion with the pull of inertia, leaning you off to the side. Repeat both sides rhythmically – in a kneeling, balancing movement - it helps to strengthen core stability while working joints and stretching limbs.

Deer Prance

Try it: Young stags will often stamp a hoof in warning. I've witnessed it as a show of vigor and vitality in a stag when a young doe enters a wooded area; or as a gesture to defend territory -- a stag will stamp each foreleg and sometimes move forward with each hoof stamp. Marc Bekoff, author and behaviouralist, observed the elk prance as high stepping practice might help them outpace predators in deep snow or to work their kicking muscles for defense. In PyM, there are a few ways to do this and it is best to start from visualization. In dancing - try it as an offensive and somewhat audacious movement akin to the Flamenco dancers proud quick step to emulate moose, reindeer, or caribou: Chest opened with a straight back, chin high with a wide-browed gaze, lean forward menacingly and lift to step a foot forward sharply in warning, and repeat moving forward slowly with precision. Or, more gentile, with the shyness of Key deer:

Try It: Standing upright, lift a leg, point your toes and tap in front of you twice before placing your foot down to move forward. Repeat on the other side. Interpretations can be added to dancing in animal characterizations although, high-stepping Russians on parade may come to mind.

Try these other mammal postures from the eastern tradition:
Asanas (traditional yoga)
Camel (*Utrasana*), Downward-Facing Dog (*Adho Mukha Svanasana*), Upward-Facing Dog *(Urdhva Mukha Svanasana),* Lion (*Simhasana*).

Chill Acclaim for Xenarthrans

Xenarthrans are an ancient clade of placentals that appeared in the Paleocene Era around 59 million years ago. They include species of giant armadillos the size of small cars and giant sloths that stood 15 feet tall. Today, tree sloths, armadillos and anteaters comprise the now relatively small group species in the Xenarthra family lineage. The species in this group are known as a slow, deliberate group and having some of the lowest metabolic rates of all mammalian species.

Ground-dwelling sloths evolved in South America and evolved to immense sizes as giants there; they then spread to North America adapting to different environments. Some species evolved as mostly ground-dwelling species in the grassland plains, others were arboreal and a few were semi-aquatic. The slur in the common name "sloth" is indicative of their inherent movements. It belies the species' versatility and evolutionary fortitude through the ages. The slow-moving, largely ground-dwelling herbivores once ate grasses, shrubs, yucca and tree foliage in safe, open fields and meadows. Giant sloths ambled along on their knuckles with long claws turned inward occasionally retreating to climb amazon-sized trees. The morphology of their hip bones reveal that the ground sloths often propped themselves up to squat on their haunches while foraging on leaf foliage above. All the ground-dwelling and swimming, semi-aquatic species are extinct. Today, only six species remain of the smaller, arboreal species in the world, and they survive very much on the edge. All six are threatened as their habitats have been reduced to small remote areas and islands in the tropical rainforest regions of South America where animal trade poaching is difficult to control.

Tree sloths are the biospheres' only inverted (inversion moving) quadrupeds. Their strictly arboreal limbs are adapted only for clinging and grasping branches which involves only the tensile strength in limbs. Without extensor muscles to compress for extending their limbs in broad-based movement, opening outwardly to reposition a limb is a matter of relaxing their flexor muscles. We have 12 extensor muscles in the forearm for wrist and hand manipulations. Imagine having no triceps or hamstrings with which to balance inward pull with outwardly motions. Without extensors to protract in directing muscle action while walking, arboreal sloths must literally relax-drag themselves across the flat ground. All six sloth species remaining today have little more than half the muscle mass of other mammals and all of the extant sloth species weigh less than 20 pounds individually. When a species has not evolved for movement, it is reason enough to require so little food to live on with metabolism and digestion also extremely slow. Sloth evolution through the ages is quite astounding as tree sloths are the only extant descendants from the massive five-ton giant sloths that earlier had roamed continents.

Enter the Carnivores

Always attendant where there are ungulate grazers, predators will come and go. Through millions of years, one of the most successful predacious mammals is the cat. F*elidae*, the feline family species are found on almost every continent, in the hottest deserts and the coldest remote regions of Siberia. They can be counted among the most cunning and fierce of all predators, and yet the feline family also includes a species living sedately in our homes. Cats all hail from the *Carnivora* order and along with their cousins the wolves, from the *Canis* family, the mammal order of species also includes the bear, weasel, elephant seal and raccoon families.

While the short-legged wolf and the long-legged giraffe may move limbs in similar fashion when walking, their gaits differ particularly in the predator species at speed, along with the aforementioned ungulates. The gait of a sprinting cheetah is vastly different when it is walking, stalking and trotting; yet its gait will never match that of a galloping horse. The subtle variance in four-legged locomotion testifies to their individually honed evolution, evident in the rhythmic nature of movement. For 50 million years now, the grasslands have engendered a broad biodiversity in moving migratory interplay, made possible only on the wild, unfettered plains.

One factor that affects quadrupedal gaits are the flex/extension positions of an animal's spinal movement that drives how center of gravity shifts. This is especially evident in ambush predators. When predatory animals initiate a burst of speed in attack, the quick forward limb reach inevitably lowers their center of gravity.

The fastest four-limbed animal ever recorded is of course, a feline, the intrepid spotted cheetah. According to Wikipedia,they are capable of attaining a running speed of 112 kilometers an hour (70mph) for short durations. Consider this account of a cheetah's morphology in a sprint by zoologist Milton Hildebrand: *"The tight binding of the tibia and the fibula restrict rotation about the lower leg, thus stabilizing the animal throughout the sprint... The pendulum-like motion of the scapula increases the stride length and assists in shock absorption. The extension of the vertebral column can add as much as 76 cm (30 in) to the length of a stride."* (Hildebrand, M., 1961)

    A cheetah's running body is stabilized in forward motion. Its body is quick, flexible, strong, and built to handle propelled landings of the limbs that touch the ground so widely that more than half the time in a full-on run a cheetah's four limbs are simultaneously airborne. (Taylor, M.E., 1989) The distance a cheetah covers while completely airborne exceeds twice their body length!

    Feline movements are often characterized as fluid, measured and controlled. When prey is centered in the stare of their golden eyes, the rapt intent extends from head to tail with every muscle poised, calculating and deliberated. They are formidable top predators. Even when the common household cat is engaged, its movements are perfect to intentions, so much so that it will appear embarrassed by any slight miscalculation. There is much to emulate in feline movements and much fun to be had in the postural attitudes when embodying felines. Below, try beginning with their awesome limb range and spinal stretch fluidity. Imagine a cheetah chasing down a fast and fleet gazelle, a worthy prey. In a sprint, the cheetah spine undulates from head to tip of tail in a graceful steady rhythm. Then try to reach that extension extremity in our spines and limbs also.

Cheetah Core

Cheetahs are a gregarious cat species and socialize in groups in and out of the breeding season. They hunt mainly during the day; yet after sunset, their excellent night vision and sense of smell demands that all other animals be wary. Their historical ranges have been immensely reduced and of what little remains, 76% of their territory is currently on unprotected lands. They are now a vulnerable species for extinction. They are rarely capable of living among humans as their mortality rate is high when living in captivity.

Cheetah photo by Malene Thyssen

Try It: First, we mimic the curving movement along the cheetah spine. On hands and knees, exhale and tuck in abdominals to strongly curl up through the spine. Optional: engage in *uddiyana*[1] at the end of the exhale to further collapse the base of lungs and abdominals. Hold the breath out for six counts, then begin to slowly lower down by sinking hips back. Begin a slow inhale. On reaching the calves of the lower legs, arms should be straight ahead forward, hips pressing down and the back stretched long. Continue to slowly inhale keeping internal muscles contracted (also optional - engage in *mula bandha*[2]). Again hold in *mula bandha* for six counts on the full inhale. Exhale, bend elbows and rise up, keeping the chest and hips low in moving forward and arching the spine down first in extension, then with breath, flexion to arch the back. When your breath is full once more, briefly engage *uddiyana* (6 counts) and keep scapula pressing down and chest open. Repeat with another long slow exhale, curling in and repeat. Our exaggerated movements of spinal extension and flexion in rolling motions are indicative of the length of movement the long cheetah spine moves through in a run. After a few deliberate undulations increase the speed of motion and omit *uddiyana*, but maintain *mula bandha* throughout. Try the rolls also going in the opposite direction and inhaling on the arch (instead of exhaling). Gracefully exhale on the low creep forward towards extension. It's more effective to move as you breathe. Imagine you've a tail and it is also moving in line with the slowed motion of the spine. The undulating motions of spinal rolling can also be performed sitting or standing.

---

[1] An upward pull in with abdominal lock
[2] Squeeze and lift the floor of the perineum in an energetic lock

Cheetah Stride

In a run, a cheetah will maximize its limb reach to the full extent possible. To emulate the fullness of the stride length and explore the range of movement comparable in leg flexion and extension, take it slowly. From the starting position on hands and knees we move in motion which requires stabilization. Follow this three-posture stretch to help envision the flexibility, reach and thrust of a cheetah.

Try It: 1. Begin from a straight plank (push-up) posture: on the balls of your feet, straight legs hip distance apart. Lift the right leg up off the ground and bend the knee in towards the right shoulder, practice bringing the bent knee in under the chest a few times from plank. Add to each flexion a slight kick from the knee. Then if available to you, bring the right knee to the outside of the shoulder, and hold briefly. After the warm-up, place your foot down and forward on the floor, beyond the outside of the right hand in a long lunge. Take a minute to stretch the groin down gently. The limb stretch almost matches cheetah sprint range although with practice, further reach is attainable. Feel free to drop your chest down inside the thigh and come down onto elbows to release pressure on the wrists; hold for a couple of minutes to relax and stretch the connective tissues in the posture.

2. Next in the posture, extend the right foot out and forward as far as possible, 45 degrees from the right wrist. Shift fully forward to further extend the left leg to stretch. Gently does it. Modify by lowering the left knee on the ground. Bend at the waist, and again lower the chest to come onto elbows to the left of the right knee. Gently push your right thigh out rotating to the full extent in the femur head. Hold the posture to stretch ligaments and increase flexibility in the hip fascia. Imagine running with this extended range of motion. Play with the flexibility of the hip socket by moving the knee as a cheetah, quickly adjusting the angle of the limb as needed in turns to  closely follow prey. Keep the foot flat on the ground when moving your leg side to side from the midline to work in ankle flexibility as well. Relax and move in slow motion to explore the **Cheetah Stride** in strong, stable and flexible long-leg extensions. This will stretch hip flexors, psoas, ankles, hamstrings and other connective tissues of the low back and hip. To release, shift your weight back and up slightly to lift the leg and straighten it back into plank. Repeat the above with the left leg forward.

   3. Try capturing the Cheetah Stride with more movement (advanced). Begin on hands and knees in a squat. First, lift hips to fold and thrust the left leg forward between hands, circle the leg around to the back and into a squat. Then, immediately shift over and lean on the left thigh raising the right hand up to fold the right leg under your body, around and back. Alternate circling the legs in and around side to side in a crouch will quickly drive home the weight of energetic expenditure in the cheetah sprint. Momentum, once begun, helps. Lean forward by quickly placing hands down following the thrust through and out to the front. While none of us will ever come close to the 22-foot airborne strides a cheetah achieves in their mighty movements, it may lend a sense of appreciation to their magnificence and the evolutionary conditions that make speed and agility so beautifully matched in a predator/prey balance.
  Quadrupedal extensions, contractions, twists, flex abilities, spring actions, stabilization, pacing, and fine motor tuning may all be practiced in emulating animal movements which predate hominin species. Many of today's practiced animal movements by Mike Fitch, Guido Portal, Cameron Shayne can be viewed on the internet and many others who have sought to emulate arthropods, mammals, primate and insect movements with awesome fluidity and choreography - check them out on YouTube. Especially check out the compilation of animal movements presented by Rudy Cabrera called **Animal/Movement Flow**. They will help to envision the quadruped movements of felines, sloths and otters, and arthropodal crab and spider movements, plus many primate motions. All are accomplished movement characterizations with which to emulate.

Stalking Moves

   Typical human movement in most lifestyles do little to keep primate-evolved shoulder girdles moving fluidly, we would do well to learn from the motions of a cat stalking prey. A good place to practice the stalking movement is right after practicing **Lizard Pump** (Amphibian chapter), and just before or after arm stretching in **Sea Star, Anguilla**. Lie face forward propped up in *Sphinx*, resting on elbows directly beneath shoulders with the back and legs relaxed. Keep the head and neck relaxed and aligned with the spine and shoulder blades low. Steadily rotate shoulders off-set from one another – one moves up as the other moves down. Rotate them as a cat in their full rotation, forward, down and back up in smooth rolling motions. Visualize the slow, quiet descent of the paws quietly pacing after the prey. Make sure to open the collarbone wide and drop the scapula fully downward for cervical stretch; also try rotating shoulders in the opposite direction (backward direction) to open further across the breast area. Also, if you exaggerate the movement into a swaying body motion down into the waist from moving side to side; it also lubricates the lumbar vertebrae and shoulders more deeply to loosen laterally at the arm sockets.

Leaping Leopard

You may remember in **Tom and Jerry** cartoons where Tom is depicted as a hapless cat in a constant struggle with a wily mouse, Jerry. They engage in relentless *gotcha* antics. Tom would leap onto a table edge only to discover he'd landed on a loose table runner and he'd frantically scramble to grab the slipping runner as it tumbles hopelessly from his grasp and down he'd plunge. Leopards and elusive mountain lions spring to many times their length in a single leap.

Try it: With forearms bent and digits poised like claws extended, spring forward from a crouched posture from bent legs. Lift the arms menacingly as you jump out, ready to claw and strike with an awful *Hiss!*

A wise and keen observer, Ed McGaa, an Ogala Sioux, in the book *Nature's Way* peppered his lessons with wisdom from stories of wild animals. Of cats, he said, "there is nothing more sought after by a wild animal than the freedom to roam (which) is likely to be subdued…(because)true freedom scares others, especially in those who are in control". His insight for human interrelationships -- "Both male and female lions hunt, both care for the young… (both) are free individuals… those who hold female and male energy in balance are likely to be more peaceful than those who favor one over the other."

Early *Felidae* species were short-legged and bent at the joints and reached running speeds considerably slower than the wild feline species today. The bent configuration in their joints indicates that muscle leveraging was designed for maneuvering into burrows and climbing trees. Forty-three million years ago, the *Carnivora* order split into the *feliforme* mammals, the cats and *caniforms,* the many wolf-like animals. The *canids* then split into two groups, the fox species and wolf species which now also include coyotes, jackals, dingoes and dogs. *Canid* groups are known for their close-knit societal ties, patience with young and their social cooperation in hunting collectively. As for dogs, I think we may also appreciate their loyalty and playfulness, as in the puppy play here.

Playful Puppy

If you've ever witnessed two puppies meeting together in a park, you'll recognize this stance. It is unmistakable as a gesture in many species, from hyenas to great apes as an invitational "Let's play together and have fun". It can be accompanied with stalking, pouncing and head shaking motions.

Try It: First, lower down into the posture on hands and knees. Come down onto elbows and lower the chest sliding the elbows forward and curving the upper back gently down. Keep thighs vertical so hips remain high relative to the head and shoulders. Keep the head gently lifted. Play with this exaggerated extension in the upper spine to wag your 'tail' with a mischievous grin daring others to join in. Compress and move the vertebrae with pup play.

As both cats and dogs belong to the same *Carnivora* order *Canid*, they are cousins and share similarities in body plans and sitting postures. To sit like they do, we need to stretch the calf muscles and Achilles tendons, so - Do you know *Dog Squat*? If not, here ya go!

Dog Squat

Upright balance is always improved with healthy flexible ankles by lengthening the Achilles tendons behind the heels in stretch.

Try It: Begin in a low squat with knees deeply bent. Then, hands brace on the floor ahead to extend a leg straight back, flex the foot and toes. Keep the toes flexed with the heel pushed back to extend the Achilles and gently pulse the leg straight back to gently stretch ankle tendons with each backward thrust. The rhythmic stretch and release will gently lengthen the tendons. Now you're ready for the *Dog* Squat stretch.

Step 2: From the extended posture above, straighten toes down on the ground and bend the straight knee of the extended leg placing it onto the ground also, then lift it up slightly to bring the opposite foot back beneath you under the (crouched) hip as far as possible. Your foot position should be as far back beneath you where the foot is flat and fully grounded. This positions the thigh and knee close on the chest. Ideally, the foot is further back than perpendicular on the ground. Keeping it flat, sink the hips down and begin to bend forward from the low pelvis over the bent leg to push the thigh low stretching calf muscles and ankles. Proceed slowly, the tendons are connective so they do not carry much leeway for stretch, it takes practice to ease the tissues. Release by leaning back. Repeat the same lunge as above on the opposite leg and after warming to the pulses, fold over on the opposite calf and ankle. Try to hold the stretch at least a minute for each leg calf in this posture relaxing down over the bent leg.

Step 3: *Dog Squat*. Squat down on both legs and position feet in a slightly outward angle, drop the knees down to the ground or as far as they will descend keeping feet flat. Try to keep the heels down and crouch over on the thighs. Folding forward in squats is beneficial to flush organs and the reproductive system while compressing hamstrings, calves, knees and ankles.

Another family of species to emerge from *Carnivora* lineage is the genus *Ursavus,* bear family. Observations of bear movements in PyM follow:

Bear Swagger

Try It: Squat down onto the balls of the feet and slightly lean forward, widen arms out and place both hands on the ground with flexed wrists turned slightly inward, like bear paws. Bear paws are rarely flat with their long claws so curl fingers; elbows are rounded outward. Brace on the metatarsal of the feet and lower knees down to within an inch or two above the ground. This will move your center of gravity forward shifting more weight onto the chest and shoulders. Explore their quadrupedal movement on your shortened haunches by swaying from side to side shifting weight from paw to paw into a swagger; perhaps lift an arm open your chest and a swipe menacing paw. Try moving about on the balls of flexed feet, abdominals tucked firmly in and knees bent deeply just inside forelimbs to initiate forward motion. The range in movement of feet and ankles is largely constrained but try walking forward. Modify to ease from the kneeling posture onto knees to work the chest and shoulders only. Bears are essentially quadrupeds but will often raise their bodies to stand on hindlimbs.

One day along a wild river, I had the pleasure of witnessing a bear in the same Boat pose as pictured by the tawny Black Bear below as she plays on bearing a balance:

Bear Boat

Try It: Begin sitting upright and extend legs forward. Bend the right knee in towards the chest and grasp the right toes with hands, as seen here. Then straighten the knee and pull the leg up in close to the chest while keeping the left leg grounded, straight or comfortably bent. Hold and lower when ready.

Repeat on the other side. Sitting upright with legs on the ground, bend the left knee into the chest and hold onto left toes, slowly straighten the knee and extend the leg up and in. Be sure to keep your right leg relaxed and down, as this bear appears to enjoy

Next, complete the posture in *Bear Boat*. Seated with both feet extended out, reach forward and grab onto feet. Bend the knees up then straighten them out to the sides. Lean back slightly on sitz bones as the legs come up and comfortably balance, arms straightened. Ta-dah

Try It: In the *Bear Boat* posture above, holding firmly onto the feet, roll your posture forward and back – as I witnessed the bear rock to and fro, seemingly quite pleased to do so. Enjoy having as much fun as bears do!

Although appearing a little awkward to us on the land - if you have ever watched sea lions playing in among the rising bubbles and floating strands of kelp – there's a graceful fluidity in their circling, twisting movements. They, like all pinnipeds, are as fluid as the ocean itself.

Walrus

Genetic origins of pinnipeds (walrus, sea lions, fur seals, and seals) suggest that they descended from a mammalian ancestor most closely related to bears, the genus having diverged 50 million years ago. Pinnipeds worldwide now comprise only three remaining families; of those - the walrus is the last remaining species of its family. In the evolutionary split, their mammalian limbs once made for walking evolved independent reverse-convergent swimming flippers. (Lento, G.M et al., 1995) Their fore flippers move independently while hind limb flippers terminate joined to power their swim movements and massive bodies. Walruses propel through the seawater with flexible maneuvers with fore flippers predominantly used for directional rudder control. (Berta, A., 2006) On land, the walrus pinnipeds have a distinctive lift-and-waddle scooting undulation, rather like a rolling shuffle. (English, A.W.2009) John Wayne, the former country western actor, ambled in a similar fashion walking. Walrus locomotion might seem less awkward if we are cognizant of the fact that their locomotion moves over a ton of blubber - often over two feet thick on their bony frames held on two flippers and pushed from behind.

Try It: To prepare, lie down and come up onto your elbows into *Sphinx*. Move hands from beneath the shoulders about a foot diagonally out to each side, palms flat and fingers spread. Keep the hips grounded and press down into your hands to lift up and straighten the arms fully if possible, do not shrug in shoulders. Lift the head high and lengthen along the spine from the lumbar through the cervical vertebrae. Release down.

Step 2: Initiate movement in the low back and belly by pressing into abdominals and ribs and undulate the spine, lifting up from the low back up through to the nape of your neck, chin rising up last. Begin rolling again in the abdominals to create a continuous undulating motion. Let the motion flex down from the cervical (neck) spine to the lumbar spine. Undulate the upper body forward perhaps 20 to 30 rolls. Try changing the rolling direction to undulate backwards; much like a dog moves its body forward to bury a bone with its nose. Tuck, drop and extend the head to swoop forward. Imagine a walrus and move as they do - come up on your hands (angled slightly outward as flippers) and undulate then lift one flipper and the other. Check out the ***Adelaide Walrus Workout*** on YouTube to exercise with a walrus leading in push-ups, lateral stretches, leg lifts and more, alongside a walrus.

More Traditional Asanas (traditional yoga)

Half Boat Pose (*Ardha Navasana*), Head to Knee Pose (*Janusirsasana*), Forward Bend on a Leg Bent Back (*Trianga Mukhaikapada Pascimottanasana*)

One of the most ubiquitous of mammals is the attention-grabbing squirrel species. This conspicuous species is widespread throughout the world. They enjoy success on every continent except Antarctica. Their quick, agile movements, little manipulative digits and playfulness are a joy to emulate. Given their dexterity and acrobatic abilities, like otters, they are delightful social flycatchers of our human attention and wonder.

Squirrel's Saturday Night Live

Instruction suggestions for this particular mammal are to seek your own personal freeform versions in movement. However, I've found that creative expressions are easily facilitated with some funky music should you require accompaniment to motivate you to get in the groove.Try "*Staying Alive*". Feel the rhythm and let your body interpret how to find and best emulate your Red Squirrel.

Eurasian Red Squirrel

Skill is Built

Ginger Rogers and Fred Astaire aside - simply observing a dance for most of us does not mean that we can also immediately dance the steps or have ability to emulate the skill required. Seeing how an animal moves only allows us to visually memorize the motions in general; skill and emulation requires practice. Choreographing creative expressions takes time and repetition to mentally and physically develop. Using visualization of course, improves delivery, accuracy and eventually, with spontaneity, the movement expression, timing and technique. It is with repetitive practice that memorization can transform into the skilled physically -based associations rather than a dependency on mental constructs. Practice is required to become proficient in anything we do, including our access to expression. When skill becomes explicit there is a palpable easing in the effort that is required. On reaching the level where skill requires little conscious effort and becomes more easily accessible, skill is responsive moment to moment because it is body memorized and spontaneous. Then it is only a matter of fine tuning to resonate dynamically and absorb what is happening externally. Subtle details become more noticed.

Moving as a pure membrane differs from moving with stiff but semi-flexible chitin, and carrying a shell differs from having interior bones for stability in motion. Movements may direct how swimming as a shark might differ from swimming in slick integument rather than with whale blubber buoyancy. These and other aspects affect detailed expression and requires some imaginative thought to "fill in the spaces" for more than mimicry by adding knowledge and visualization. Indeed, the forms and movement representations must occur first in our minds before it's possible to trust that our movements will mirror another species in practice. Folded over a pillow in *Turtle*, we have to imagine the heaviness of a hard turtle shell; and detail the feeling radiating laterally down the spine in the sinuous slither as a snake.

Can't wrap toes around a tree branch like the primates could? Stand and move on a foam roller; it not only strengthens the muscles and tissues in the foot arches, it might help you to feel the primal feet of our ancestors. Creatively use touch to better sense how a particular body as a completed form where there is no firm exterior to provide you with any direct feedback, as in *Flapping Fish*. Posture and imagination may fill in the gaps for the body plan of a fish, to feel a closed tail or several more arms, or even experience the loss of bones. Costumes such as Cirque apparel or having the appropriate surroundings or environment for practice can support making it real. Appreciate the species you emulate in the environment that has shaped their movements;

it might open another facet to enhance the creature movements more completely. If the workout hopping like a ***Rabbit Running*** underwater doesn't leave you with an intimate appreciation for a hare's abilities… nothing will. As a single celled organism, it's hard not to feel intimacy with the water surroundings-- it's all around you in temperature, viscosity, slip, buoyancy, welcome it as becoming part of you.

Once you begin to know favored species, feel free to play around with choreographing them together, moving from one species into another. In the water, try out some progressions moving spontaneously as you may feel in the water, perhaps diving down to glide in ***Beaver,*** barrel over at the surface into ***Otter Roll,*** then undulate back in ***Shark,*** float roundly as a ***Jellyfish,*** then turn to a side-winding ***Water Snake*** or a few full body flexions and extension in ***Nautilus Pump*** and finish as a vigorous ***Running Rabbit***, or another ***Beaver*** glide beneath the surface to set the stage for emerging in the shallows for amphibian fun. Fill yourself with expressive primordial animal movements, shape them and weave them together in whatever way feels right to you bodily. You can't go wrong if led by listening to how your body wants to move and play. At the most basic level, engagement identifying with other species opens new dynamics to an inherited past to participate in the true immediacy of the world.

Emulating other species may surprise you in many ways. If not, perhaps the journey back through geologic time will. Some may easily identify with other species and tap into an ancient primordial well where creative expression just emerges and flows directly. Setting the stage in a natural environment or terrain is an option to stir the creative juices. Imaginations are powerful and observation and visualization feed the senses in how to move and morph as other creatures.

Whether restfully meditating in ***Serpent***, enjoying the weight of your ***Elephant Trunk*** swaying back and forth, or seeking relief in a tense workplace in an ***Emperor Penguin*** neck roll, or perhaps folded in repose breathing as a ***Frog*** to slowly quieten the body and mind; **PyM** practice can be full of meaningful inspiration and is best when it comes from the heart. By mimicking and emulating other species' actions, the more aware we become of connection with other species and thee organic cells within.

References

Bekoff, M., & Pierce, J. (2017). *The animals' agenda: Freedom, compassion, and coexistence in the Human Age*. Beacon Press.

Berta, A. , Sumich , J. L. , and Kovacs , K. M. (2006). "Marine Mammals: Evolutionary Biology," 2nd ed. Elsevier, San Diego, CA.

Bertram, J. E., & Gutmann, A. (2009). Motions of the running horse and cheetah revisited: fundamental mechanics of the transverse and rotary gallop. Journal of the Royal Society Interface, 6(35), 549-559.

Bofarull, A.M., Royo, A.A., Fernandez, M.H., Ortiz-Jaurequizar, E.,Morales, J., 2008. Influence of continental history on the ecological specialization and macroevolutionary processes in the mammalian assemblage of South America: Differences between small and large mammals, BMC Evolutionary Biology, Vol.8.

Brannen, P., 2017. *The Ends of the World: Volcanic Apocalypses, Lethal Oceans And Our Quest To Understand Earth's Past Mass Extinctions.* Simon and Schuster, NewYork.

Brusatte, S. Zhe-Xi Luo, 2016. The Rise of Mammals, *Scientific American,* 30-35.

English, A. W. (2009). Limb movements and locomotor function in the California sea lion (*Zalophus californianus*). *Journal of Zoology*. 178 (3): 341–364.

Fraser, C. (2009). *Rewilding the world: Dispatches from the conservation revolution*. Macmillan Press.

Fröbisch, J., & Reisz, R. R. (2009). The Late Permian herbivore Suminia and the early evolution of arboreality in terrestrial vertebrate ecosystems. *Proceedings of the Royal Society B: Biological Sciences*, *276*(1673), 3611-3618.

Hildebrand, M. (1989). The quadrupedal gaits of vertebrates. *Bioscience*, *39*(11), 766.

Hildebrand, M. (1961). Further studies on locomotion of the cheetah. *Journal of mammalogy*, *42*(1), 84-91.

Jones, K. E., Dickson, B. V., Angielczyk, K. D., Pierce, S. E., 2021. Adaptive Landscapes Challenge the "lateral-to-sagittal" Paradigm for Mammalian Vertebral Evolution, Current Biology.

Lento, G. M., Hickson, R. E., Chambers, G. K., & Penny, D. (1995). Use of spectral analysis to test hypotheses on the origin of pinnipeds. Molecular Biology and Evolution, 12(1), 28-52.

Li, J., Huang, J-P, Sukumaran, J., Knowles, L.L., (2018) Microevolutionary processes impact macroevolutionary patterns, BMC Evolutionary Biology, Vol. 18.

McGaa, E., 2004. Nature's Way: Native Wisdom for Living in Balance with the Earth. *HarperCollins Publishers*, New York.

Padian, K. (2015). Dinosaur up in the air. Nature, 521(7550), 40-41.

Sahney S.; Benton M.J. (2008). "Recovery from the most profound mass extinction of all time". Proceedings of the Royal Society B: Biological Sciences. 275 (1636): 759–65.

Shubin, N., 2008. *Your Inner Fish: a journey into the 3.5-billion-year history of the human body*. Vintage Books.

Soulé, M., Gilpin, M., Conway, W., & Foose, T. (1986). The millenium ark: how long a voyage, how many staterooms, how many passengers?. *Zoo biology*, 5(2), 101-113.

Taylor, M. E. (1989). Locomotor adaptations by carnivores. In Carnivore behavior, ecology, and evolution (pp. 382-409). Springer, Boston, MA.

Vrba, E.S., Fernandez, M.H., (2005) Macroevolutionary Processes and Biomic Specialization: Testing the Resource-use Hypothesis, Evolutionary Ecology, Vol. 19.

CHAPTER 6

Primates to Hominins

In this series of exercises, we stand at the threshold of our primate family of *Hominidae* with kindred cousins. The common reference to *hominid* refers to the family of apes and from which the species of mankind, the *hominins* descended. Current evidence holds that the taxonomic primate order is traceable to a lineage of small, furry terrestrial shrew-like mammals appearing 85 to 55 million years ago; however, fossil discoveries may push that date even further back. We do know that the ground-dwelling mammals survived past the last major extinction and primates arose as distinct mammalian groups in forested regions. The evolutionary history of the primates reveals that they diversified widely and rapidly into many ecological niches across the planet. They comprise one of the most diversified of mammal groups found in a variety of challenging and capricious ecosystems.

There is much scientific evidence confirming that primates are ancestors of hominins, the early human species that began to evolve from the apes around 8 million years ago. The most compelling is that all but 1% of DNA sequenced *Homo sapient* genes are shared precisely with ancestral great apes. Hominid gorillas, orangutans, bonobos and chimpanzees are our kin as their genes carry very few subtle differences. Visually, our hominin limb structure: shoulders, pelvis, hands and feet are obviously analogous. Facial expressions and gestures are also often easily understood cross-species, not only in shared approaches, emotional displays and temperaments but in the ability to recognize intent and behaviour at a glance. We identify with similar responses and react to fellow feelings instantly, comprehending intentions and actions cross-species, such as how a sibling might show compassion or how anger is being felt. Communication between the species has its limitations yet has been enhanced through sign language. Do our ears not prick up on hearing the wild calls of our cousins? Not the sports fanatic ones, but calls from the jungle should we be fortunate enough to hear them in the wild.

Hominid evolution has had a long and lengthy history of speciation with numerous species spread far and wide. During the earth's transformations over hundreds of thousands of years, the deepening complexity of the arboreal ecosystems influenced primate variations in their anatomical evolution, populations and speciation. The devastating effects of a massive asteroid impact 66 million years ago resulted in oxygen-depleted seas and an atmosphere flooded with carbon dioxide for 10 million years. The overheated earth was inhospitable except near the Polar regions. However, forests and jungle ecosystems worldwide eventually began to usher in a new miscellany in plant evolution providing repositories for food along and protective habitat by the Eocene. Forest habitats and climatic swings resulted in growing diversity of food sources with flowering and fruiting angiosperm plants and trees ready-made to further insect evolution as pollinators. A slow drift of the continents also played a definitive role in reshaping geological landscapes and hydrological configurations which further nourished the land and oceans with abundant bio-complexity and diversity. The result was a continuum of tree species covering the land under forest canopies interspersed by meadows, savannahs and wide open plains. In the rainy, temperate regions, vegetation grew ever taller and more dense, trees reaching higher in competition for the sun's energy. Beneath, the undergrowth grew impossibly thick as jungle, moist soils became rich in humus and loamy with all the decomposing plant life. In such rich environments, the preeminent arboreal primate mammals were in the company of marsupial lions, giant ground sloths, mammoths, dire wolves, panthers, giant armadillos, glyptodonts, camels, saber-tooth tigers and other feline *smilodont* species.

The earliest known primate was a ground-dwelling quadruped, *Torrejonia* that lived 63 million years ago, a furry mammal with opposed thumbs for grasping and climbing. However, there have been no other discoveries of primates until the Eocene era some 52 million years ago when primate fossils began appearing frequently at dig sites around the world. The records indicate that clinger and leaper species were the first primates in the primal Eocene forests. They preceded the brachiating monkeys that appeared in the late Oligocene and Miocene, moving through forests swinging branch to branch in arm-over-arm locomotion. And so began the 52 million span of *simian* evolutionary history whereupon hundreds of primate species ramified into the differing niche primate species that led to us.

An Arboreal Way of Life

Among evolutionary scientists there is some discussion about how the arboreal habitats may have influenced the evolution and locomotion of primate species based on adaptations size-related to what they encountered in the forests. Early movements through a forested environment might have affected how quadrupedal mammals evolved in the undergrowth. Most species living in arboreal regions today are in general, lighter and more agile than the ground-dwelling quadrupedal herding animals of the savannahs and grass plains. As the forests expanded on territory across land, the small and mid-

sized primordial terrestrial-bound quadruped mammals, if threatened by predators, may have retreated to the more protective and defensible forest boundaries. As some species adapted to the growing arboreal regions, their limbs, joints and finger digits also changed to enhance their crawling, climbing, clinging and leaping abilities. The first successful arboreal vertical clinger and leaper species and distant ancestors of today's galagos, tarsiers and lemurs diversified adaptations in a series of distinctly stepped anatomical modifications. Primate fossils reveal lighter bodies with longer limbs, flexible elbow and knee joints for moving and balancing with more abductive and extensor capacity, likely to reposition the center of gravity often required in arboreal movements. (Grand, 1968) (Schmitt, 2003) Longer forelimbs often provided extra mobility in joints for swinging branch to branch and with improved grasping ability, for suspension.

The primary finger digit in forest primates evolved more angled in opposition to the other digits and useful as thumbs for grip in climbing and clinging. The opposable primate thumb first appeared around 47 million years ago. In some species, the thumb was also elongated and equipped with a claw for extra grip. (Cartmill, M.,1974) Their tree climbing motions also brought about significant modifications in the joints of arms, wrists and feet that varied in some anatomical configurations within the different species. Between primate groups, the differences were especially pronounced in the humeral arm and wrist pronation to affect range of motion, and in pelvic joints. In the primate leaper species for example, the mode of locomotion through trees required that the hind legs deliver strong propulsive force as necessary to spring from branch to branch. Habitual leaper species have sitz bones with longer ischia that are oriented more orthograde forward. They also have deeper knee joints and muscle extensors to enable rapid-fire flex and extension in hind legs. (Smith and Savage, 1956)

The evolution of prehensile tails appeared early in primate evolution and is thought to have improved balance in leaps and in foraging to stabilize primates in clinging and suspensory postures. Primate morphology, as mentioned, has been characterized by many anatomical changes that have appeared, disappeared and reappeared again over time; which undoubtedly applies to primate prehensile tails, especially in the leaper and clinger primates. Old World primates of today, the tailless macaques, gibbons, colobines, golden snub-nosed monkeys, red-shanked doucs, mandrills and baboons -- all descended from ancestors with prehensile tails. Evolution can be just as dynamic as ecosystems are given the space and time to respond to changes occurring in an environment.

Leaping Lemur

Over the course of nearly 52 million years primate family species have evolved morphologies and characteristics from adaptations, transforming, converging and reappearing many times over. Each new adaptation may have been prompted by a change in their environment, a different tack in their locomotive technique, a new change in food sources or feeding habits; however most ancient characteristics are fairly represented in the extant species today. Primate morphologies have culminated with great variety, refining and tuning quite unique sensory features also, many of which were carried to our near-hominid cousins.

The arboreal habitats shaped many primate aerial, locomotive and balancing abilities in crawling, pulling, grasping, climbing, swinging, suspending, leaping and twisting movements. Their quick reflexes and acuity of their binocular vision were a result of sensory demands intrinsic to life in jungles and forests. Evidence points to commonalities shared with other non-primate species, particularly in arboreal marsupials which have a similar shape in the thorax and abdominal viscera, opposable thumbs and very similar spinal structures. Comparatively, primates have long been the undisputed masters of slack-line, aerial, trapeze and high-wire acrobatics. Employing various modes of suspension, brachiation, bipedal balance, twist and spin, they perform surprisingly quick actions well suited to life above ground. Imagine the high degree of visual assessment primates calculate in their speedy locomotion through a dense, tangled maze of jungle overgrowth; tree limbs jutting at different angles with the slippery moss laden coverings on branches, all in unknowable conditions of variable strength and fragility. Often it demanded lightning speed sensory reflexes. Primate survival often meant speedy retreats from predators requiring heightened senses attuned to the silent threats of stealth pursuers lurking on branches and shadows. It only took inattention for flight from one threat and into the jaws of another. The arboreal environment demanded evolution in primate defenses with the heightening of cognitive and sensory demands and safety in numbers and actions. Senses that were closely matched to equally acute, sensitive, responsive, perceptive and lightning-fast attacks of other primates, snakes, birds and various feline predators.

The acuity in panicked flights predicated that slight miscalculations of balance or grip were not an option where each leap and landing demands split second assessment. Assessing angle, size and structural integrity of vines and branches, clearance and pathway adjustments with swing inertia, scanning for likely pathways, judging beam and material slip in the dark, damp, slick fungal, moss and lichen-laden growth. Seems impossible, but body mapping the environment as much as possible while fleeing demanded that exactitude. It had to be intuitive to calculate reach, grip timing, weight displacement and shifts in balance. At high velocities, each forward leap or pitch in swing carries a variable momentum and in order to mitigate jump thrust and control weight on impact -- primate neural and physical senses needed to be attuned and alert to every detail. Consider it then also add in grip ability of a clinging infant!

Primates evolved the necessary visual, reactive and motor abilities for their arboreal habitat bounds in dark, tangled, overgrown jungles. We are the result of their evolutionary abilities with elevated acuity, sensory precision, pressure receptors to enhance touch and grip, quick motor and reflex responses, and more than adequate proprioceptive sensing and interoceptive feedback. The motor control, flexibility and balance in motion require a new level in neurological reflexes. While hominins, including our direct-lineage ancestors of the *Homo* species, evolved brain functions away from the visual-based neural acuity and agility that are so necessary in the wild, humans still retain much of the complexity as inherited sensory motor characteristics. As primate descendants, many of us are endowed with quick and flexible reflex attributes, *n'est pas*?

Brachiation, the ability to propel between branches using arm-over-arm movements, developed fairly early in primate morphologies to characterize certain species with extended musculoskeletal length and a higher range of mobility in their forelimbs joints. Some brachiating primate species exhibit exceptional rotational capacities in arms and a highly stable elbow. (Fleagle and Lieberman, 2021) The gibbon is a good example with forelimbs quite unequal in length to hindlimbs; they exhibit exceptional rotation in shoulders, elbows and wrists. However, brachiation is not typically accessible to humans post their childhood; but for a time, swinging from rings rung to rung is possible and great fun over short distances.

Gibbon

Climbing motions are contralateral in which forelimbs alternately reach and pull assisted by the adjacent hindlimbs initially occurred in the swim movements of tetrapods and in mammalian quadruped gaits. It is most pronounced however, in climbing and is the signature locomotive movement of arboreal animals. Primates coordinate contralateral motions with their adjacent limbs to reach, pull, stabilize and push upward to generate forward thrust vertically. One needs only add an alternating twist to introduce swinging brachiation. Curiously, contralateral movements appear instinctive in human infants as their lateral crawling progresses into contralateral and particularly when pulling to upright positions by enlisting the support of a standing post or chair leg, reaching hand over hand to stand upright on baby fat legs. All in all, we hominins inherited many sensory locomotive characteristics and traits from the many hominid adaptations in arboreal habitats.

Gibbons are the fastest arboreal mammals living today, moving at record speeds brachiating limb over limb; they have been clocked covering distances up 50 feet at speeds of 34 mph before pausing and leaping across spans more than 20 feet wide. Their current global status is now threatened, endangered due to destruction and loss of jungle habitat and encroachment on their rainforest territories.

There's no better way to practice our given primate abilities than to play as they do. In fact, human anatomy benefits from demands imposed by stretching, lengthening and using the agility in our nerve, circulatory, tissue and bone structure evolved from simian ancestors. By the age of seven, most of us will have lost the fluid Tarzan brachiating of primates in swinging vine to vine (or ring to ring). Our ground-dwelling, bipedal, movement-conservative lifestyles build only on the balance and fluidity of our walking gait and other weight-bearing motions of the lower body. The muscular bulk in our buttocks evolved from a habitual mode of walking works to ensure an upright build as a trade-off in transitioning from arboreal quadrupedalism to terrestrial bipedalism. Whether, as Darwin asserted in 1871 speculating that bipedalism evolved in order to gather and carry food which occupied use of hands, we cannot know. We do know that bipedalism evolved in spurts and starts, unevenly in different hominin species. (McHenry, 2009) (Lovejoy, 1981) *Homo sapiens* inherited much of the primate flexibility and range of motion in our joints and limbs and have further evolved forelimb and hand dexterity beyond the capacities attained by primates and the earlier hominins. Our limb evolution has expanded upper body arm usage and the manipulative abilities of finger digits. For example, the third metacarpal styloid now enables our hand bones to lock into the wrist bones which allows for greater force in the grasp of thumbs and fingers. (Ward, C.V. et al., 2013) We also have a highly functional forelimb design with good rotational motion in shoulders, elbows, wrists, and thumbs adding to the strength and manipulation required for making and using complex tools.

Primate Play

Try It: When ready and sufficiently limber, find a bar or parallel bars you can hang from, a pair of rings, a rope, secure horizontal branch, parachute cloth panel or sturdy vine. Enjoy hanging, pulling, climbing, swaying and clinging, twisting and generally "acting out like a monkey".

As you play, take a moment to consider the advances primates have contributed to human movements, their penchant for climbing and leaping. Over millions of years they raised the cognitive bar with elaborate sensory physiology and have defined many of our underlying social characteristics that go beyond instinct. In the upper canopies of forests and jungles, primate species pushed the limits in climbing, clinging and leaping with their flexible, quick, fluid, lithe and strong bodies.

Primate caveat: While hominins genetically split from great apes almost 10 million years ago and share many sensory and musculoskeletal traits and characteristics, there are of course, differences. Primates are primarily herbivores with diet subsistence dependent on leaves and shoots, seeds, fruits, flowers, insects and worms. Ape primates are more ground-dwelling species; they characteristically use one or two hands for gathering food which may have contributed to more orthograde postures with more time spent on the ground. As a result, their arms are typically longer, stronger and brawnier than their hind legs due to their history and semi-arboreal lifestyle spent climbing, hanging and foraging. Bonobos and chimpanzees frequently brachiate from branch to branch rather than coordinating their movements on hind limbs to traverse tree branches. Chimps and low land gorillas typically leave the forest floor and retreat up into the trees at nightfall for better protection but spend more time in the undergrowth floor. Yet male silverbacks have more gorilla arm strength than do 20 human adults. Human forelimbs are comparatively shorter and proportionately less strong. While we do retain some suspension ability in our shoulders, our hominin hands are now quite different. (Skinner, M.M., et al., 2015)) Two-hand suspension for any period of time has become less useful in our bipedal lifestyles. Unless a seasoned young rock climber, human hands generally cannot sustain such strenuous usage. Human hands have evolved away from the primate strength in grasp and cling capacity. (Marzke, M. and Marzke, R, 2000) Suspension depends not only on grip strength but the condition of shoulders, their strength and flexibility. So, if you are young, strong and confident – play to the limits! Hang and swing, brace and brachiate the pectoral muscles, triceps, lateral extensors and pronators, your serratus anterior, trapezius and rhomboids. The stronger and better balanced the connective tissues and muscle attachments are on a young bony frame, the better. For the rest, it is more beneficial to maintain health in arms and shoulders through stretch and weight training.

In the following series of exercises, the focus is on the shoulder girdle and arms - the connective tissues and muscles inherited from primates that give us twist, extension and flexibility. The exercises help to balance the tone and maintain flexibility in the muscles, ligaments and tendon tissues which directly affect not only the shoulder girdle and posture, but condition the upper body. They are for everyone to balance the push-pull, abduct/adduct aspects in a framework of contrast working on the serratus anterior and rhomboid musculature and the trapezius in relation to the pectoralis minor.

Shoulder Stretch

Sitting or Standing:

1. To begin with rotator cuff and other medial rotators, bring arms straight out at sides from the body. Rotate the extended arms slowly around turning in one direction at the shoulder sockets, and then rotate the other direction, hands turning around in full rotation. Start with the palms up and opened with thumbs out from the fingers to better sense the full rotation, rotate palms to the front, down and back. You may try this also lying down on a roller, arms are bent outward at 90 degrees, palms open – rotate fully up around and fully downward on the floor.

2. Arm circles – place fingertips on the tops of the shoulders and rotate the elbows around in wide circles. Then rotate the arms relatively straight in a wide overhead swim stroke. Then holding a strap or thin towel behind you with arms fully extended up above the head, move the arms straight behind as far as is possible and lower the arms 30 to 45 degrees down beyond the back. Your hand grip should be at least two to four feet apart on the towel or strap, depending on the level of comfort. Raise the arms above the head and bring them straight forward, then rotate them up and around and down behind, and again, up and around -- repeat eight times.

3. With one arm leading with the strap, make circles above the head in deep-angle sweeps using the whole upper body to work on lateral strength. Rotate from the hips and knees around first to the right, then left. Change direction.

To assure a comfortable flexibility in the overhead extension of the arms, first note how high the arms may rise. In raising an arm up straight, can you keep the other shoulder blade down and back? If there's any arm or neck strain, back off a little and be cautious in advancing the stretch. The connective tissues may need more temperate progression to improve range of motion. Build on stretches by extending the time in postures for longer and longer periods and tissues will accommodate safely over time.

Suspension Extensions

1. Lay supine face down in a *Sphinx* posture - lower the chest down and slide elbows forward until they are alongside the head to stretch triceps, bend forearms back behind to add further stretch also in the deltoids. If comfortable, turn the head to one side on the mat or bed to relax the upper arm and shoulder muscles, first on one side, and then turn to the other side and relax the opposite arm. This arm stretch is quite comfortable as a floor exercise or in bed (where pillows may prop up as needed to protect against overstretching the shoulder girdle). Ease into the posture slowly if shoulders are constricted. Hold the stretch for two to five minutes, each side.

2. Return to a facedown position then come up onto elbows to thread the right arm through and under the left armpit across the chest, between the clavicle and sternum. Slowly lay back down onto the folded arm to stretch the rhomboid and trapezius muscles. Gently turn the head to place the cheek down. Next, bring the opposite arm (left) along the left side body, with the palm up. Hold the posture for two minutes. Repeat with the left arm pinned under to deeply stretch and compress shoulder connective tissues on the other side. This helps to restore flexibility and circulation of the connective tissues in the back and posterior shoulder girdle.

3. Return to *Sphinx* and lay down again with the right arm extended out 90 degrees from the side body. Next rotate the core body in the same direction to the side as the open arm to stretch tissues across the chest and front and compress the girdle in the back. This simultaneously opens the chest out and squeezes the scapula, shoulder blades, together. Next, raise the left arm to bring it back behind also. If possible, join the two hands together behind the back. Relax the head down comfortably on the floor or on a soft support.

Variations

1. Begin kneeling on knees, place blocks or something similar well in front of you side-by-side (if your neck is long, leave a couple of inches

of space between blocks to brace the top of the head). Place bent elbows securely on top of the blocks and lower the chest down until your head rests halfway between the blocks. Relax the neck downward in the block opening to allow for extension in the triceps and relax forearms.

2. To test wrist pronation, sit on your haunches and flatten the palms on the ground next to hips, then lift the hands, rotating them around in little steps, around in one direction as far as they rotate, then stop and go the other direction in little steps on the wrists. Bend wrists under, palms facing upward and begin to step around on the backs of folded wrists and repeat the rotation circling to apply gentle pressure and stretch on the back sides of wrists: walk them around, circling in one direction and then the other. Go easy to sense just how much forward weight to place on them.

3. Traditional strengthening postures for the back and shoulder girdle muscles are typically practiced through isotonic extension. For example, when extending arms overhead in the traditional yoga Warrior 3 (*Virabhadrasana III)* or Locust Pose (*Salabhasana*).

Try It: Lay down on the torso with arms straight and parallel above your head, fully extended forward, legs also parallel and stretched long. Lift both legs simultaneously pressing the abdominals and torso firmly down, then lift the head, shoulders and arms off the ground. Keep neck vertebrae lengthened aligned with the curving of the spine, raise the arms even higher and begin pumping them up and down high above the ribs and waist.

4. **Advanced:** Reclining Hero Pose (*Supta Viransana*). Begin seated, bend the knees deeply bringing the lower legs close in and angled back alongside your thighs, with heels beside the hips. The folded legs form a "saddle" (If too uncomfortable, try it with only one leg bent folded back, the other straight forward). Still seated, gently lower the upper body back down to the floor (place the head on blocks or pillow) and stretch the upper thighs. Use a large pillow or bolster to support the lower back and to prevent overstretching the thighs. In a comfortably reclined position, raise arms above the head and clasp the elbows relaxing them above. Proceed easefully. Take care, if lateral muscles are tight, raising arms overhead can cause hyperextension by overarching the spine.

A good rule of thumb for improved upright posture is to maintain an open chest with shoulder blades tucked in together and down, away from the base of the neck. Habits in human lifestyles have a tendency to frequently cause a hunching over from slouch sitting. When poor postures become habitual, imbalance in oppositional muscle sets occurs, especially as we become lax. The above posture, bringing shoulder blades together behind, elbows at the sides; it automatically rotates the chest open. Neck/head positioning is easy when neck muscles under the chin are held in to support an erect head - well balanced and upright on the shoulder girdle.

Traditional Yoga Asanas for Upper Body Flexibility and Strength

Cat-Cow (Chakravakasana), *Triangle* (Trikonasana) and *Revolved Triangle* (Parivrtta triknonasana), *Great Mudra* (Mahamudra), *Mountain Pose* (Tadasana), *Chair Pose* (Utkatasana), *Dancer Pose* (Natarajasana), *Cow-Faced Pose* (Gomukhasana), *Gate-Latch Pose* (Parighasana), *Bow Pose* (Dhanurasana), *Crane Pose* (Bakasana) and other bird poses such as *Crow, Rooster, Eagle, Scorpion* (Vrschikasana) and Warrior III (*Virabhadrasana III).*

Hail to Hominids

With an evolutionary history spanning over 55 million years, our ancestral primates are a highly successful and adaptable mammalian family group. For millions of years their numerous species throughout the world were especially densely distributed in the warmer arboreal regions and climes. Unfortunately, in recent years the world's primate populations have been reduced to a small fraction of their former numbers. Most species in fact, are threatened today with extinction. Beginning as early as the 1800s, monkeys, apes and other primate species have fought a losing battle to retain the territorial ranges of their previous generational populations. Every year they have been further driven from their natural habitats due to deforestation, road building, human settlements, agriculture, and from rampant destruction caused by tribal and civil wars, wild fires and other climate-induced changes. They have been mercilessly hunted and trapped by poachers for bush meat and captured for research subjugation, confined in animal zoos and subjected to pet trade.

Orangutan

Hominid genetics are also shared alongside hominins as our kin which also puts them at risk for Coronavirus and other human diseases and ailments, including diabetes and trauma. Our closest hominid ancestors are chimpanzees, bonobos, orangutans, and gorillas, all of whom are now facing more and more genetic isolation in smaller and smaller groups constrained in unconnected territorial areas. Every year, primate species are less numerous in their temperate forests, mountains and savannas with very few primate groups found outside the tropics.

Habitat destruction is at the forefront of the problem. What typically begins with a road cut through the jungle, roads inevitably mean that forests will be cut and cleared, the land then parsed and parceled for human use and dwellings. In the last ten years, 76% of all primate species have lost habitat regions due to agriculture expansion alone. (ICUN) Deforestation claims most of primate territory as the inroad incursions and destruction go unchecked and losses are realized only after the fact; especially in the dense jungle habitats where damage is evident by satellite. Worldwide, more than 60% of all known 448 primate species are close to complete annihilation. It is unfortunate that most of the primates' natural habitats are in regions where there are high levels of poverty, inadequate awareness and education, local official corruption, lack of accountability and political instability. Primates are systematically killed or removed from their habitats at a more rapid rate in underdeveloped regions in the world; more than 90% of all primate species are disappearing due to widespread poaching. (IUCN online data, 2019, 2020) What will it take to ensure that primates prosper in their historical regions? Without sustained, enforceable land-use initiatives, effective governing measures, transparency and accountability, and local education; it is conceivable that all primates living in natural habitats will become extinct in our lifetime. Within a few generations, it is likely that no great apes will still be living in any of their hereditary habitats, even with the tireless campaigning for protection from conservationists and advocate primatologists such as Jane Goodall.

All creatures on the planet merit honor; especially those that are 99% like us - the apes and primates whose evolution has defined and refined so many of our hominin characteristics; surely they deserve special recognition from us. We owe the ability to ride mountain bikes pell-mell through the twists and tangles of forest trails to them, our split-second reflexes in batting a ball flying towards us at 98 mph, and the graceful fluidity and dexterity in arms, elbows, wrists, fingers plus opposable thumbs to tool materials, all of it to ancestral primates. They, not us, were the ancestral mammalian group to develop and refine many of the social and cooperative, defensive and offensive characteristics indicative in our species; they care for one another, learn from one another, use tools, fight and play in groups together. We are like them and they are like us. Should we not honor primates at the very least for *how* we came to be a species? No matter whether we now feel that they are "not quite up to snuff" comparably, since they *are* the ones in the cages; does that mean their inferiority deserves only our disregard? *Homo sapiens* happen to be the last hominin species remaining on the earth. How sad it would be if our evolutionary legacy to our birthplace is to fail to restrict our own species to ensure the habitat necessary for our ancestors to live. It is tantamount to shirking responsibility to defend a grandmother's right to live. Or shall we go down in history as the only *Homo* species that selfishly evolved only to know and care for our own kind?

Our social minds draw us together as if we are one mind on the world, but also protect us from those we don't wish to believe have much mind worth considering.
~ **Melanie Challenger, How To Be an Animal, 2021**

Knuckle-Walking

Try It 1st Modified on a Roller: With straight legs crossed one atop the other and seated behind a foam roller, begin by rolling on the lower hamstring (back of leg) from just above the knee to below the buttocks. Curl hands under to put the upper body weight on the second hand knuckles and straightened arms to lift up enough to roll back and forward on the roller. Roll tuck inward pulling in on the abdominals to swing the upper body back and forth between the arms.

Try It: Legs on primates are typically shorter on all the great ape species than the length of their arms. Here's how you can emulate great ape ancestors - begin standing with knees bent quite low to the ground to offset the length discrepancy, or begin by kneeling - it's easier to access the same ape walk. Let the arms hang down where they fall forward, curl in the thumb and fingers and try a little gentle knuckle-walking on a carpeted or other soft surface. Next, place the knuckles down ahead slightly forward, tuck in abdominals and lift up on the arms to swing the knees forward (or hop the feet). Bring knees down a little forward between the arms. Again, plant the knuckles and swing forward to move like an ape. If the movement is easy, also sway from side to side, push out your jaw, and pucker and protrude your lower lip. Try alternating the knuckled movements contralaterally, and with opposite knee movements, as chimps will often do. Knuckle-walking on feet is more difficult and requires upper-body strength and firmly held abdominals to fully flex feet for clearance. Locomotion in this manner will strengthen muscles from toes to neck and everything in between. If a carpeted or a soft surface is not available to you, try wrapping knuckles with socks or a soft cloth.

…we err, and greatly err. For the animal shall not be measured by man. In a world older and more complete than ours they move finished and complete, gifted with extensions of the sense we have lost or never attained, living by voices we shall never hear.
~ **Marc Bekoff, Animal Manifesto**

As far as we know, no early species of hominin habitually used knuckle-walking as do chimps and modern apes use the forelimbs in quadrupedal walking. Yet it feels good to do so. We are after all, every one, simply apes needing to remind ourselves that we are related. Humans are just one more species in the hominin family that evolved from the hominids, recently. So think about it, ease up and play with the fact that you are an...

Apeman

However structurally similar to the great apes we are, the carriage of our posture is markedly different. Humans have repositioned limbs relative to an upright frame influencing the angle of hips, feet and knees, chest and shoulders to the spine. Feel and witness the differences by physically returning into posturing as an ape.

Try It: Standing - widen the knees out wider than the hips and bend them out slightly rotating from hip sockets. This will lower the torso, lean forward and push the buttocks back and let the arms hang down, curl your toes. The belly should be repositioned over thighs to allow the lower ribs to open. Keep the upper chest open and head aligned with the spine, do not over exaggerate the arch in the low back -- just enough to thrust the lower ribs forward. Ape arms are longer and heavier, hold them wider than the thighs and rotated inwardly with elbows rounded out from the sides in a loose shrug, curl fingers. Visualize your forehead as broad across the face; tilt the chin in with a slight jut in the lower jaw. Have fun with the posture, swaggering with side to side deliberation like a stiff trail cowboy should give you a real sense of this ancestor. Raise your arms and stagger!
Oo-ou oo-oo–ouh - aawh!

Have fun as you move to the tunes of The Kinks from 1970 in their song

- *I Am An Apeman*:

I'm an ape man, I'm an ape apeman
I'm an ape man I'm a King Kong man I'm ape apeman
I'm an ape man
Cos compared to the sun that sits in the sky
Compared to the clouds as they roll by
Compared to the bugs and the spiders and flies
I am an ape man

In man's evolution he has created the cities and
The motor traffic rumble, but give me half a chance
And I'd be taking off my clothes and living in the jungle
cos the only time that I feel at ease
Is swinging up and down in a coconut tree
Oh what a life of luxury to be like an ape man

I'm an ape, I'm an ape ape man, I'm an ape man
I'm a King Kong man, I'm a Voo-Doo man
I'm an ape man

Once comfortable emulating a species you have only slightly evolved away from, ask yourself this question: was acting out as an ape any less comfortable than other PyM emulations simply because the mimicry required so few minor postural adjustments to your natural posture and movements? Is it possible that the smaller the difference might instill a greater (more competitive) disapproval not because they are different but are so similar?

Climbing, leaping, and clinging primate hips are not human hip design: their position relative to the spine is more outwardly lateral, adapted for climbing narrow branches and consequently have more rotation in the hips, especially when in a more upright posture. As a result, it is faster for apes to move across ground by modifying a more sideways motion when traversing terrain on foot. As the series of images below show, locomotion of arboreal primates is more of a sideways hop and skipping motion. Be careful when trying this, it's not easy and requires some practice. The sideways motion continuously requires our use of lift and momentum assistance from arms. It is necessary to swing the lagging leg sideways then lifting the leading leg, hop both legs apart to plant both feet down almost simultaneously to the side. It is definitely more fun and easier if you practice from a hanging rope or other suspensory aerial material with a wide swing available. With a twist and hop, skip and feet plant wide and bent, repeat.

From The Gap by T. Suddendorf

Hominins, Stepping Stones to Us

Humans are a *Homo sapient* species in the same genus as *Homo Neanderthalis, Homo Habilis, Homo Erectus, Homo Ergaster, Homo Denisova, Homo Rudolfensis* and *Homo Florensis,* to name a few; all were taxonomic *Homo* species thought to have descended from *Australopithecus*. There are many earlier hominin species not directly related to the *Homo* genus but were anatomically bipedal and upright adapting to life on the savannah, some also semi-arboreal.

Seven million years ago, the earth's climate underwent some substantial cataclysmic upheavals. Frequent, closely spaced global ice ages alternated with long periods of drought causing many of the vast arboreal forests to shrink in many regions on earth. The stressors in the forested regions may have contributed to the hominid to hominin evolution by shifting the new species onto the plains. Physiologically the early hominins were more ape than human and the record is far from complete. Data on the known early hominin species indicate there was quite uneven anatomical evolution between hominin species taking many trial adaptations for hominid/hominins to fully descend from the forests as bipedal. Pinpointing a timeline in the evolution of bipedalism in early non-human hominins is unclear; however what fossil evidence there is supports bipedalism as an early evolving characteristic.

Discoveries of hominin fossils dating 4.4 million years to 3.9 million years ago reveal that most species had far less suspensory anatomical features than their chimpanzee and bonobo predecessors. One of the earliest hominin species, *Ardipithecus ramidus,* were diurnal and only occasionally were bipedal by retaining their principal walking in trees on horizontal boughs. However ,they had more frontal forward motion in gait with greater extension in knee joints indicating a semi-upright stance. (Tuttle, R.H., 1981) *Ardipithecus* had a large divergent, opposing big toe indicative of habitual tree climbing; yet the species was semi-arboreal as the teeth show they also fed on grains and berries from the savannah. (Lovejoy, 2009) (White et al., 2009) Research on hominin groups with more upright bipedal postures was just one aspect in adapting to the plains landscape and activities gathering and later in hunting food. *Australopithecus afarensis* is considered our prehistoric ancestral species from Africa, although not classified as a *Homo* species. The fossilized remains of a skeleton named Lucy led to uncovering details leading to our species origination. The *Australopithecus* species lived from 3.85 million to 2.95 million years ago and habitually walked on two flattened feet fully upright with arm swing which confers gait speed and minimizes energetic expense. She and others of her kind had long arms with more forward-facing shoulder joints, also strong arms and hands well suited for tree-climbing as optional. (Green, Alemseged, 2012)

Since 1994, there have been a number of new hominin species discovered around the world adding to our knowledge of hominin evolution. There have been a surprising number of confirmed hominin species which now number over 20, with more being identified currently. The fossil discoveries globally make it clear that going back 3.5 million years ago multiple hominin species walked the earth concurrently; although it is doubtful that they encountered one another. (Kate Wong, 2020) The record shows that bipedalism was firmly habitual in *Australopithecus sediba*, a hominin that lived 2 million years ago in South Africa and shares several morphological characteristics in common with the hominin genus *Homo*. However, the species had an ape heel bone with a modern ankle. Their feet suggest a tendency to hyper-pronate, walking on feet rolled inward. It is another indication that bipedalism emerged in hominin species unevenly and as late as 2 million years ago. However hominin fossilized remains do indicate a progressive trend in bipedal movement that drove hominin toes into smaller, closer digits and elongated their feet in adapting to more forward rocking motion. Not only did feet adapt for more thrust off the metatarsal balls of the feet, but a more aligned posture in walking upright. Paleontologists are still drafting a clearer picture of the many unrelated hominin species with widely varied morphologies.

When the *Homo* species in the hominin lineage first appeared, they were distinguished as a genus of different species also. Their morphology and limb proportions indicate that *Homo* anatomies were fully bipedal and upright although some retained distinct signatures of apes such as curved toe phalanges. The oldest fossils in the *Homo* lineage appeared around 2.3 million years ago with *Homo Habilis*. *Homo Habilis* are the first known hominin species to have fashioned tools (Oldowan). (Leakey et al., 1964)(Susman, Stern, 1982) Their fossil evidence also reveals a larger brain case than in all other previous hominin species.

Homo Erectus appeared about 1.9 million years ago and holds the record for the longest surviving species in the *Homo* genus thus far, of course including *Homo sapiens*. *Homo erectus* walked the earth for 1.5 million years, they are known to have migrated vast distances across Asia and Indonesia, Africa, and north to the Black Sea. They were the first "humanlike" *Homo* species, taller with shorter arms and they walked fully upright. *Homo erectus* were resourceful in toolmaking (Acheulean) and in their use of a wide variety of natural materials. They also importantly, controlled fire and cooked food. (Goren-Inbar et. al., 2004) (Pruetz, LaDuke, 2010) *Homo erectus* fashioned shelters for group protection, used tools for hunting and defense, and ate a variety of foods including meat. (Lepre, C.J. 2011) (Faisal, A. et al., 2010) Not only did their knowledge of using fire provide them warmth and drove animals and insects away, but cooked food provided more nutrition in digesting tuber plants, starch, and seeds. (Wrangham, R.W., 2009) *Homo erectus* was astonishingly migratory and inhabited a wide variety of terrestrial environments in different climes.

Other hominins of the *Homo* lineage species include a jungle pygmy species found on an island, *Homo floresensis,* and an earlier *Homo luzonensis* species that died out only 50,000 years ago, an islander also. Pygmy hominin species changed little over time as forest dwellers comparably. The *Homo floresensis* species only died out a mere 15,000 years ago. Another European *Homo* species, *Neanderthalensis* went extinct only 17,000 years ago. Another close relative living at the same period in history as the Neanderthals, were *Homo Denisovans*. Little is known about them and they died out, it is thought between 30,000 and 50,000 years ago. More recent 2021 hominin discoveries currently underway indicate the possible inclusion of two new *Homo* species.

Homo hominin species made huge evolutionary strides through controlling fire, fashioning tools, building shelters, hunting, farming and cooking more digestible, more sustaining protein. By improving the human condition, living and provisioning together and later, communicating with language expanded their sociability leading to the development of cultural cooperation and cohesion for greater expansion, protection, and defense with division of labor. Eventually, hominins found it possible to further harness the physics of their environment as a part of the living enterprise and with division of labor formed the first rudimentary culture. (Stock, 2008) As hominin brains progressed away from visual processing and into communicating through representation and the use of abstract ideas, together they forged commonly understood realities among one another. The use of symbols in *Homo sapient* communication has expanded a shared knowledge base in more and more complex ways. All of the above has played into the rapid acceleration in our brain size, capacity and intellectual prowess. (Ko, K.H., 2016) The possibilities are endless to become who and what we may in the world.

Physical Trade-offs

In the years of derivative history leading to *Homo Sapiens*, our inherited physiology from apes has varied little. We share limbs and joints that are similarly proportioned, share the same design in muscle structure that extend, twist, flex and abduct; ligaments and tendons that girdle shoulders and arms to externally rotate the humerus and stabilize the jointed sockets and the scapula to rotate and abduct the upper body. Apes share the same muscles as ours to lift arms and adduct and restrict against extreme adduction, the same pronators to rotate forearms, and similar muscles which stretch, flex and abduct arms distally, extend the wrist and extend fingers. Even the proportionate sizes are similar in large and small muscles, ligaments and tendons in our shoulder and leg girdles that join to work together in our back, chest, waist, hips and legs including all the lateral support muscles which connect the ribs and spine.

Primate morphology has afforded our bodies not only a wide range of motion but attitudes of strength with the stabilized flexibility to move, balance and support pulling, twisting, clinging and swing motions. Our shoulder structures are similar enough to primates to sustain climbing mobility and suspension. Many of us as children loved the idea of living in a treehouse and swinging from vine to vine through the forest like Tarzan and Jane. However *Homo sapient* forelimbs are designed for speed and accuracy in throwing, catching, spinning, bouncing and object manipulation. In general, shoulder architecture and peripheral limb isotonic strength no longer support lengthy periods of clinging and swinging. Yet we have retained the stable architecture in the core body with further girdling of the internal organs to support an upright spine. Our orthograde posture is now built for bipedal locomotive stability. As hominins left arboreal life for the savannah, morphologies advanced towards endurance running. In doing so, the trade-off for lighter, more gracile bodies and running stamina was to lose the strength of our ape ancestors with each successive *Homo* species over a span of 3 million years. (Bramble, D.M., Liebermann, D.E., 2004)(Walker, A., 2009)

Physically, *Homo Sapiens* carry more muscle strength in our legs with longer stride extension for locomotive mobility and sustaining running speeds. The narrowed, upright human frame has resulted in more efficient bipedal walking gaits and better suited for long-distance running. The femur head in the thigh bones have become thicker, more robust with a greater load bearing capacity in support of the fully upright frame. The femur is angled more inwardly from the hip to the knee joint – a distinguishing feature away from the outward leg orientation of apes. The girdling at the pelvis bridge the hips and supports upper body weight and stabilize movements in our upright posture. The *Homo* pelvic bowl ilium is now shortened and more deeply curved for connective tissues to pull the femur forward. And the ischium, connected to the ilium now extends dorsally to the back of the leg to align the forward orientation, rather than laterally as in apes. (Grabowski et. al., 2011) (Lovejoy et al., 2009) Hominins have retained substantial twist in the spine with remarkably mobile upper body movement considering their evolution towards improved upright stability, for that we may thank primate evolution. (Robinson, J.T, 1972)

The first living cells of bony vertebrae 400 million years ago derived from minerals in the sea. Bone composition is as integral to sustaining function now as it was then. Strength and resiliency in the human spinal column can result in a smooth walking gait, flexibility and balance. A slack line or tight-rope walker must have well-informed, stable nerves for balance. Sensing tension, elasticity and other factors of balance is apparent in how stability mitigates flexibility where both factors must work together to confer balance in the body. Somatic author Emilie Conrad wrote about the interplay of these two factors that guide balance in human movement. While both are necessary, a caveat is that one may compromise the other - too much stabilization compromises flexibility (i.e. weight-lifting without stretch) and flexibility must reconcile with stability. She was neatly succinct in the body's need for stretching... *"Stabilization is vital for efficiency but it becomes rigid when uninformed by new probabilities"*. (Conrad, E.,2012)

Sixty years ago scientists confirmed that evolution of the human musculoskeletal systems had traded physical strength (of primates) for running speed, throwing ability and hand manipulation. (Maynard Smith, J., Savage, R.J.G., 1956) (Shipman,P., Walker, A., 1989) Our evolution in the anatomy of joints and connective architecture has also replaced physical strength for mechanical and manipulative advantages. (Scholz, M.N.,et al., 2006). More importantly, humans have a species-unique ability to deliberately separate the work action of different muscle sets. (Walker, A., 2009) The placement of directing physical action within the body affords us the possibility of more selective control with less stress on the certain parts of the body and can give us more leveraging in manipulation. It has allowed us new physical abilities such as sign language, yoga, team sports, dance, charades and other physical expressions to fortify health. However, it is not as practiced as it could be to improve our physiology... Practice using muscle sets deliberately in opposition is the "yin-yang" of Hatha yoga which involves concentrating on relaxing certain muscle sets while using others to stabilize and activate poses; it thereby invigorates selective body parts and channels energy in the body, directing flow not only energetically and fluidly, but dynamically. It is a main component in somatic therapies as a factor to support physical expression.

To maintain physical health, flexibility and bone strength, it is essential to all vertebrates to maintain integrity and strength in the spine. Human vertebral column ligaments and tendons hold considerably less fluid than do the surrounding muscles and doing twists in particular will keep the spine refreshed and fluid. Unless the vertebrae and joints have adequate fluids to maintain intracellular nutrient flow to hydrate connective tissues, stagnation will reduce fluidity to the cartilage in bones and can result in inflammation and weakened, debilitating movements. Connective tissues hold onto body wastes and if dehydrated, cause thinning and compression between vertebral discs and skeletal joints. To maintain bone condition with a healthy composition, thickness, elasticity and range of movement, we need to move, stretch and load. The spinal column is central to all moving vertebrate species and we are no different. In human anatomy, an important internal fluid system is contained in cerebrospinal fluid that moves up and down bathing the spinal cord and the human brain. While the dura mater assiduously filters these fluids in reaching the brain, the cerebrospinal fluid nourishes the central nervous system and in part helps to constitute a kind of hydraulic suspension to absorb impacts to the spine. Young, growing human bodies stop adding fluid to the cerebrospinal fluid reservoir by the age of 24 years when physical growth ends. At that point, the only way to keep vertebral discs fit is to "juice" them through movement. In moving the spine, the intercellular fluids circulate the cerebrospinal fluid bath to keep the spinal column healthy. Since movement and stretch acts to compress and release vertebrae and the intra-tissues, it also supports drainage into the lymph system. Flushing out dead and dying cells consistently always maintains better health so new cells may grow more easily. Keeping connective tissues happy requires consistent and regular stretch and twists, especially through the spinal column between the two large girdling fulcrums which defines our four-limbed *Homo sapient* morphology. Our primate and hominin ancestors have passed down the elegance of a natural curve in the vertebrae giving it an awesome characteristic of flexibility with easy, graceful body motions. With twists and other inclinations, we can honour our kin, right down to the celerity in the swing of our hips.

Come on, Let's Do the Twist

Try it: If standing upright, round your arms down in front at the pelvic bowl and weave your fingertips together comfortably below. With your feet apart and firmly planted, rotate the pelvis around 20 times swinging in one direction, then rotate in the opposite direction 20 times. Modify in sitting or with support (a sturdy chair back is ideal).

2. Gently swing open arms twisting side to side from the hips. If seated, be sure to lift up through the spine before engaging twist motions. Then place hands strategically to brace either in a standing or seated twist (one hand behind the chair, one hand on the outside of the knee) and hold the twist momentarily, then twist and hold in the opposite direction.

3. Seated on the floor with legs crossed or spread wide, lift up from the hips and turning to one side, inhale fully and on the exhale bend down over the thigh with a straight back, aim your head towards the outside of the knee and hold briefly. Lift upright, and inhale up and forward, then twist and exhale down over to the other knee. This will laterally stretch in the lower back and spine. Continue side to side, 10 to 20 repetitions.

4. From the seated position, bend in the right knee and lay it down open to the side, then straighten the left leg out and away in the opposite direction from the bent knee. Turn to the right and bend down over the right thigh. Keep moving low to the ground across the floor and keep the tailbone firmly grounded. Play with micro-pulses across the floor to stretch the vertebrae of the low lumbar spine. Be sure to do the same with the left knee bent on the other side.

5. Lay down supine facing up, raise arms flat out at 90 degrees. Bend the right knee and press it into your chest and using the left hand, hold and guide the bent knee across the chest to the side near or touching the floor.

Keep the right shoulder pulled down and close to the floor, hold in the compression twist. Repeat the same, twisting on the opposite side.

6. Next, bend in both knees to your chest, arms again flat and perpendicular on the floor. Keep knees together and twist them together over to the right. If available, straighten the upper (left) leg and hold the ankle or toes in the right hand to twist in hamstring stretch. Hold the stretch, then bend both knees in together again and twist them over to the left. Extend the upper leg. Continue and hold.

7. Advanced. From the twist posture given above on the right side and holding the toes of the left straight leg in the right hand, bend the knee of the lower right leg back behind you and reach to grab the right foot with the left hand to further deepen the twist. Use a strap or towel to loop the foot if it is not possible to reach the foot. Hold the stretch. Repeat on the other side.

Spinal twists should initiate from the low back moving from the locus in the nexus of the organs and elimination. All major locomotive movements are dependent on this stable foundation area in the core of our bodies. With the spine grounded deeply in the low sacrum, or "sacred fulcrum" of all core movements, it provides a baseline for the lift in the upright carriage of the body. Each of us has unique, genetically-endowed signatures in our individual proportions and dimensions, yet we all share the same joints as junctions to bend our limbs in movement. No matter what our inherent size and proportion, there are a variety of balanced postures that are available to us. It requires energy to optimize the connective, muscular contrasts to maintain balance in a given frame. With that in mind, I encourage you to explore, strengthen and find the cruxes and apexes within. Do so in honor of the beauty of the energetic, connective, and muscular form of the species.

Homo sapiens ~ Us

As hominin ancestors evolved and set our species' precedent with lighter, more streamlined and upright carriages, the barrel-chested ribcages flattened especially front and back to more suitable upright postures with longitudinal arm movements. Initially, these structural adaptations reflected hominin occupations on the savannahs in throwing weapons, manipulating and fabricating tooled weaponry, and in running to hunt. As a result, the human frame is predominantly open and balanced in an upright stance with the scapulae and shoulders held further back and together opening the chest and collar bone. Human bipedal locomotion consumes less energy moving over distances due to efficiency of an upright frame and compact torso. From the ground upward, *Homo sapient* legs are generally longer and fleeter than hominin species of the past; they are structured for walking distances and sprinting. Our inherent running capability is evident in a prominent gluteus maximus, strong psoas musculature and hamstrings. (Bramble,D.M., Lieberman, D.E., 2004) However, nothing has changed from quite so much as the structure of our feet. Human feet range greatly in size and shape from person to person but are uniform in their functional design. Ground locomotion has evolved hominin feet away from the pronated grasping of tree climbing, clinging and leaping of primates. Human toe digits are now proportionately smaller and more narrowly spaced, evenly aligned and they have less curl structurally. And around 1.8 million years ago, *Homo* feet were modified with arches to further enhance running ability and which has evolved the spring in our step. The arched foot design modification improved running performance and also modified ankles to be more robust. There's also more curvature in the human spinal column for impact resistance to our now upright bone structure which is supported by redundant, interwoven connective tissues and muscles with enough mechanical strength to stabilize and distribute weight in lateral movements. We enjoy a wide range in joint rotational ability, extension and flexion in the spine and limbs which easily can control leveraging manipulation, crawling, climbing, twisting, jumping, spiraling and undulation from our fingers to toes.

Foot Series:

If possible, awaken the undersides of feet on a soft, springy, curved or uneven surface. Walking on a foam roller is ideal. The compression stepping and rolling will invigorate the 25 bones in the feet and ankles to their former, primordial condition. Try moving to music on a full or half foam roller along a wall or other support for balance. After stretching the connective tissues and energizing your foot structure on the soft, rounded surface; take a seat and enjoy the following foot manipulations.

Try it: Seated, lift the right foot and place it atop the left knee to the side just above the ankle. You may also do this sitting on the ground with your back propped up and the left leg straight out. You need however, to be able to grasp your foot with the opposite hand. The following self-massage of the feet will be more enjoyable with less friction if you add a dab of moisturizing cream.

1. Intertwine the fingers of the left hand through toes of the right foot to grasp it firmly. Lightly hold above the right ankle with the right hand to stabilize the ankle and then use the left hand to circle the foot at the ankle 20 times in one direction, 20 in the other.

2. With the forefinger and middle finger of the left hand together, hook them around the right big toe and lift the foot upward towards your head

to stretch the connective tissues of the ankle. Raise the leg up 20 seconds to stretch the big toe, foot, ankle and hip joint.

    3.   Return the foot down onto the knee and use fingers, knuckles or the base of the thumb to massage the centerline of the sole, from the metatarsal (ball of the foot) to the heel. Wherever there is tension in the arch, gently massage longer to help it release.

    4.   Then deeply squeeze and stroke the base of the heel to release the daily pressure of walking.

    5.   Continuing, reach down with right hand and cup across the top of the right foot at the ankle, with long downward strokes down the top of the foot to the toes, press firmly but smoothly to bend the foot back in extension pointing the foot and toes downward, *en pointe,* to stretch the tissues of the upper ankle. Repeat strokes up to 20 times from the ankle and hold toes under briefly.

    6.   Finally with the right hand, reach to hold the toes up to flex them firmly. Again massage the underside along the foot sole centerline with the left hand.

    7.   Massage other areas as needed, then switch to position the left foot across the right knee and repeat all of the above on the left foot.

Our inherently supple *Homo* skeletal frames support some extreme flexibilities front to back and toe to head in folds, extension, flexion, lateral twisting, adduction and abduction. With upright bipedal bone structures, one of our morphological advantages in human movement resides in cross-sectional integration of structural symmetry in crossover postures by adjoining the peripheral limbs on a flexible spine. Such inherent symmetry can be exceedingly graceful also in flowing movements. Our given propensity to bend, fold and twist with balance may seem curiously contorted and impossible except in some individuals, those as flexible as Gumby and as poised as Buster Keaton. In September 2012 in New York City, I watched a street performer share his talent as a contortionist by fitting his 5.3 foot frame into a tiny transparent cube less than the length of his femur with room to close the door.

A Homo sapient Inclusive

The constant flux in individual physical health comes from the various physical parts and functions within our multi-celled bodies. We inherited the hormonal cadences of our emotions and the mineral composition of our blood, the chemical and cellular complexity of our immune and reproductive systems, the constant molecular transports and intracellular signaling, the electrically charged exchanges of our nervous system and all the other physical processes, actions and transformations occurring with each breath; nearly all were systematized first in other species. Each of our cells carry the passages and stories of distant predecessors - from the fluidity of jellies and the matrix of sponges, the muscles of molluscs and the bones of fish, the appendages of tetrapods, and from the joints of primates to the hands of hominins. Humans are free from the restraints and constraints of many long-ago evolutionary rites of passage. Consider what limitations from the past have been overcome through struggle, mutual dependency and cooperative action, wholesale collaborations, sacrifice and last ditch efforts. For every bone that forms a skeleton, the cells contain all the now forgotten possibilities that came from trial and error along with the fortitude of shaping a pathway. Every stabilizing tendon and ligament that pulls on a muscle was a mere predilection of another species' movements. Each new function made systemic in our multicellular predecessors brought with it fresh capacities with which to forge a new species. Each new advance was a step in evolution to instigate, complicate, regenerate, annihilate, commensurate, aggregate or invigorate with others the surroundings to reshape their living system, both internal and external. All the innovation that has been expressed in the billions of years leading to a human frame that can successfully function in a living system(s) took inconceivably countless generations of creative vitality of life on a life-giving planet.

Our years alive are possible only because cells participate to function organically in their roles, many of which were taken on billions of years ago. Cells constantly need to replicate themselves, to store energy, move, grow and die until the final moment of breakdown and corporeal expiration. Cell evolution brought life that is overwhelmingly self-directed, autonomous, symbiotic and homogeneous in balancing and sustaining all the systems to perpetuate their living systems. All are made by cells that contract, expand, die, and regenerate with pre-ordained roles in a dance to constantly replace themselves in multi-celled cycles. We are not what we think we are, we are each of us a multicellular conglomeration…a conglomeration of cells that completely replenishes itself every seven years to maintain our health through molecular and interstitial communications. Imagine the coding that would require to maintain a living, growing, collective body; the busyness within each of us in the rush of life and death cycling.

"**many of the answers we seek already exist and are part of the greater creativity – and generosity – of nature. That should give us hope because we are not alone in our struggle for wholeness.**"
~ **Kristin Ohlsen**, *Sweet inTooth and Claw*

A Homo sapient Exclusive

Nothing can quite move us to feel flexibility energetically like dancing does. Music and rhythm can be felt viscerally in our bodies so to make it happen, turn it on and attune inward… Whether standing, sitting, or supine ~ Find the Riff and just Move!

Try It: Explore ways of moving, feel the fluidity within and the energetic components that awaken with movement. Roll and sway to the rhythm – feel it and let it grow larger in motions; add more in and play to another sub beat, follow your own riff and rhythm – nothing is awkward, don't think, just focus on expressing and move, any way that pleases or releases, let it out from within what feels right to move you - let your body lead you.

Play through whatever emotions bubble up - whatever arises… work them through viscerally as the music pumps your soul. Music partner! Dance with the tempo, feel the tones, let the instruments play and lead you along in the down beat and up beats letting them manipulate you through the rhythmic raggedy rages and shallow drifts. No matter how you feel physically, think of your body as fluid and the dancing endorphins will remind you of another perspective of its aliveness without much thought.

Just remember: All life forms must move and flow! Swing and Step, Spin and Prance, Kick and Duck, Roll and Shake, Wiggle and Twist, Bend and Turn, Hop and Rock, Undulate and Express… to another, to yourself, to the world!

References

Bekoff, M. (2010). *The animal manifesto: Six reasons for expanding our compassion footprint*. New World Library.

Bramble, D.M., Lieberman, D.E, 2004. Endurance running and the evolution of *Homo.* Nature 432:345-352

Brusatte, S. Zhe-Xi Luo, June 2016, The Rise of Mammals, *Scientific American,* 30-35.

Conrad, E., 2012. Life on Land: The Story of Continuum, the World-Renowned Self-Discovery and Movement Method. North Atlantic Books

Darwin, Charles, 1871, The Descent of Man and Selection in Relation to Sex. Murray Pub., London, U.K.

Faisal, A. et al., 2010. The manipulative complexity of lower Paleolithic stone toolmaking. PLoS ONE 5(11): e13718

Fleagle, J. G., Lieberman, D. E., 2021. 15 Major Transformations in the Evolution of Primate Locomotion. In: Dial, K., Shubin, N. and Brainerd, E. ed. *Great Transformations in Vertebrate Evolution*. Chicago: University of Chicago Press, pp. 257-280.

Grabowski, M. W., Polk, J. D., & Roseman, C. C. (2011). Divergent patterns of integration and reduced constraint in the human hip and the origins of bipedalism. *Evolution: International Journal of Organic Evolution*, 65(5), 1336-1356.

Grand, T. (1968). Functional anatomy of upper limb. *Bibliotheca Primatologica*, (7), 104.

Green, D.J., Alemseged, Z., 2012. *Australopithecus afarensis* scapular ontogeny, function, and the role of climbing in human evolution. Science 338(6106): 514-7.

Hare, B., Woods, V., 2020. Survival of the Friendliest, *Scientific American,* September, 58-63.

Hodge, A.M. 2011, Meet Your Newest Ancestor, *Scientific American.*

Ko, Kwang Hyun, 2016. Origins of human intelligence: The chain of tool-making and brain evolution. *Anthropological Notebooks* 22(1): 5-22.

Leakey, L., et al., 1964. A new species of the genus *Homo* from Olduvai gorge. Nature. 202:7-9.

Lepre, C.J. et al., 2011. An earlier origin for the Acheulian. Nature 477 (7362): 82

Lovejoy, C.O., Suwa, G., Spurlock, L., Asfaw, B., & White, T. D. (2009). The pelvis and femur of Ardipithecus ramidus: the emergence of upright walking. *Science,* 326(5949).

Maynard Smith, J., Savage, R.J.G., 1956. Some locomotory adaptations in mammals. Journal of the Linnean Society of London. 62:603-622.

Marzke M., Marzke, R., 2000. Evolution of the human hand: Approaches to acquiring, analyzing and interpreting the anatomical evidence. *Journal of Anatomy 197* (1), 121-140.

McGowan, P. J., Traylor-Holzer, K., & Leus, K. (2017). IUCN guidelines for determining when and how ex situ management should be used in species conservation. *Conservation Letters, 10*(3), 361-366.

McHenry, H.M., 2009, Human Evolution. In *Evolution: The First Four Billion Years.* Belknap Press of Harvard University Press. Cambridge, MA.

Ohlsen, K., 2022, Sweet in Tooth and Claw: Stories of Generosity and Cooperation in the Natural World.

Robinson, J. T. (1972). *Early hominid posture and locomotion.* University of Chicago Press.

Schmitt, D. (2003). Substrate size and primate forelimb mechanics: implications for understanding the evolution of primate locomotion. *International Journal of Primatology, 24* (5), 1023-1036.

Scholtz, M.N. et al., 2006. Vertical jumping performance of bonobo (*Pan paniscus*) suggests superior muscle properties. Proceedings of the Royal Society of London. 273:2177-2184.

Shipman, P., Walker, A., 1989. The costs of becoming a predator. Journal of Human Evolution 18:373-392.

Skinner, M.M. et al.,2015, Human Evolution: Human-like hand use in *Australopithecus africanus.* Science 347 (6220): 395-9.

Smith, J. M., & Savage, R. J. (1956). Some locomotory adaptations in mammals. *Zoological Journal of the Linnean Society, 42*(288), 603-622.

Stock, J.T., 2008. Are humans still evolving? *EMBO* Reports 9 (1S): S51-54.

Suddendorf, T., 2013 The Gap: The Science of What Separates Us from Other Animals. Basic Books. New York, NY.

Susman, R.L., Stern, J.T., 1982. Functional morphology of *Homo habilis.* Science 217:931-4.

Susman, R. L., Jungers, W. L., & Stern Jr, J. T. (1982). The functional morphology of the accessory interosseous muscle in the gibbon hand: determination of locomotor and manipulatory compromises. *Journal of Anatomy*, *134* (Pt 1), 111.

Tuttle, R.H., 1981 Evolution of hominid bipedalism and prehensile capabilities doi.org/10.1098/rstb.1981.0016

Walker, A. (2009). The strength of great apes and the speed of humans. *Current Anthropology*, *50*(2), 229-234.

Ward, C. V. (2013). Postural and locomotor adaptations of Australopithecus species. In *The paleobiology of Australopithecus* (pp. 235-245). Springer, Dordrecht.

White, T.D. et al., 2009. *Ardipithecus ramidus* and the paleobiology of early hominids. Science 326 (5949):76-86.

Wong, K., 2020 The First Story, *Scientific American,* March, 68-73

Wong, K., 2020, The Origin of Us, *Scientific American,* September, 66-72

Wrangham, R.W., 2009. Catching Fire: How Cooking Made Us Human. Basic Books: New York, NY.

Young, R.W., 2003. Evolution of the Human Hand: the role of throwing and clubbing. Journal of Anatomy

CHAPTER 7

Mimicry, Emulation and Embodiment

Primordial yogic Movement is based on the observation and study of body plans and the biomechanics of movement, organic integuments such as shell, chitin, membrane, skin types; along with other motive aspects of physicality. Emulating the forms and movements of various species in history-based progressions informs us of material, structural and locomotive characteristics that have made them significant in response to the living systems in play at the time. A principle point in PyM is that every living species exists as a result of reciprocity in and with its environment. While the exercises in PyM are provided to expand a repertoire of animal movements and progressions in workouts, expressing through mimicry, emulation and embodiment is meant to engender relationships. They are only examples; other species may present a whole catalog of possible forms, swim strokes, exercises, postures and motions to choreograph movements in progressions that make sense and hold meaning to you. With mimicry alone, the workouts will be more expressive when the experience broadens a deeper understanding of past history. You may find there's a spectrum in skill reflected by how much of yourself you put into characterizing other species. Or perhaps, that some forms and movements will lend themselves more easily to imitation and emulation, simply perhaps because the species' specifics reach deeper into the imagination. While engaging in PyM, the more knowledgeable you are of the species you imitate, the more likely that that knowledge will influence your creative expressions in the propulsive forces at play.

A Doorway through Imagination

In the year 2019, scientists uncovered the earliest figurative cave art known to date. On the island of Sulawesi in Indonesia, a single entrance tucked high above ground under a remote cliff, prehistoric cave images were discovered. The entrance was accessible only by a tall ladder, the interior paintings on the cave walls depicted tribal hunting scenes by hominins living 43,900 years ago. This latest discovery today claims title to the oldest human art known. It exceeds the 40,000 year-old cave painting found in Borneo and a 39,000 to 40,000 year-old sculpted half-lion, half-human figurine discovered in a cave in Germany. There have been many such ancient artifacts uncovered around the globe including petroglyphs in the Americas, cave paintings of Caceres, Altamira, El Castillo, Lascaux, Niaux and Chauvet in Europe, and prehistoric art in Africa and Australia, and now in Indonesia. The Sulawesi discovery will most likely not remain the last. The remote and challenging location of the Sulawesi paintings tend to confirm the fact that much of the early hominin artwork was carefully placed in often difficult locations where the entrances were hard to access. Many prehistoric caves reveal no traces of human habitation and were kept separate as sacred places. At the Sulawesi site, the paintings appear to be carefully positioned and applied to utilize the natural shapes and surfaces of the rock conforming in order to enhance the animal shapes and shading, perhaps even to enhance an illusion of movement in the paintings.

David Lewis-Williams, in his book *The Mind in the Cave*, argues that the early subterranean art by hominins were designed to celebrate the animals they depended on and possibly to connect them spiritually by honouring them in celebration for the abundance they brought. However the true intentions of the artists are not verifiable in any of the petroglyphs, sculptures and cave paintings. Were they meant to stir memories, to mark an event or discovery, honor a geographical area or an animal characteristic, or to invoke an emotional or spiritual response in viewers, or perhaps all of the above? However, it is likely that the renderings held meaning for the hominins simply by the fact that they took trouble to insure the paintings preservation in remote, inaccessible safe places.

Images at the Sulawesi site depict a group of hunters brandishing spears or ropes. Some of the hunters were depicted as animals, perhaps wearing a costume. One warrior has a tail, another wears the image of a beak. (K. Wong, 2020) However speculative the reasons may be for the warriors or hunters to engage in expressing an animal or bird, they are depicted as endowed with animal characteristics. One thing is certain, by creatively adorning or endowing the warriors as animal figures, the hominin artist painted the hunters as depicted with an abstract association; this is a uniquely hominin trait. Expressing abstract associations are meant to convey a meaning, a narrative or a characteristic that is intentional through the representational imagery. Almost 44,000 years ago hominins had an ability to artistically represent images to depict hunting scenes as narrative. They also had a unique ability to visually and symbolically communicate artistically to represent the encounters in such a way that intended to relay dynamism by also shaping the figures on rock contours in such a way as to make them emerge from the rock shapes.

The artists in Sulawesi in drawing an interpretative perspective by wearing bird beaks or an animal tail intended to convey an underlying surrealistic meaning in doing so, as it goes beyond realism to express a view of symbolic adornment as adding something imagined. Whether early hominin cave paintings were intended to honour, memorialize, instruct, celebrate or record; they depicted a narrative of meaning. The *Homo* artists 43,000 years ago or even 17,000 years ago may not have had more than grunting abilities in their verbal discourse, yet their depictions in art reveal a uniquely human urge to creatively express symbolic ideas of life.

Is the urge not just as primal today for us to communicate and express creatively as it was for hominins 44,000 or more years ago? Many mammal and avian species copy and mimic one another also; they team up and co-operate together in a single purpose, to hunt, learn the use of tools and tooling and even instruct on usage. However, the cortical parts in the cerebral neural circuitry of primate ancestors that involve creative assessment and planning, such higher-order cognitive functioning has become particularly enlarged in the human species. (Pinel. P. et. al., 2007) (Sherwood, C.C., 2018) As far as we know, no other species use such a variety of verbal and non-verbal tools in creative ways, such as paint and movement to communicate symbolic and abstract meanings. Such expressive abilities may not only be the métier of dreamers but an evolutionary driver.

Mirror, Mirror, in the Hall

As infants and children, we learn our skills from family members and others around us. By 3 to 5 months of age as infants, we can exercise a good degree of control over our movements and are beginning to define emotional states in others. Developing awareness as a distinct self, separate and distinguishable from others is typically firmly established by age 5. By then, we have a good sense of self and others because our neural connections have rapidly built trillions of synaptic linkages with which to sense our individuality from perspectives. This mammalian process of autonomy is built on observations of others to help us make sense of our reactions to what others are doing, feeling and acting on. And by comparing, we connect reasoning to response and actions. Observation also builds our ability to mimic others, a learning process which in turn, is associated with reasoning and emotional states. In watching others, we empathize by processing and imitating not only actions but the feelings they carry. Our neural circuitry is wired to sense, communicate, respond, comprehend and mimic others, building on our knowledge in experiencing the world around us. The associative cortical regions link up and mature relatively late in postnatal development and are more numerous compared to primates. They are the locus for imitating and learning new skills.

The neurons in our brains that "light up" when we observe to learn and imitate are called mirror neurons. The term refers to the neurons which code the actions of others we observe which then can inform our own actions and our ability to mimic the actions of others. They were first discovered in the premotor cortex in macaque monkeys, a group of gregarious Old World monkeys, a class of primates that include the inimitable snow monkeys of Japan. (Winters, A.F., 2008) Researchers found that mirror neurons discharge actively both when a monkey is observing another monkey doing something and also when attempts are made to imitate the action. Over time those particular neurons become hardwired by preselecting the necessary motor responses to mimic in learning based on interactions. The same neurons exist and fire similarly in us. If you have ever found yourself unconsciously moving or doing something in a way that imitates another, you've engaged a neurological response of synchronicity. (Rizzolatti et al., 1997) Yet mirror neurons are only the tip of the iceberg. When we see another's smile - our mirror neurons fire with the feelings associated with smiling and because we have a neural mapping of smiles already cataloged in our memory banks which trigger an impulse to smile back in response, and it makes us feel good to do so. It is a felt empathetic response and has expanded from the increased hominin cranial capacity during the past six million years. During that time the *Homo* brain has evolved with widely distributed cortical association regions, with the most accelerated growth having occurred in the last 200,000 years. (Zhang, J., 2003) (Neubert, et. al, 2014) Imitation is comparatively easy for us thanks to our mammalian brain evolution with primates playing their part in laying down the neural hardware.

Recent research exploring our deeper sense of connection to others can occur when we observe others. Researchers have found that mirror neurons and other association regions consistently fire when we observe emotionally laden movements to affect similar reactive states in us. This happens simply by witnessing another's movements and gestures. The American Dance Therapy Association (ADTA) set out to determine whether emotionally-charged movement expressions would raise analogous emotions in observers. Working with Dance/Movement Therapy (DMT) students in NYC, the study was designed to measure our recognition accuracy in emotional performances expressed by dancers and whether their postures and movements induced similar affective states. Participants were randomly assigned to either of two categories, those who emulated the emotions in dance movements and those who observed the performance. The findings confirmed that becoming aware of a performance with emotional content by another does induce a sympathetic response of similarly felt emotional responses in the observers. We are no different than other species in that we are neurologically wired to detect the emotional content from observations in order to reveal a deepened sense of others. As a eusocial hominin species however, body expression is very much a part of the subtle signalling we may engage in with one another. Our associative neural circuitry has a unique signature in the human psyche to identify with others well beyond mimicry. Learning from our ability to mirror others, we can also sense resonance with others consciously and subconsciously in expressing and comprehending abstract concepts. Imitation is the root of empathy. While empathy may be accessible to everyone at one time or another, given the complexity and restraints possible in our cultures, modern humans may not necessarily accept, value and actively devalue their ability as useful; especially in poker games.

The ability to imagine is a necessary precursor to expressing or rendering a representational image; and as a keystone in the experiential learning process, biologically it derives from mimicry. To imitate takes a prominent role in constructing and relaying events and stories, relating meanings and expressing physically. Although neural speeds inherited from fast-moving arboreal primates was substantive; human delivery often carry the subtle feint and jab of abstractions and innuendo to creatively juggle plots and the subplots even as the narrator interprets and gauges what is happening simultaneously to ad lib situationally.

As mentioned earlier, we pre-simulate observations to review them comparatively in our minds to help ascertain whether our perceptions moment by moment are accurate. Early in education, preschool, primary school and the like, we are encouraged to draw and depict experiences such as past activities during the holidays. In recalling our experiences, we depict and draw them in ways to communicate the events, our findings and feelings in the interpretations; whether or not they are recognizable by others. We assimilate not only other persons and places, also values, concepts and feelings. We draft our ideas in storytelling, paint, and in movement. We can express a tree or fire by visualizing a tree blowing in the wind or recalling fire as it dances; we only have to decide how to express a particular image in mind with our bodies. It is through the complex association neocortical circuitry where perceptions and comparative actions are visualized imaginatively for proprioceptive physical expression.

Proprioception

Throughout earth history lifeforms typically have progressed towards more and more complexity in organism's sensory systems. From the earliest pathways that fed primitive chemotaxis sensing on a molecular level to the complex neural processes centralized in vertebrate senses - neurological networking in invertebrates and vertebrates have become a richly elaborate. As they expanded into more interconnected interactive systems, conspicuous sensory changes occurred. Avian, invertebrate and mammalian cortical circuitry varies widely depending on how a particular species use their senses in the world. For example, in bears and canines, the cortical region delivers far more powerful information for sensing smells. Senses are specific to the task of echolocation in whales, for infrared detection in bats, and from sound detection in elephants, to name a few.

In the last chapter on primates and hominins - I mentioned that primates evolved much of their sensory systems from adapting to arboreal locomotion moving at high speeds through the tangled complexity of dangerous forests and jungles. The regions in the brain for our senses are traceable to our primate ancestors and likely set the stage for *Homo* species to have enhanced, fast extrapolation and interpolation abilities. When a baseball pitch is delivered as a 95 mph curveball with spin and is complemented by a batter's split second decision to swing or not requires quick assessment to initiate the contact in advance, or not. It is through our inherited sensory reflexes and spatial detection that humans assess fast-changing, fluid representations with physical reaction. One very important sensing mechanism that both primates and hominins share is proprioception. It is sensing corporeal placement and action engaged in the physical body. Proprioceptive perception is externally oriented; it is knowing at any given time where and how to position your body relative to where it is and what it is doing or is about to do. Sometimes when distracted and clumsy, proprioception may not seem as though it's highly functional or physically there, but it's always aware as necessary consciously. We might stumble, but it can catch or direct a fall. Proprioception is our body's feedback loop to where we are physically at all times. The neural network of proprioception is centered associatively in the cortical region of the brain and constantly monitors factors of moving and movement in the immediate environment. Proprioception body maps in real time how to move within the perceived and pertinent spatial parameters. For example, it subconsciously moves the hand as an extension of the mouse to move a cursor on a computer screen. There are even distinct fibers in our spinal cord for proprioceptive nerve transmissions. They are the nerves that sense body and peripheral limb positions and are poised to direct skeletomuscular motor neurons to move the body as needed 24/7. They transmit sensations that travel up from the body to the sensory mapping centers in the cortex of the brain to confer and direct action downward to move connective tissues and muscles. Proprioception senses position, agility and strength in locomotive movements; from the fingers to toes and body posture, it models and maps how and where to move to keep our body aware.

Proprioception works side by side with another sense, interoception, which senses bodily feelings that arise internally. Arousal, shortness of breath, an itch or stomach upset, all come from our primate-derived interoceptive response system. Just as extrapolation goes handily with interpolation, so it is with the senses mapped in the body - proprioception and interoception are neural mechanisms evolved as part of our neural architecture; and very much involved in body expression. Our unique neural circuitry may not have the ability to physically change appearance to mimic a sea snake, octopus or cuttlefish, but in movement expression, we rely heavily on proprioception and interoception to get it right.

Interoception, Wired to Feel

Wikipedia conveniently points out a comparative difference between imitation and emulation -- "to **emulate** is to attempt to equal or be the same as, while **imitate** is to follow as a model or a pattern; to make a copy, counterpart or semblance". I typically think of imitation as mirroring or mimicry, a spontaneous attempt to copy an action after observation. Whereas emulation as defined, requires practiced repetition to develop the muscle memory necessary to engage a feeling of reciprocity. By enveloping the details of another "as the same as", our expressions incorporate the other forming participation or partnership.

To progress from following another's movements in mimicry, emulating is more than just copying from observations. It requires another sense we possess in our cortical architecture, that of interoception. Interoception is the sense of what is being felt on the inside. It's sensing hunger before the stomach growls, of thirst, anxiety, optimism, depression, and other feelings that arise in us and bubble to the surface of our awareness. Interoception is neurologically wired in our brains and overlaps with the circuitry involved in proprioceptive sensing. The crossover joins both our physical awareness with emotional and other internal states. The two co-emerge to sense and monitor how we are feeling about what we are doing. Neuroanatomists say the primary neural juncture of these two sensing systems coalesce in the right frontal insula of the human cortex, although there are also associated circuitry in three other brain regions, including the mapping region in the anterior cingulate. As mentioned earlier, *Homo sapiens* are unique in having widely distributed cortical association regions connected in large-scale overlapping networks. Depending on the feelings being felt, neurons are activated in the frontal insula, anterior cingulate, and other regions when experiencing psyche or physical pain; but the frontal insula is a main juncture especially when feeling rejection, shame, grieving or joyful states. The right frontal insula region is where intereoception and proprioception sensory networks strongly associate internal felt states and the physicality of body mapping.

Interoception not only cross-links with proprioception; it also picks up on homeostatic states, on sensations arising from our homeostatic autonomous regulatory states. Here's how these sensory aspects might inform us. Let's say that you had a disastrous argument with your partner whereupon you storm out to go run off the frustration energetically. On venturing out, your body temperature takes in the data from outside weather conditions. It is cold and rainy and your internal homeostatic regulation adjusts to keep you comfortable by adding more core blood circulation; interoception picks up on this and delivers more data awareness: how anger in your present state of mind is pushing your lungs to breathe harder than is usual. Meanwhile, proprioceptive senses keep you aware of how easy it is to slip and modify your movements over the various wet surfaces while running. Interoceptive senses inform you of thirst and homeostatic responses regulating internal resources are marshaled autonomously for thirst and shortness of breath which may or may not motivate you to mitigate the exertion. The sensory facets of proprioception and interoception from exertion and homeostatic taxing may begin a slow release in your psychic state of tension. The awareness of what is being experienced, of the cold, anger, pain, strain, thirst, exhaustion and energetic release can also easily be linguistically expressed to another person running alongside with you.

Our brain's neural circuitry evolved to map the external environment, guide motor and other responses, inform of internal feelings and emotions, and use abstract thinking and analysis with linguistic processing; which are all wired together into perception. Neuroanatomical research using MRI brain scans confirm that our interoceptive neurobiology is a signature of *Homo sapient* neural complexity. Proprioceptive and interoceptive circuitry is elaborate, and allows us to wrap our minds around complex abstract concepts and visualize physical movements in expressions. We can dance, interpret, imagine, represent, infer, depict, predict and co-create ideas or different facets of an idea to share concepts with subtlety and finesse. We can breathe life into meaning and comprehend abstract meanings from others. It's a trait to value in our species, an awesome hominin gift to use to create, express, and symbolize. From storytelling to city planning and fine art to architecture, our cultures are founded on these psychophysical skills. Talented painters, graphic artists and designers, sculpture and kinetic artists and performers of music, dance and theatre are all endowed with the neurological complexity necessary to skillfully depict, express, render and perform. Expression has advanced from the realm of mimicry into a human realm to include emulation and embodiment.

Empathy Matters

Defining interoceptive sensing is neatly identified in a book by Sandra and Matthew Blakeslee, *The Body Has a Mind of Its Own: How Body Maps in Your Brain Help You Do (Almost) Everything Better*. Drawing on an interesting study conducted at the Institute for Cognitive Neuroscience at University College in London by a neurobiologist on cognitive mapping, Hugo Critchley. Critchley explored how emotional sensitivity relates to physical neuroanatomy. His research discovered that the thicker a person's gray matter is in the right frontal insula, the more empathetic they were towards others. Further testing then confirmed that those persons with thicker gray matter were also consistently better at reading their own internal emotions and to attuning to the emotional states of others; much more so than those that had lesser amounts of gray matter in that region of the brain. The right frontal insula region is where interoception and proprioception sensory networks strongly associate our internal sensing with how the body maps. It is therefore fair to say that the New Age adage advocating we "get in touch" with our bodies actually does have real validity in the neurological maintenance of health. Feeling empathy for others directly reinforces being more in touch with sensing our own emotional states.

Another neurological study found that those who meditate regularly also have thicker gray matter in the right frontal insula, a likely result of the practice to cultivate internal awareness and equanimity. (Lazar, S.W. et al., 2005)

Feelings of distrust, shame, lust, composure, arousal, embarrassment, joy, abandonment, deceit, love, approval, disdain, guilt, humiliation are emotions that activate neurons in the insula of the brain. They light up when we feel disgust at the actions of an untrustworthy politician, experience contempt from oppression, or when our nerves jitter like butterflies, or when welled up with pride from achievement. And just as neural pathways are reinforced with repetition to affect how we perceive, so too does the circuitry from patterns that deepen to predispose and engrain awareness(es) along certain psychophysical sensory pathways. Not only are thoughts physically processed, but as our internal emotions are also neurological processed, they also inform us perceptually in a perspective.

The heightening of nuance in hominin psychophysical neural/cortical architecture also implies another aspect for us as a species. Having a sympathetic/empathetic awareness of others can directly help us in our conscious and automatic responses that involve cooperation or reciprocity in partnerships or as a team. Simply by synchronizing closely with others in coordinating teamwork, such as in participatory movements required in sports or dance, having a sense of affinity with others can easily promote a more cohesive camaraderie among participants. Engendering a felt sense of group belonging from training and body mapping with others directly stimulates responses in what scientists call "self-other blurring", a scientific term for feeling such collective cohesion that the line separating self and others' sense of individuality is obscured by the cohesiveness. Ivana Konvalinka, a cognitive scientist at the Technical University in Denmark describes the blurring as "a weakening of boundaries between self and other. When we become attuned to others' actions, whether consciously or not, (and) we integrate them with our own". (Zaraska, M. 2020) It implies that not only do proprioceptive/interoceptive actions and responses body map 'outside' objects such as a baseball bat or a car mapped as an extension of the physical self when driving; but in teams, we incorporate into our zone of subconscious attention other members that collectively, we integrate into a single field of perception.

Yet, opening out to integrate others however common may not be accessible to everyone. Additionally, as with all our individual human perspectives, we might also choose to selectively dampen our feelings willfully and culturally. To empathize or stigmatize, that is the question facing each of us daily. As complex a highly cultural species as we are, the dark side of desire is to dominate, manipulate and oppress others which exists as easily as reaching out, cooperating, and respecting the rights and boundaries of others. We individually decide which to claim for ourselves and whether to nurture one another, or not.

A Sharing Sense

Belgian scientist Bernard Rimé has extensively studied and researched human sociability and communication. For over a decade, in eight studies involving more than a thousand respondents ranging in age from 12 to 72 years, Rimé found that 88-96% of participants regularly engaged in sharing the emotional episodes of events in their lives with someone else. (Rimé, B., Philippot, P., Boca, S., and Mesquita, 1992) This is not surprising as I'm sure we can agree that narrating many of the events in life with others is fairly typical and commonplace when people gather together. Rimè's interest also extended to the impacts sharing had on the individual and on others.

Generally speaking, communicating socially is encouraged in most human cultures as a way to gather useful information, help others to release concerns and emotions empathetically. Rimé's research reveals a human characteristic and a social need to communicate personal impressions with others as a part of human neurological development. Sharing emotional events can impart a cohesive resonance in sensing solidarity with others. It is an adjunct in human communication to engender cooperation, empathize and a method to reach out and openly engage in understanding through reciprocity. Sharing emotions imparts a shared commonality that can emerge through reciprocal interaction listening and expressing.

We, like many other mammal species, create social and cultural mechanisms to adapt to, adjust, position and parlay social order and hierarchy. Many "social" creatures often create behaviors to improve survival strategy or otherwise confer advantage to the benefit of a group or a species. We are no different - we communicate, organize, structure, inform and tweak our social systems and institutions, most often to improve community and ourselves. But the hominin need to share ourselves with others goes beyond pack intelligence or establishing "pecking order", it goes beyond cooperating together for protection, or coordinating a hunt together or even communal sharing of a feast together. Rimé's research revealed there's a social need for affirmation that comes from the reciprocity of sharing our emotional lives and a health-related need to be understood by others.

Historically, human cultures traditionally communicate in sharing individual stories and traditions in order to promote a sense of common ground and to reaffirm or reinforce a sense of collective identity. Identifying and belonging is a fundamental social motivation. Actions which elicit strong feelings of cohesion and togetherness can also enhance a sense of wholeness to counterbalance the other disparate social urges. Sharing pertinent information, stories, testimonials and expressions in personal engagement is a form of building trust between individuals, tribes, ethnic groups, nations and other collective groups and species. They stand as a pillar in our cultural learning and teaching institutions. However for some in our societies, past experiences can make it an uncomfortable journey to trust others and an even further stretch for them to share of themselves and openly express with others.

Expression as Trust

We all carry life's ready-made running narratives from our individual perspectives. When emotional responses are triggered, the responses are generally automatic. We are predisposed to react from a spontaneous neural pathway of a running narrative. Typically, an emotionally-driven response is an old, neural rut that dictates what can be seen and how the world is experienced. Getting unstuck from those repetitive and automatic reactions that have settled in is often cited by psychologists and psychotherapists as at the core of their professional work. Methods to battle triggered responses may include the widening of its context or by diminishing its importance. There is always hope that triggered emotions can be moderated by expanding an outlook or by encompassing other perspectives which will eventually diminish a narrowed view.

The field of somatic psychology and dance movement therapy (DMT) frequently focuses on movement expression as a therapeutic method to work through blocked and triggered reactive thoughts with experiential actions to explore alternatives through the release of emotions. There is a substantial body of DMT research that supports the theory that emotional constraints can be eased with movement expression to affect a palpable change in participants. But what if we do not trust our proprioceptive/interoceptive senses enough to let them flow? What if we cannot trust our bodies when awkward in movement and feel uncomfortable when our perspectives don't value physical expression? The quality of human life is directly related to how much interest we have in it and directly, in what the limits we impose from mental attitudes and habits. Author Thomas Ots once wrote, *"man is the only being capable of opposing himself, negating himself, setting limits to his own life forces, and to making himself the object of pure (disembodied) thought."* (Ots,T., 1994) Sadly, our firmest inhibitors to sharing are those driven by our internal perspectives.

A very interesting five-year DMT study conducted at a drug-rehabilitation clinic set out to investigate how emotions are processed in dance therapy by a select group of non-aggressive patients diagnosed as severely depressed with low self-esteem and having a long history of drug abuse with at least one clinically-diagnosed psychiatric disorder. Moreover, the study included substance addicted participants who exhibited a complex defensive structure and whose awareness of self was impaired and severely fragmented.

The investigator, Diane Thomson, stated that initially in the experiential training the "participants were intimidated by moving spontaneously, fearing they would lose control and be embarrassed", she reported that "movements by participants were restricted and slow with little or no intention and a passive use of weight"… their breathing was "shallow or held, inhibiting a natural flow of emotions". But as Thomson worked with the group, over the course of a couple of years, increasing self-awareness began to emerge in the participants' physical feelings. They began to identify with the sensations they were experiencing. Thomson found that emotive states were slowly being accessed by the participants. Slowly, the movement expression practice began to generate in each individual participant a sense of trust in their own physical and emotional state. She also found that on expanding the dance activities, the participants began to relate more easily to other group members. Finally, her research showed a sense of cohesion developed as a collective group through sharing the organized theme expressions. Thomson's study readily confirmed that movement expression provides an experiential avenue through many of the mental blockages of participants through their very severe, emotionally latent restrictions. Movement expression provided a passage past the containment of emotions and opened their self-perceptions to different outlooks to initiate improvements in self-confidence. (Thomson, D., 2005) Through years of accumulating mental stress and tension, the physical body can become a repository for those mental states held in psychologically whereupon the body eventually learns to close off physical areas that affect emotional states. It takes training to reopen the habitual physical blockages so that the body may heal and respond to movement in a more healthy opened state.

Whether young or old, DMT research confirms that practice of movement expression can deepen both proprioceptive and interoceptive sensing in individuals. (Hoban, S., 2000). There are the obvious positive effects from engaging in a movement practices which increase physical awareness and heighten a sense of mastery in coordination and balance, not the least of which causes improvement in confidence and self-esteem. (Hanna, 1995) There's no doubt it takes much courage to assuage uneasy or turbulent inner thoughts and feelings when externalizing and moving expressively. Exposure is intimately felt; especially when unsure that expressing might exceed self-imposed boundaries and loosen protective boundaries. If not accepted "publicly" as an appropriate behavior, there is often worry that personal expression may reveal more of oneself than might be acceptable. Yet everyone is self-exposing when dancing and since everyone is expressing in movement, exposure of the self-image we uphold tends to be arbitrary to feeling sensations in dance and movement. That perfect storm of body awareness colliding with mental metaphors is why movement expression is so good for us and so directly affects a sense of wellness and of completeness in body and mind. Confronting and expanding the body's limits, blockages and predispositions can open us to expand our perceptions and grow. If only all of us were to open to the freedom it offers!

"Live and love your questions. Dance them fully to the best of your ability, and one day, perhaps without even noticing it, you'll dance yourself into their answers"
~ **Rainer Maria Rilke (1885-1926)**

As a part of this study, I conducted surveys of dance participants who met for informal, freeform, weekly dance sessions in my local area. (Core Connexion, Ecstatic Dance, and TransDance) The quantitative survey questionnaire online first established the demographic information about the dancer's gender, number of years of dance experience and weekly frequency of involvement in dance expression sessions. After setting demographics, the qualitative portion of the survey focused primarily on the felt experience and elicited more descriptive responses from the participants' personal experiences in dance expression. I also questioned whether dance helped to process their emotions and on the importance of metaphor in dance themes, and if there were perceptual changes in well-being. While the responses differed, participants seemed to agree that expressive dance facilitated emotional discovery and did much to release their emotions and energetic benefits. Statistically significant was that over 95 percent affirmed that expressive dance helped them to process emotions they carried onto the dance floor. The following comments from respondents highlight how emotions affected movement expression:

"I dance with my emotions. They are part of me and so they naturally are a part of the dance that I create. Dance helps me move through emotional states, and transform emotions, e.g from sadness to gratitude, appreciation, and love."

"I try to dance out my emotions. As I focus, become aware of my feelings I sometimes try to dance them."

"It connects me with rhythm, allows me to work through emotions and can relieve a mental state; it brings me into present moment awareness."

"I feel that dance connects people within that dance community, and also that the positive emotional states achieved through dance can spill over into more positive interactions that I have with others in general."

(Movement expression)" elevates a sense of being in the moment, of feeling free and light."

Sometimes, we simply have to get out of our own way to become an instrument of expression. To allow thoughts and emotions to flow, preparation by observing others can often serve to reassure as first attempts are made. It is possible for everyone to eventually reach a place where inner feelings and outer perspectives can be assuaged to move beyond concerns of physicality and awkwardness. I cannot improve on this statement by another participant:

"It has taught me to trust myself in each moment, to trust that my body will know what to do and I don't have to think too hard. TRUST."

Movement expression can be opportunities to replace habitual self-perceptions with wider perspectives that neutralize or diminish closely-held narratives. Individuals in many indigenous groups have traditionally engaged in practices which directly instigate a loss or a change in self-image in the hope of gaining insights through renewing or establishing deeper connection through vision quests, spiritual dances, sweat lodge ceremonies and right-of-passage rituals. Primordial yogic Movement practice is another method to similarly connect the individual self to the past in movement expression.

Emulation

Expressing other animals deepens with the knowledge of the subject at hand. Building a repertoire of images with which to express how a particular species moves, feels, communicates, and reacts can be brought to mind in expression. Yet, attuning to the facets that make a species unique also does something else; it establishes openness to reciprocity in understanding what makes another tick.

In the wild I often attempt to imitate the songs of birds. If you have never tried "talking back" in their language, you'll be surprised by how birds react. Many bird calls are actually within my range of my whistling and more often than not, the bird I imitate seems to truly care that their notes, sequencing and tones are correctly performed although they also may be considering the timbre and more; I don't know as it would require music training on my part. Sometimes though, when my whistling call sounds are perfectly attuned and matched to their song, the bird will ante up with new variations. This is when it transitions into sharing the moment with another species as I emulate the new song variations; and by having a mutually identified common ground, the relating promotes relationship from reciprocity.

The mid-century philosopher Maurice Merleau-Ponty (1908-1963) recognized that perception changes its function when something is related in a new perspective. He proposed that if a "closed" concept is seen in a little different way to reveal another facet previously unseen in the concept, then how the concept relates to us widens. As a result, a prior perspective is then perceived with more clarity or perhaps more deeply to reveal a fuller, more descriptive meaning to the observer. When that happens, mimicking and sharing by vocalizing (bird song), both parties communicating will then engage in a reciprocal interaction by acknowledging a change in the interplay; this can also happen when merging the imaginative with imagined expression.

Practicing a form or movement in PyM co-creates a dynamic of engagement through identifying with another species in emulation. For example, assessing and rendering an expression in the range of movement of a cheetah femur may well be imagined in different ways. It can be expressed as a stretch which requires positioning and time enough to relax the connective tissue incrementally until a satisfactory personal edge of extension is found, or by expressing a cheetah sprint in motion. For myself, accepting that the low crouching forward leg swings from a tucked posture requires a degree of strength and tone of youth; I modify the kicks straight back and swing out to the side. The modification results in a more brief range of movement, I still affect the same contoured curves of the spine as a factor of essence in a cheetah. While the movements may not imitate, the emulation is still applicable from visualizing a coupling to the cheetah locomotive dynamic that characterize a running cheetah. The forms and motions characterize aspects of an animal that make them unique in evolution. All things are equal in emulating with different perspectives to re-create a species, if their evolution and context brings more meaning in expression. If the sensations feel honest and true, then the characterizations symbolized in meanings to experience another species in expression will benefit you and honor the other mutually. Imagined visual emulations places all on equal parity through your efforts to recognize and associate more closely with others to guide expressions of resonance. This can be seen more clearly in the innocent creativity of children.

Children are untainted by cultural prejudices created by the fear of otherness. They are free of social protocol that (neither) dismisses or demeans the position of animals in our lives.
~ Animal Grace, 2000, by Mary Lou Randour

Children seem to intuit that animals are our kin by identifying with other species. They easily develop feelings for animals they come in contact with to form real and imagined friendships whether the animal is living or representational, as stuffed animals. Animals are typically viewed as those equal in kinship, completely worthy of affection and even imbued with a fullness of identity and often a sense of wonder and mystery. As children grow up however,  that kinship is lost within the contexts of acculturation, shared family values of maturity and new interests in which leave our initial kinship and reciprocity behind as less important.

As adults, our existence often leaves little way forward to return to the kind of innocent imaginative kinship that we once had with other species. We ask much of ourselves and our lives, yet a turtle or a frog asks nothing to be what they are. Even the most life-hardened of humans may produce a flicker of a grin in recalling or seeing a puppy or kitten in play – rump high, tail wagging in the air, with sudden leaps and eyes bright with the sparkle of fun. Typically an association to access a thread of inner innocence remains available to most of us. Yet simultaneously, our culture allows each of us to choose whether to hear only what we wish to hear and see only what we wish to see. So consider what might happen if we were all to follow an evolutionary journey down the primordial rabbit hole? By exploring the past scheme to our arrival on earth, a doorway might open to a wider and more spacious view of ourselves. Unless confident that the world could never have as wide a stream of consciousness as once experienced in childhood, PyM practice might be a method to reconnect; not to the world of mankind but to a primordial crucible that is dynamic in meaning. It would require a turn from off the old worn cultural road of human-wrought existence and to travel connected in time by listening to and identifying with older, wiser, more complete species, to realize true equality; we are them and they are us.

Remote from universal nature, and living by complicated artifice, man in civilization surveys the creature through the glass of his knowledge and sees thereby a feather magnified and the whole (bird) image in distortion. We patronize them for their incompleteness, for their tragic fate of having taken form so far below ourselves. And therein we err, and greatly err. For the animal shall not be measured by man. In a world older and more complete than ours they move finished and complete, gifted with extensions of the sense we have lost or never attained, living by voices we shall never hear.

~ Marc Bekoff, 2010

Recently I practiced as many organisms and animals as possible which took me from water to land and back again. Embracing, expressing, working and embodying different elements, forms and movements as the evolutionary passages sprang up by listening to where the spontaneity would lead. I found the cephalopod workout so energizing that downshifting with amphibian movements in the shallows were great fun as the lumbering motions modified and then engaged my revelry of the more contemporary locomotive movements of mammalian species. It fired my imagination from growing awareness of linkages while travelling along an evolutionary path. Whether lying supine as an organism, moving to express a characteristic swagger or predatory advantage, the movements co-created with a resonating dynamism; an associative aspect of kinship and the upshot to deeper connection.

The PyM framework is simple and can be initiated from any starting point in an evolutionary trajectory. If on land, curl up and imagine the amazing journey of cell life. See yourself as separate from the world by a thin, flexible hydrophilic membrane, an absorbent outer skin. The simplest of organisms react to the merest of influences in the surroundings, sensing food, predators, pressure, chemical and atmospheric change. Move with micro=movements, twitch, grow and morph, temporarily. A cell's first movements are from electrical potential fluctuations in the cell membrane, from internal/external contractions that power axons to move flagellum and cilium; or as in a muscle set. Move from the internal core in and out; expanding on one side and feeling the other side moving too. Lower a shoulder then the other and so forth to "creep" along, curling in, and expanding out. Imagine cilia growing on the thin covering of membrane like a breeze felt on skin. The cell membrane is operable - hydrophilic, allowing molecules to pass in and out to maintain internal metabolic equilibrium, just as it has expanded into the autonomic homeostatic systems within you. Think of growing an appendage, a flagellum perhaps. Laying down supine on your back and use legs as flagella, together as a tail or two. Can it move you? Undulating or spiraling, in kicks or sweeps… and if it attaches, how might your weight shift and balance in movement; remember your whole body flows so what parts might stabilize and what factors play in motions? Early primordial lifeforms had only soft exteriors; then evolved hardened exteriors that constricted some flexibility. Future primordial species then found more flexibility and strength in solutions centered from an interlocking stiffened central chord, as in one of the first such organisms, trilobites. Experiment with form as a Flapping Fish, roll into Lizard Pump, laterally stretch vertebrae in Serpent and pause at Crocodile to open hips, vertebral discs and shoulders; then on to emulate the once ubiquitous amphibians. In transitioning into movements of amphibians and into the push-pull motions necessary to evolve limbs on land, first slow the lateral fish motions to find stability on the substrate below. Test balance and buoyancy in the liquid environment where the smallest shifts in weight placement may waiver your control. The fragile, tottering edge of a buoyancy and stasis plays with ability to move in the shallows and improves on land. Try a flutter with appendages; an internal circling, a slight twist to discover the edge of falling from balance. Think of where skeletal fulcrums are placed, the positioning of joints, where bone divides to add flexibility and fold for comfort adding smoothness in movements; or thicken to add stability and rotation in linking joints. Consider the balances at stake in the contrasts. As in winged birds, how structures influence drag or lift and can affect forward motion and reaction factors. Or in mammals, the wiggle and hop, and sideways sweeps or limb kicks. Questioning provides endless ways to choreograph your practice within elemental parameters to guide chronological and choreographic options, where does it take you? Emulation is getting a sense of how to perceive other species in a relational way. Opening to a perceptual practice of PyM allows for opportunity to relate dynamically in the vital immediacy of the world. At the most basic level, we engage perceptively when connected to the physical, evolutionary history of the planet. The more knowledgeable about the life and the constructs of other organisms, the easier it is to emulate.

Embodiment

Most body-based skills such as martial arts have distinct plateaus in proficiency. A martial arts novice may view his or her skill limitations as insufficient knowledge. The insufficiency may reside in a lack of adequate knowledge or in the physical performance (inadequate muscle memorization). All experiential training requires support physically in the idea held in the mind. In the intermediate phase, a martial arts practitioner may see his or her limitations as a lack of skill to confidently demonstrate their learned knowledge fully. The practiced knowledge allows for creativity and physical expression as thought through, but can be obviated or confused when confronted with outside interaction. The final phase to acquiring physical/mental proficiency in a skill is when the self is blurred and one's skilled responses are mostly reflexive. Skill is then embodied. It is attained only after the phases of learning mimicry and emulation. It is how a martial arts master might view skill as relative only to the quality of the awareness in each moment. Where perceptions are direct and responsive; skilled mastery feels fluid and connected as openly receptive and attuning where improvisation is accessible as responses are well-internalized and somatically available in the dynamic of the immediate.

In embodiment, a mime depicts imaginary spaces and paces to create a reality from gestures and expressions of emotions to tell a story, whether of helplessness, villainy, heroism and more. A mime may choose to climb a ladder with confidence or in fear; he might show scheming with a simple twist of an imaginary mustache and shiftiness in eye movements; or he may use an imaginary bow tie as a final touch of formality to add prestige before welcoming an honorary. A mime may shoot an imaginary arrow and also react to its impact. Miming is embodiment that melds together elements of movement expression in a creatively shared, reciprocal reality with an audience.

Embodying requires a totality of presence. It goes beyond identifying with another because we do that especially with our minds and we are not just what we think -- we are what we do and feel.

The nature and experiences of the mind is structured by our individual neural circuitry, which presents a conditioned lens through which we view ourselves and the world. That is just a part of what we are, we are also our physicality and emotional body. Embodiment requires the whole of what we are, not just the ability to wrap our minds around the concept of another but from attuning the body viscerally -from practice.

The root of compassion is passion. When we are passionate about something, our whole field of perception opens to it in an emotion-associated response. If the source of passion is empathy towards another then the passion is commensurate and embodiment is directed by feelings.

Some careers are built on a person's ability to embody. Actors and actresses constantly forfeit self-narrative to embody another character. You could argue that embodiment of other species is unlikely to be quite as deep an experience as embodying a human being, but those trained certainly come close. Take a look at the French film *Molière* where the actor, M. Romain Duris gives a laudable performance as a spirited horse. However, other species are unique in their nature to the environments they were born to, and in such cases may be seen to carry the weight of anthropomorphism. We simply cannot comprehend the experience of other species as much as may be possible as the subtlety and detail an actress can glean from a well-known, well-documented figurehead of her own species. Yet while we may more easily embody another person's behavioural and emotional mindset if like-minded, a portrayal of Caligula may carry no empathy to make it a compassionate performance it may still be a passionate one. Only with empathy that is not antithetical to the other are we able to entrain expressively from much farther afield such as when emulating another species.

Embodiment with empathy shapes a new reality, larger than the individual species involved. Embodied compassion is an openness to absorb the feelings of another. Like mixing sugar into water, understanding and empathy dissolves the two together to become sugar water energy. The process melds both entities together into one another, yet takes nothing from either.

Another way to look at embodying compassion is to imagine you are a stream. Life experiences of the past can make one cold, and colder still, until the narratives that flow across the mind become rigid and frozen in life passages. Like a freezing stream, on the surface we may exhibit a solid exterior held in place by time and the cold frigidity of experience. But since we live, we all still flow darkly beneath the frozen exterior and on the surface there can be moments when we may break free to swirl and eddy openly. Yet if it is possible to encircle and flow in order to envelop another in empathy, the heat of the warming embrace can thaw even the most hardened exterior by absorbing each other in interplay and embarking on a sharing experience. Once practiced, solidity and flow may be linked as needed, whenever there is a wish to relate and connect.

Empathy might also be the catalyst to cause two independent elements to react together to form a compounded understanding, one to the other. Then, embodiment of another can be an emergent experience, as in an "Ah-ha!" moment, where a new relationship is possible for both. And finally, perspectives and perceptions can be altered with empathetic embodiment as a type of reductionist method to slowly sense personal affiliation with another species.

However our empathy is manifested and our passion is embodied, author Melanie Challenger in her book *How To Be an Animal*, reminds us the underlying principle is that *"what unites the different routes to the human experience of empathy is the willingness to think about someone or something else and match our behaviour to what the other needs."* (Challenger, M., 2021)

Research has shown that people who believe that the human species is a superior species compared with other creatures on earth are generally less willing to favor space equally for those they deem inferior. However, those same individuals can be swayed in their narratives of superiority and hierarchy when presented with just how similar their emotions and behaviours are to those of other species. In effect, research has shown that when animals are "elevated" by emphasizing the similarities with our species, perspectives towards other nonhuman species will typically soften to become more empathetic. (Bastian et al., 2012) (Costello, K., Hodson, G., 2010) Decades before the research, author E.O. Wilson, a zoobiologist and also a keen observer of humankind once said that, *"to the degree that we come to understand other organisms, we will place greater value on them and ourselves"*. The above studies show that empathy for nonhumans also translates into empathy toward other people. And prejudice against other beings because they are not our own species often translates to prejudice against inferior groups, such as immigrants.

I think it fair to say that embodiment requires at least a modicum of empathizing to relate effectively. Yet it also requires that imaginations extend beyond the boundaries of internalized narrative for perception to creatively envision another's experience in the world. To effectively help a traumatized animal or a psychologically wounded one, the best way is to attempt to witness from the perspective of empathy. Individual perceptions are not only embedded with certain personifications of a species, those views are formed through contexts from which thoughts of them arise. Shared commonalities - of pain, joy, social order, frustration and confusion are all emotional states that can be recognized across many species, just as differences may also be as recognizable; yet sensing resonance can be largely projected and bound perceptions and perspectives.

Pursuing an evolutionary dance through the past confronts us in vast distances of time and space with the contexts of chosen species which have bearing. While we may feel more intimately connected with those species we share a closer kinship with, they may seem more accessible to us at least partly because our similar four-limbed biology more closely matches theirs. It is prudent to remind ourselves:

> **The organism and the environment are not actually separately determined... The environment is not a structure imposed on living beings from the outside but is in fact a creation of those beings. The environment is not an autonomous process but reflection of the biology of the species..**
> **~ Richard Lewontin**

PyM can be modified to what you want it to be. Each time, you decide through intention and engagement, whether as mimicry to exercise in a series of movements, a moving meditation, spontaneous, free-form choreography or as a method to deepen understanding of how your body moves and why. Whatever, I suggest you allow the species to inform you in the practice. Acknowledge that each evolved organism is imbued with a spirit and history of life on earth; they all carry the burden and glory of the earth, its growing pains, passages, triumphs and tragedies. Each one has been beautified by having life and each, has enriched diversity of living systems and the landscapes. An ancient evolutionary heritage is there to claim and explore, take it to where it may lead. PyM is good groundwork to allow your soul an opportunity to respond and reconnect in reciprocity, where transformations, insight and meanings may flow and heal. You never know, primordial memories may awaken and attune to new awareness as just the ticket for insights to organically flow. Open to it. Take it from a fellow hominin; whittling defensives down to simply breathing in a vital, living and ancient earth story is a journey worth taking.

Strut like a Crane, Shimmy like a Snake…

A good way to begin PyM practice is with touch and sensing inwardly, conscious of breath, focusing physical awareness and getting comfortable. With the knowledge we are all just bone, blood, fluid, and tissue - purely physical beings, no different than any other physical being wrought by the earth and formed through billions of years of challenge and change.

There are many different ways to choreograph movements and forms of other species together into compositions. Structural forms and movements can be mixed and synergized with other species' exercises in any order that feels right to you. Some movements just blend together more easily to segway from one creature to another. Your creative composing may also be influenced or dictated by your immediate surroundings, in different landscapes and vary in bodies of water. Make the environment a part of the interplay just as nature and living systems have always been integral to evolution. Think of the world and yourself as non-static and complete as a dynamic in evolving life.

If inspired co-creating, infuse the physical manifestations with observations and ideas to open others to new interpretative expressions. Accept and honour what you feel. And in the spirit of wikipedic cooperation, share your ideas collectively.

There are also arthropod and insect movements to explore, strange locomotive movements of bizarre microbes and denizens of the deep ocean, a vast catalog of body plans awaiting expression. Have you ever seen a **Scorpion** stance? I have. Margaret, a very accomplished Shadow Yoga teacher once demonstrated her version: From a plank position, she bent and bracing on parallel forearms with fingers flat, shifted her weight onto the upper body. Leaning well forward on the forearms she sprang to lift her legs and torso upwards overhead with a gentle kick. Balancing upside down on forearms on the ground and curved in extension from head to toes, she then intertwined her legs like the tail of a scorpion, bending one foot as the stinger! Most of us will never achieve the postures and movements we imagine, yet the visualization at unattainable heights makes us appreciate them all the more. A perceptive practice embraces experimentation as tailor-specific. Imagining a species' evolution and attributes is good for the soul as a new way to see nature and leave "people" narratives behind. Sublimating the human species as one among many is an aspect of the journey.

PyM is easily incorporated into lifestyles. If you swim the conventional stroke workouts, try incorporating some PyM movements into the mix and bump it up a notch. It's dynamic and spontaneous to twist like a sea lion, undulate like a dolphin, and flutter like the jellies; flap like a beaver and barrel roll like an otter, and even more fun when blending one to play into another.

Simply shake up your lane-bound routine by circling the pool jetting as an octopus or side winding as a river snake and take in a view of the embankment. If more comfortable in shallow waters, play as a crab with stiff pivoting motions using buoyancy and the wave action or try standing as a heron, holding one foot up to wager balance and control, or experiment with less weight restriction in water with animal locomotive motions such as in **Running Rabbit**. Imagine being a fish in the shallows floundering up from the depths on fragile fins (elbows) that are not yet limbs and drag a tail. Imagine how that fish might slowly evolve into an amphibian: a belly-dragging salamander or transition from a tadpole to a frog. Dig in the sand with your elbows to experience how a sea turtle makes a hole to lay her eggs. Try beginning a journey onto land as a belly-dragging amphibian, then transition to a high-walking reptile, follow strengthening the limbs into the mammalian real with the sway and round-bottomed play of **Bear Swagger**, play as a wily weasel, or hang-ten as a tree sloth. Divert the evolutionary journey from four legged back to the ocean as a breaching whale or underwater penguin. Play as it evokes significance, render what feels appropriate and good, take joy to be more than yourself to witness a different side of life and being alive in meaningful, healthy ways. Spun in star dust and born through multiple stages in fire and ice, the earth's history illuminates many ways to Get a New View, Shed your Skin, Grow extra Tentacles, Flap your Wings, Widen the Horizon, Sprout a Tail and Share in Connection -- especially when matted together as Slime Mold!

TWIXT AND TWEEN

Is there difference in twixt and tween?
Divining mystery in the seen?
A mirrored light of eye convenes
A stick of snake, a shell of sand
A clod of frog, a wisp of thee?

Can sight transcend the twixt and tween?
Where fear and hope may dwell as deemed
Are bats not only shadow dreams?
A boulder of bear, a log o' gator
A charging breast defines a power seen

What notions play the twixt and tween?
Emotion bodied in the keen?
A breath is blown in spirits seen
A rock of tortoise, a tree of sloth
A leaf of butterfly or moth?

References

Achterberg, J., 2002, *Imagery in Healing:* Shamanism and Modern Medicine. Shambala Publications: Boston, MA.

Bastian, B., Costello, K., Loughnan, S., & Hodson, G. (2012). When closing the human–animal divide expands moral concern: The importance of framing. *Social Psychological and Personality Science, 3*(4), 421-42

Berger, M.R., 1972, Bodily Experience and Expression of Emotion, *Writings on Body Movement and Communication,* Monograph No. 2, 1972, American Dance Therapy Association, Columbia, MD.

Blakeslee, S. and Blakeslee, M., 2007, *The Body Has a Mind of Its Own*, Random House, Inc.: New York, USA.

Buck, D., 1987, *The Dance of Life,* Paragon House: New York, USA.

Challenger, M., 2021, *How To Be an Animal*, Penguin Books, London, U.K.

Costello, K., & Hodson, G. (2010). Exploring the roots of dehumanization: The role of animal— human similarity in promoting immigrant humanization. *Group Processes & Intergroup Relations*, 13(1), 3-22.

Craig, (Bud) A.D. (2003), Interoception: the sense of the physiological condition of the body. Current Opinion in Neurobiology, Vol. 13, Iss. 4, (500-505).

Craig, A.D. (2002). How do you feel? Interoception: the sense of the physiological condition of the body. National Review in Neuroscience 3, 655–666

Critchley, H.D., Wiens, S., Rohstein, P., Ohman, A., Dolan, R.J. (2004), Neural systems supporting interoceptive awareness, Nature Neuroscience 7 (189-195)

Ehrenreich, B.,2006, *Dancing In The Streets,* Metropolitan Books: Henry Holt & Co.: New York, NY.

Freberg, L. A., 2006. *Discovering Biological Psychology,* Houghton Mifflin Co.: New York, NY.

Hanna J. L. (1995). The Power of Dance: Health and Healing. *The Journal of Alternative and Complementary Medicine.* 1(4), 323-331.

Hoban, S. (2000). Motion and Emotion: the dance therapy experience. *Nursing Homes, 49*:11, 33-34.

Jacobson, E., 1938, *Progressive Relaxation,* University Chicago Press: Chicago, IL.

Katz, R., 1982, *Boiling Energy,* Harvard University Press: Cambridge, MA.

Ko, Kwang Hyun, 2016. Origins of human intelligence: The chain of tool-making and brain evolution. *Anthropological Notebooks* 22 (1): 5-22.

Lazar, S. W., Kerr, C. E., Wasserman, R. H., Gray, J. R., Greve, D. N., Treadway, M. T., McGarvey, M., Quinn, B. T., Dusek, J. A., Benson, H., Rauch, S. L., Moore, C. I., & Fischl, B. (2005). Meditation experience is associated with increased cortical thickness. *Neuroreport, 16* (17), (1893–1897).

Leonard, G., 2006, *The Silent Pulse: A Search for the Perfect Rhythm in All of Us,* revised edition. Gibbs Smith: Salt Lake City, UT.

Leonard, W. R., & Robertson, M. L. (1992). Nutritional requirements and human evolution: a bioenergetics model. *American Journal of Human Biology, 4* (2), 179-195.

Lewis, T.,1974, The Lives of a Cell, Bantam Books.

Lewis-Williams, D. J., & Clottes, J. (1998). The mind in the cave—The cave in the mind: Altered consciousness in the Upper Paleolithic. *Anthropology of Consciousness, 9* (1), 13-21.

Lewontin, R. (1983) The organism as the subject and object of evolution. *Scientia 118:63-82.*

Merleau-Ponty, M. (1963) The *Structure of Behavior.* Trans. Alden Fisher. Boston, MA: Beacon Press.

Navarrete, A., Van Schaik, C. P., & Isler, K. (2011). Energetics and the evolution of human brain size. *Nature, 480*(7375), 91-93.

Neubert, F. X., Mars, R. B., Thomas, A. G., Sallet, J., & Rushworth, M. F. (2014). Comparison of human ventral frontal cortex areas for cognitive control and language with areas in monkey frontal cortex. *Neuron, 81*(3), 700-713.

Ots, T., 1994, The Silenced Body - the expressive Leib: On the dialectic of mind and life in Chinese cathartic healing, *Embodiment and Experience: The Existential Ground of Culture and Self,*(pp. 116-136). Cambridge University Press: Cambridge, MA.

Pert, C., 1997, *Molecules of Emotion,* Touchstone Books: New York, NY.

Pinel, P., Thirion, B., Meriaux, S., Jobert, A., Serres, J., Le Bihan, D.,... & Dehaene, S. (2007). Fast reproducible identification and large-scale databasing of individual functional cognitive networks. *BMC neuroscience, 8* (1), 1-18.

Rimé, B., Philippot, P., Boca, S., Mesquita, B., 1992. Long Lasting Cognitive and Social Consequences of Emotion: Social Sharing and Rumination, *European Review of Social Psychology, Vol. 3, pp. 225-258*

Rizzolatti, G., & Fabbri-Destro, M. (2010). Mirror neurons: from discovery to autism. *Experimental brain research, 200* (3), 223-237.

Roth, G., & Loudon, J. (1998). *Maps to ecstasy: A healing journey for the untamed spirit*. New World Library.

Scheffer, V. B. (1983). *Spires of Form: Glimpses of Evolution*. University of Washington Press.

Sherwood, C. C. (2018). Are we wired differently? *Scientific American,* 319(3), 60-63.

Sointu, E., 2006. Healing bodies, feeling bodies: Embodiment and alternative and complimentary health practices. *Social Theory & Health,* 4 (3), pp.203-220. www.palgrave-journals.com/sth

Thomson, D.H.,1997, *Dance/Movement Therapy with the Dual-Diagnosed: A Vehicle to the Self in the Service of Recovery,* Journal of Dance Therapy, 19:1, pp.63-79.

Varela, F. (1991), *The Embodied Mind*. Cambridge, MA: The MIT Press.

Wilson, Edward O., 1986. *Biophilia.* Harvard University Press

Winters, A.F., 2008, *Emotion, Embodiment, and Mirror Neurons in Dance/Movement Therapy: A Connection Across Disciplines,* American Journal of Dance Therapy, Vol. 30, pp. 84-105.

Wong, K.,2020, The Origin of Us, *Scientific American,* September, 66-72.

Zaraska, M. (2020). All together now. *Scientific American, 323*(4), 64-69.

Zhang, J. (2003). Evolution of the human ASPM gene, a major determinant of brain size. *Genetics, 165*(4), 2063-2070.

CHAPTER 8

Just another Species

Just as we see how an animal evolves its locomotive characteristics in response to its surroundings, so too do our *Homo sapient* bodies grow to express within the confines of the physical and sociocultural parameters of our world. Today, I think it fair to say that the mechanisms of acculturation shape us as whimsical and fickle movers of our species' evolution. *Homo sapiens* of 20,000 years ago were certainly not as we are now. Scientists who study hominin evolution point to evidence that the initial acceleration in brain size occurred after hominins began tool-making and fire control, along with language processing that followed. (Flinn, M.V., 2005) (Stock, J.T., 2008) Hominin brain evolution and the species sociability facilitated ability to deduce situations and creatively strategize, develop tools for hunting and methods of transport, work out defense methods and shelter together by modifying habitat; they all were social manifestations that required foresight, planning and implementation. Scanning technology has shown that our genome has altered not only human brain size but in neurological, skeletal and metabolic ways based on lifestyle and dietary changes, social availability, medical and tech advances, language-processing, changes in physical demand, animal domestication and density of populations. (Voight, B.F. et al., 2006)(Greco, L.,1997).

Today, it is widely accepted that most high functioning species, especially us, are better defined through "intelligence-through-culture" theory through our cultures of language and learning, the degree of cooperative and gregarious behaviours of members, and tool innovation. (Reader, S.M., Laland, K.N., 2003) The theory was developed after researchers discovered that great apes born and reared in a rich learning and social environment in captivity made greater use of tools and resources in more creative and innovate ways to solve problems than did like individuals who were wild-caught or those living in wild habitats. (Van Schaik, C., 2006)

Scientists who study hominin evolution mainly attribute the biological increase in hominin brain size to tool-making and fire control that occurred along with language processing. Language communication skills and the eusocial cohesion of the Homo species that has characterized our evolution also defined and reinforced acculturated learning and solidified a different human physicality with manipulative skills. Yet the same sociability that has advanced successful hominin teamwork and pushed mankind into an exceptional species actually follows a long lineage of successful, interdependent cooperative and systemic techniques founded long ago in microbial organisms and evolved socially in other species. Beginning with the microbial cells' methodology of storing energy to protein manipulation, with techniques to harness energy and devise signaling systems, from cooperative teaming and mutual partnering with their defensive and resource-shared networking -- all formed a basis for the later social subtleties of the more "complex" multicellular species to function collectively. More than survival methodologies yet less than cultural, they serve to co-create living systems.

Well before human descent from apes, essential life-giving techniques of dispatch, symbiosis, mutual and commensal relationships existed; some in cooperative pacts governed in collective covenants with networking unions and bound without contract, all organic. Even before the first multi-celled organism, microbes had protein production and transportation for sharing resources, receptivity and signaling, methods to alter flow and motion mechanics, scaffolding, and various forms of defense and regulatory processes – as social cells. Perhaps among one of the very first synergies of life beyond the genetic exchange of information occurred with the gestation of a "different" bacterium (non-lethal and energetic) within a host single cell organism. It was ingested but not digested, to become the beginning of an endosymbiotic partnering wherein a microbe functioned only as part of a host organism and reproduced as such. This is how a cell nucleus evolved as a living energy producing and regulatory storage unit within a eukaryotic cell. (Margulis, L., 1998) Once partnerships brought groups together, then exciting things were possible, Cambrian like. There were other partnerships from microbial beginnings - photosynthesizing chloroplasts in algae, fungal and plant endo and external symbioses, bacterial symbionts in soils, in the oceans, and in every multicellular intestines, including ours. In the scope of opportunity, a little over a billion years doubled, is time enough for life to figure out all sorts of things. Moving from states only as a mindless microbial consumer of energy - to absorbing partners and creatively taking on differing roles together so each cooperative formation conferred less encumbrance, more advantage or maintained a balance? (Ah, but what do I know of cells? Very little - I only have to see around me and within me and wonder - Wow, do they really do all THAT!) Symbiotic relationships and partnerships are at the root of all evolutionary creativity. Whether biological, behavioural, social or as a creative hybridization, symbiosis has ushered in cooperative and commensurate responses in organisms and have continued as the environmental, ecological, systemic and interspecies behavioural relationships grew more complex.

Some may assert that symbiosis is essentially defined in terms that make socially adaptive behaviours unqualified as biologically-derived. Yet cooperative rules apply at watering holes around the world consistently when shared by different species. From the clumping of microbes to the sharing of resources (and nutrients) all species are, in some way, woven by acts of reciprocation and synergy. Fundamentally, it is easier to think of cells as encoding certain behavioural tendencies which were used to form new morphologies (multicellular life); from evolutionary impulses that play out cooperatively -- just as social behaviours do, given the chance. E.O. Wilson defines hominin eusociality as human behaviour balanced by cooperative elements:

The pathway to eusociality was charted by a contest between selection based on the relative success of individuals within groups versus relative success among groups. The strategies of this game were written as a complicated mix of closely calibrated altruism, cooperation, competition, domination, reciprocity, defection and deceit.

~ Wilson, Biophilia.

As an up-and-coming hominin species, human cohesion in their environment has not been particularly exceptional. Given the amount of brainpower, time and money spent in trying to understand the mysteries of relationships and devise processes to harness biological mechanisms of nature, the results of our labors are not that impressive - and animal domestication hardly counts. Few of our technologies support sustainable, life-giving systems and rarely are more productive than they are wasteful. Our *Homo sapient* eusocial cohesion has generated most "intelligence-through-culture" paradigms as dual-edge swords. Acculturation can either provide cohesion, cooperation and creativity to know and investigate aspects of human nature or they can just as easily have nothing to do with the human species as a whole or our place in the world. Culture can produce artifice as easily as it can produce charitable, authentic, responsive organizations with relationships that function to clarify and benefit us socially. Unfortunately, the human world is now littered with options, the majority of which are worthless sociocultural trends in human societies that have no tangible benefit to any species, for individuals or communities and produce only waste for future cleanup. Essentially, they are acculturations that have no soul.

In human societies, cultural norms generally reflect current cultural and economic perceptions and perspectives. Yet we rarely recognize them when they are toxic and detrimental to us to the world and other species, especially when what is customary is culturally accepted as institutional. For example, a typically acceptable norm by governing bodies is to use incentives in order to create market advantage. While this can often be a good thing; the dark side is to use incentives such as subsidies to prop up markets and as platforms for political favoritism and financial perk, directing preferential treatment that is couched in procedural and regulatory organization. All can be acceptably lobbied to influence others and all clearly legal and upstanding as bright displays in the facade of cultural acceptance. Whereas; on the other side of equally accepted behaviour , even accepted as "the will of the people" – oppression of the weak, deceit of the few, hidden hands in manipulation, blackmail, theft, political upheavals and appointments, takeovers and totalitarianism, cronyism, and the escalation of war, to name a few on the darker side. Giving access to make power moves with little or no accountability often insulates both the perpetrators and their mandates. Their authority alone can isolate them from transparency, accountability and other aspects inherent in more beneficent social flexibility such as reciprocal equality, teamwork, public access, check factors on power and other rebalancing influences that regulate living systems as living.

The same unique neurological factors in our evolution that make our species so astonishingly imaginative, intelligent, responsive, independent, cohesive, and caring as a social species; also lies at the root of our fragmentation. Promulgated by disseminating acculturation as rights of the individual (including corporate ownership!) wherein we may "rightfully" not only consume but overconsume to the public and environmental detriment – of course, completely justifiable and legal as entitlement. It can lay at the foundation of institutionalized addiction, wasteful accumulation, ecological destruction and resource depletion simply from having "right-to-use" status. Not only have we accepted nonconformity, but partisanship, narcissism, oppression and other selfish behaviours of social disorder, we admire them. All are culturally perpetrated rather than biologically felt. Melanie Challenger writes "*What is unusual about our species is that we've been able to use more and more energy without having to evolve into a different species. We've achieved this through a combination of social learning, complex culture, and technologies. We don't have to speciate to gain the claws of an allosaurus; we can share information to design a warhead*" (Challenger, M., 2021) While human division is as individually biological as the neural networks in our heads, our social missteps and inability to see beyond bias is almost exclusively culturally wrought. As a species, each of us is only separate by our individual perspectives and felt endowments.

Consider for a moment, the physicality and sensing abilities that create cognitive ability in any species. Cognition is said to be biological awareness exclusive of any existential reasoning to justify its existence. Even the most minimal awareness in any organism senses opportunity to survive to respond accordingly. Then consider why it is that so many humans have difficulty seeing that to live as a species we must provide space and protect living systems in order to insure continuance of biological life above all else, is inexplicable. The difficulty arises from culturally engrained perspectives. Yes, there are individuals in other species that exhibit self-destructive behaviours; yet human individuals lead all other species in promoting negative, self-defeating, disembodied thoughts that are both self-inflicted and from others; most often first on themselves and by extension, onto others and other species. Sharks, weeds and pests, oh my!

Contemporary culture also encourages us to look past ourselves -- to conquer space, live free, expand living spaces, compete for resources and incentivize parameters of commerce growth over species-based growth. The messaging looks to the future with the intention to *remove* constraints of living in a natural world, the antithesis to living *with* the world. A good portion of urbanites will never gain real insight into how "survival of the fittest" applies to shape life, simply because they need only to adapt to a culture-based reality created by and for us alone. Generally speaking, human efforts and endeavours are focused on extracting, harnessing and surmounting nature that tasting its true reality is now more remote and difficult to appreciate. No matter what the reasoning for altering nature may be, we all have different viewpoints and needs. We plainly have not yet evolved the vision necessary to avoid being blinded by acculturation as a cultural perspective. When we do, meanings and views may change.

In the last 50 years, just since 1972, the world's economies have expanded fourfold and global trade has increased 10 times to double the human population on earth, in *just* 50 years. Such near-sighted, only-in–my-lifetime, culture-based paradigms have wreaked astonishing harm to the biosphere, the oceans and ecosystems and most of all, to biodiversity. It doesn't take much to see that such unbridled growth is an unsustainable burden on the living systems globally - from resource depletion to waste dumping. With the exception of the temporary "one-child" policy in China, the globalized distribution of condoms, and grassroots pushing by NGOs to educate and stimulate eco-based independence, very little has been done to enforce transparency, accountability and curb human impact.

There are plenty of examples found in nature where a particular species becomes too numerous and spreads too quickly. Just look at how yeast poisons its environment from an overproduction of the byproducts of its consumption. Sound familiar? If any species (not only *Homo sapien*) strays too far from the nature of its birth and fails to co-create reciprocal relationships with others in the playing field, the outcome always points to a likely failure to co-exist. As a mechanism of self-destruction, such a life form nevertheless is a self-destructive pathogen in an impoverished environment that it alone creates. Our species has now reached 8 billion and is past the point of imposing population limitations. If it is true that our physiology no longer needs to adapt to a natural physical environment and that "intelligence-through-culture" is now the sole driver in *Homo sapient* evolution, then our cultures need to get smart and reinforce human cooperation to seek appropriate methods to increase functional paradigms modeled after open, transparent, sustainable living systems. Every cultural decision, whether through institutions, governance, media, politics, agriculture, energy, financial and technological systems - right down to the laws that influence the rights of individuals, require cohesive parameters that stimulate and mandate informed, collective perspectives to insure living systems regain the higher ground in our cultural paradigms, globally.

The pragmatic question is how to reinstate a personal sense of investment and reciprocity in this physically finite world with other species. In human communities, worldviews are shared collectively through a shared language, cultural assumptions and their history. Yet within every society, individuals vary as perspectives vary, so much so as to sometimes be indecipherable to one another. Given that often these self-definitions can fluctuate with identities and loyalties , they are further complicated by what connects: family, community, economics, mobility, history, language, culture and daily events, there are extremes at play. Is there a method to homogenize our species and yet, also insure that we indemnify and honour our differences; and motivate one another to care and plan collectively, uniformly? Frankly, we need reminders that our physical form did not arrive as a result of a passionate moment in time, but that we are members of a species - just another in the relentless pulsing of vitality in life itself.

Reintroducing the obscure notion of our evolution might just help us to rethink the direction of the species and imagine a pathway through. Individually, we tend to consider who we are in the short or near-term. We might think of our background and family upbringing in a particular place or community, or even go so far as to identify with our ethnic ancestry referring back to only a few hundred or a thousand years; and that may be as far as it extends. In thinking of ourselves in a historical context --identity only reaches as far as each individual's longest lens can focus. Whatever the perspective, what is seen as meaningful in our lives will always guide our thoughts about who we are in order to supply the signposts with which to compare, equivocate and assimilate in associations and with others socially, whether or not we consider our "group" an entity we are joined to, a part of, or separate from. PyM encourages seeing beyond all the self-definitions of near history, become more aware of the context of a lifetime of acculturation, and view with a longer lens of human evolution and life history. If, as evolution confirms, humans are just another species – we have to ask:

Are our customs, institutions and laws placing unnatural strangleholds on cultural change? If a principle in healthy living systems requires fluidity to energize, deliver, communicate, reinforce and resource with others to co-create and balance; where does that leave those who amass and stall the systems?... Those entitled individuals, corporations and creeds that by ancestry, fortune and history constrict flow of informed validity or when a real need to update the code we live by is justified to affect necessary realignment to human culture – as a departure from proprietary entitlements, or old alliances mandated by law, or an antiquated constitution that is no longer applicable; or immigration policies, land reform or domestication practices? If our institutionalized boundaries bled and morphed from timely pressures as they do in living systems, would the changes serve more effectively to rebalance human evolution in our "intelligence-through-culture" societies? Would the free flow of change produce more opportunity for productive equilibrium, just as the life of our cells within do??

The Past is a Distance Seen

Human biology relates a longer narrative, going past family and country, past ethnicity and gender, past the ancestral hominins and the Homo genus, even beyond our primate cousins and all four-limbed mammals, fish, amphibians, invertebrates and early sponges... to single cells that make up the 37.2 trillion cells of our biological self. We are just another multicellular species that has taken form through evolution as another expression of life and currently at the tail end of million on millions of years of speciation on this planet. But are we not a work in progress? Our unique bio complexity underscores the associative narratives that brim with perspectives of complexity and connection. We are a species awakening to not only a physical universe, but millions of virtual ones! At this 350,000 year juncture, Homo sapiens truly must attune to our environment, the one that is real. The bonus would be that by envisioning and enveloping a wider, more responsive and responsible collective vision, we might even touch on something that makes each of us quite unique in the earth's life history -- a knowledgeable, perpetuating, life-engendering caretaker of living systems.

It could be said that the onset of the primitive artistic renderings removed hominins from a species of yesterday and drove us to go beyond other animals into a new level of hyperconsciousness. From the earliest guttural sounds to communicate meaning for warnings, states of being, feelings, and learning with songs and storytelling; our imaginations have directly influenced the relationships we wished to define. And equally, our cultures reflect those meanings in all of us. Yet in a single lifetime, we may witness how truly heartfelt cultural historical unity with commitments to a cause and celebrations marking past achievements can be relegated as obsolete, indicative of a bygone era, and what was considered glorified heroism in one age can culturally evolve as misappropriated and worse, cast aside with disregard -- in a mere generation. Cultural moodiness can make former virtues no longer pertinent and individual humanity even regarded as a mere derisive diversion to others' entertainment. Human nature is not in flux, our cultures are. In other words, we never know which acculturated institutions will be the next to fall and which cultural flavor will lead the next generation. Sadly, leaves little in the way of awe for cynics. And yet, all cultural metaphors still boil down to the appropriation that individuals inwardly and perceptively ascribe to any one concept. Meanings are self-held and individual in their significance. Social media in the information age has affected us greatly and has done much to shape public and individual opinion, but it will also likely become an institution subjected to its own failure given enough time. Although acculturation is foundational in everyone, change can occur in personal viewpoints that form individual narratives. The culture we are making now; the institutions, laws and creeds must morph to follow. But initially, for real change to occur in hominins, most past the age of 4 must be willing first to de-signify their internal storyline within the context of new experience. Reducing self-importance also happens to be a Buddhist precept to enlightenment – in order to encompass new meanings, singularity of self must bow out.

Natural Law

The languor of elephants, the struggle of fish, the sinuous slither of snakes, the frenetic efforts of rabbits, the ferocity of wolves, and the cunning of cats. A species' behavior and individual character shapes their movements just as their movements define their intent. Evolution has shaped the altruism and playfulness in dolphins, the adaptability of octopuses, the breeding habits of corvids, and the empathy and grief displayed in elephants. (Gill, 1995; Dunbar & Shultz, 2007; Holekamp et. al., 2007) An animal does not equivocate in what it does. There are no shoulds or "coulds" - Should I eat that? Can I leap from that hill or across that chasm? No, for it typically takes only a split second to sense distinctly just doing it or search for an alternative; their instincts are directly attuned to their physical sensing of the surrounding conditions moment to moment. Animals evaluate but with little equivocation, if any, as to whether actions are possible to withstand, attempt or not, whether something is right or healthy for them or not. Our observations of animal behaviors can be trusted as true enough to the animal. We may not understand all of what we witness but characteristics are as true as what we see as abilities and behavioural reactions in reflecting the species. The feints and jabs that characterize a species are manifestations of what and who they are and present us with a clear opportunity to learn from them.

While we cannot know the innate complexity of their thinking, instincts, actions, relationships and values; singling out a particular attribute which identifies an essential aspect in the behaviour or an action can inspire expression. Our hominin ancestors and more recent ancients may have sought to emulate those characteristics they found true to the animal spirit in movement, dance and prayer in rituals for centuries. The purity of instinct in animals, unadulterated by equivocating desires, self-denial or inner aversion is testimony enough that animals feel simply what they feel, unless in service to mankind. Their exuberance, trust, loyalty, vitality, ferocity, effort, senses and abilities are traits and attributes indicative of a species' nature.

I once viewed a *Nature* program in which a naturalist documented the recent return of wolf packs to Yellowstone National Park, one of the largest national parklands in the United States. The crew followed the packs, filming them over a few years. The program happened to highlight an event which seemed to surprise the narrator, and no doubt, others involved. The unusual event was captured when one of the park's wolf packs mounted a vicious attack on a lone coyote.

Wolves and coyotes have long co-existed in the wild together and the victim was no different from any other coyote; there was no apparent logic driving the wolves' conduct in the killing. Coyotes are generally loners and warily give a wide berth to one of the parks' top predators, the wolves. They generally only approach from a safe distance to eat what might remain of a kill after a wolf pack has left the area. The victim had also habitually kept his distance and the attack occurred without any outward sign of prior provocation. One, and then more of the pack members chased and harassed the lone coyote and ended with the pack tearing the terrified victim apart and then abruptly leaving it dead. What the filmmakers found even more surprising was what they recorded after the incident. Shortly after the killing – another wolf pack in the same park area went into the attack wolves' territory and laid siege outside the aberrant attackers' pup den for days - not leaving until all the pups hiding in the den below ground had surely starved to death. It appeared as though it was a species' self-culling event whereby a wolf pack had purposefully wiped out the coyote-killing wolves' offspring for the year. Without advocating a judgment here, the siege event had all the appearance equivalent of a Nuremberg trial and the sentencing was a species' code of Natural Law implemented once it had been breached.

It may be a stretch for some especially in the West to believe that other living creatures possess moral qualities within the context of social mores and ethics. Dolphins also form strong social bonds; they name one another, play together and oversee the care of injured individuals but not just their own kind. There have been numerous reports of drowning persons assisted by dolphins and lifted up to the water surface to breathe in rescue attempts. (McCowan et al. 2000; Paulos et al. 2010) Dolphin groups have also been observed hanging around in order to protect the vulnerable divers working underwater apparently against shark attacks. Elephants are known to memorialize, show empathy, depression and grief over deceased members, exhibit leadership and care for one another; they can also be vengeful and cunning. Crows and other corvid groups are playful as they create games such as follow the leader and pass the twig. (Gill, 1995) They, and with other bird species, are known to participate in cooperative breeding (it has been calculated that 3.2% of bird species do). In the case of crows, they forego breeding independently in order to apparently follow some unknown clutch size parameter in order to follow a species rule by only cooperatively breeding with nonreproductive 'helper' crows as co–breeders. (Arnold, K.E., Owens, I.P.F., 1998)

The research on wolf packs also indicates that the number of individuals in a pack is not based on food availability, but rather, the size of a wolf pack depends on their cooperative breeding determined only by how many wolves may effectively bond in a group while withstanding competition. (Rich, L., 2012) Natural law that governs species population is also somewhat applicable in human populations. In many high density cities, women are less fecund and less willing to have offspring in places where there is overcrowding. (Jones, G.W, 2007; Brinton, M.C., Oh, E, 2019) And generally speaking, more reproductive balance is moderated where there is more education and choice available for women and where living standards may improve.

Learning to recognize and be open to Natural Law and its apparent wisdom offers a deeper, more consciously aware path antidotal to sensing and operating as a separate species from the natural world. There is a direct purity in the "rhyme and reason" of organisms, in the instincts of animals unsullied by convoluting equivocation. Imagine assessing details and actions in the world as opportunity for rebalance without splitting hairs over interpretation. Each of us has something to learn from the natural world even when perspectives are subject to the whims of sociocultural norms, paradigms and current valuations. The exuberance, trust, loyalty, vitality, sensing, teamwork, daring, prudence, care, courage, enjoyment, forgiveness, friendship, love and other emotions exhibited in other species and individuals may be at times surprising, but they're behaviors that are as trustworthy as the ability to see. Interpretation is the only variant. The ability to identify with social attributes of other species is straightforward; it is only viewpoints that may block recognition of what they tell and teach. How we relate affects how we learn from other species. Observations of animal-to-human and animal-to-animal dynamics are influenced objectively and receptively in drafting ideas of their ethical, emotional and social content, their social structure and complexity. How other species define their relationships and create their social mores can actually present us with an opportunity to gain insightful resources for our species, even if those impressions are labeled as "anthropomorphic".

Recognizing the pitfalls to anthropomorphism by adding human valuations - this one good, that one bad, of less or more value often result in perception as appraisals to narrow and for personal opinions to cloud perspectives. But clearly perspectives can widen viewpoints also…it allows us to expand. Wolves, for example, would not have such disciplined uniformity of intent in their packs without exhibiting distinct, unbound loyalty to one other as a species. Therefore, such behavior might just as easily include a species-wide version of moral equity as a given interspecies right-to-live principle and indicative of the unwritten natural law between the different species. It could also be a component of interspecies fitness to have a baseline of trust within the groups. However explained, the wolf pack exhibited a response that is well within a possible natural law of a well-evolved, million-year-old behaviour in species-to-species relationships. Of course, not all observed behaviors cross-species will always be applicable to the *Homo sapient* species. Cultures dictate that culling a future generation as responsible action to an antecedent behavior is not appropriate for our species because we hold that children should never be held responsible for parental actions either before or after they are born. It is a basic principle built into the morality of our laws.

The idea here is to open to observations of natural law as possible applications to seek to improve interspecies health, to help equate and determine functionally moral guidelines for our species to adopt honourable respect to co-exist with other species. As principled intent of humanity, natural law may provide valuable lessons to help our species establish cultural, social and governing uniformity as a basis to affect greater good. Perspectives that project the viability of natural law to guide decisions can help us to identify with life's successful stratagems that were worked out in the interrelationships of species-to-species eons ago. They include far-reaching behaviors that accurately reveal binding codes, covenants, materials, technologies and the group parameters within social relationships of many species. It should apply especially to those species nearer as kin to us and when a specific result, behavior or conduct is repeated often enough, or if found in both primordial and complex species alike. There are many ancient systems for us to better understand how Natural Law and living systems might help us address our future, including how to better assimilate the aberrant ones. Forget the diversion of the meta-universe -- it is time to observe how organisms design systems of cooperation and containment.

Cooperation and Pathogenic Containment

The Information Age has made it evident that throughout society there are those who live to diminish and hurt others; they do not purport to stand on their own endeavours but live to trample attitudes and actions that engender kindness and respect. They exhibit behaviors wantonly narcissistic, blindly self-centered and plainly selfish. Thankfully, individuals that consistently exhibit such pathogenic behaviours count only as a very small number compared to those who work in amicable relationships, partnerships, communities and groups and sublimate themselves for the benefit of others. They are the altruistic, conscientious members of our species, often thinking of others and mindful of future generations. Gratefully, the vast majority of individuals in our species enjoy feeling a part of a greater good through conscientious actions and by adoption of working ethics in relationships. Many consistently attempt to see where fallacies or false steps may lay and take the necessary steps to correct them to improve the plight of the oppressed or disadvantaged, to wipe out blight when and where it appears and "come to the rescue". By joining together they do whatever is necessary to assure a better future and will frequently devote time to research, deliberate with others, communicate and cooperate on the best courses of action to create systems and/or technologies to better sustain life and health for the future. There are those who provide avenues for aid and supplies when and where they are needed, often safeguarding the "lesser" groups, individuals and species by giving them a voice or oversee that accountability and transparency enforces responsibility human actions, they research, moderate and protect the natural balance in environments ensuring that key species are seen to have a rightful place. There are many who work to care for and restore ecological stability. They are often highly informed as first responders who are cognizant of the working perspectives necessary to rebalance and amend harmful climate, environmental and human activities.

Author Paul Hawken wrote eloquently on the efforts of these altruistic grassroots groups in **Blessed Unrest** in 2007, illuminating how leadership and cooperation in grassroots movements will arise and moves to correct environmental damage and social inequality around the world. Popular movements often bubble up in societies to push back on injustice, to counter oppressive actions on rights and freedoms, and to thwart the damaging entitlements of individuals, governments and corporations – in order to heal the wounds of the earth. Hawken paralleled the emergence of grassroots movements metaphorically with the biological system of immunity. Yes, the immune system -- the physical system that oversees, corrects and rebalances the healthy equilibrium as a living system in the body. Our immune system responds to a pathogen in several ways, first by recognizing the threat of a foreign invader and there are checks on recognition. Then appropriate steps are taken to counteract the threat, if any are required. Upon identifying whether the foreign body is a new threat or a recognizable one, the immune system responds accordingly based on whether it is benign and if inimitable, whether it can be incorporated or disposed. If non-damaging, the body's internal waste system initiates the break down, if harmful causing disruption or damage to cells, the immune system goes into a different mode by surrounding the attacker, isolating it, initiates heat with inflammation and calling on killer cells to eliminate the pathogen. The immune response boosts internal reactions as an inflammatory response along with other cellular action such as increasing white cells. T cells also additionally are produced to help fight and minimize any damaging effects by the anomalous invader so that healing may commence. Immune defense is far more complex than the above outline, but rest assured – a healthy immune system is all for one and one for all.

Drawing on biological system responses, such responsive rebalancing frequently occurs in human societies. Hawken extrapolated how grassroots activists and organizations improve their response time and resiliency with improvements in organizational connectivity to "be task-specific and focus resources precisely and frugally… linking individual actions to larger grids of knowledge that evolves and grows as needed". (Hawken, P., 2007) In effect, by modeling the immune system, Hawken advocated bringing cohesive cooperative and assistance efforts together with more focus on communicating specific tasks as in a living system, to better contain the effects of disasters and to improve coordinating relief efforts. This is just one example where biological processes can inform us with what procedures found in Natural law can be utilized as effective systems.

There are few better places to look for Natural law than in cells and cellular interactions for dispatch, particularly those that have a complex exchange for chemicals or information, circulatory and dissipation mechanisms, purposed and resilient material constructs, flow mechanisms, matrixed networks and collective behavioural responses; and particularly those that guide responses for sustainability. Cells in biological multi-celled organisms communicate to perpetuate life through cell initiation of timely death and cell replacement and growth. It is a sustaining process that rejuvenates the cellular vitality. Nearly all the cells in our bodies regenerate every 7 to 10 years on average. The exception to this consistently restorative system to sustain living occurs when cells become cancerous and work to compromise the system of health in other cells.

Researcher and psychologist Athena Aktipis of Arizona State University Cancer Evolution Center explains how the cancerous cells behave in evasive, narcissistic and uncooperative ways: "they break the rules of normal cells… they rob other cells of essential supplies, shirk their cellular jobs and pollute extracellular spaces. Cancer cells grow extra blood vessels to grab more for themselves and… by hogging resources; they replicate more quickly… and take over, unless there are mechanisms to enforce cooperation." (A. Atktipis, 2021, SciAm) The reason such actions sound familiar is that such behaviours can also happen in neighborhoods and failing nation states. The conduct can become ubiquitous in cultures where greed is not only tolerated but condoned and even encouraged. The monopolization of assets and supplies, acceptable polluting of the environment, financial embezzlement, lack of transparency in procuring land entitlements and extraction contracts, slacking off responsible accountability, and hidden schemes to manipulate societal, financial, resource and economic systems are but a few prime examples. It happens when legislators risk safety for corporate or personal gain over communities, when inequality occurs in the distribution of food, vaccines, and clean water. Disruption from damming rivers, permitting chemical fracking, unbridled fishing and hunting practices, strip mining , rampant development, and soon on the horizon -- dredging the deep ocean floor is happening now.

Cancerous pathogenic cells deplete local resources and drain health by starving the surrounding healthy cells and the blood vessels that feed them. Just as cancer cells impoverish their local environment, so too do sociopaths that impoverish a neighborhood where illegal activities that go unchecked will shrink the primary sources of commerce in local communities. Parallels may be drawn as in a cancer - pathogenic cells follow what occurs in every other living system whether biological, ecological, economic or societal – with corruption and deprivation of healthy cells (businesses/cultures) and the blood vessels (local suppliers/people/communities) that once thrived are also are compromised with the impoverishment. The morbid incursions exhaust resources, routes and supplies in the surroundings and eventually force aberrant cancer cells, parasites, or sociopathic persons in an impecunious neighborhood to move on and look elsewhere for more resource-full areas. In their wake, the surroundings once healthy with cells/commerce are left strangled, poorly and sickened, as the ruinous sociopaths who seek to demolish community benevolence, cooperation and infrastructure.

In Natural law, healthy environments share resources through mechanisms created long ago to insure biochemical growth, flora and fauna recycle nutrients and maintain systemic growth through signalling systems. Researcher and author, Suzanne Simard discovered such folds of growth in vigorous healthy forests -- from the diversity of plant species that influence sharing soil nutrients to microorganisms. Integral to the distribution and networking is the symbiosis with the underground fungi mycelium that acts as a networked system of communication and delivery. (Simard, S., 2021).

All life is built on cooperative cell life. It took billions of years for cell organisms to work out how to signal, differentiate, build receptor processes, to move effectively, sense and form symbiotic systems within the chemical and physical parameters. They are systems of cooperative covenants, processes, pacts and agreements that govern living systems. It is through their multicellular processes that organisms fill landscapes with healthy ecologies due to the underlying living codes that perpetuate life. One covenant mandates that organisms in living systems work by following uniform regulatory rules: in communications, sharing nutrients and the surrounding resources, to stimulate flow, dissipation and dispatch and more. They all translate to sensing change occurring in neighborhoods and initiate appropriate action to rally with what's happening, such as signalling to others multiply as needed, investigate and repair, to force a retreat or annihilate to prevent intractable harm from spreading. Microbial and multicellular life with biodiverse systems sustains all living systems. It's interesting to consider whether life could be considered "benevolent" as cooperatives in the billion years' reign of microbes on earth. If not, how could single cell lifeforms have successfully joined forces to design the systemic complexity they have to perpetrate the vitality of life with the creation of multicellular beings?

Likewise in the human body, healthy cells will curb excess growth and rampant proliferation; they distribute nutrients equitably and transmit chemical signals to maintain the vitality of tissues through cell health and regeneration. The life of a cell is based on its receptive communication and cooperative systems yet rely also on regulatory methods to maintain vital responses. If a few cells become cancerous in a healthy environment; the cancerous pathogens generally cannot get a foothold because the surrounding cells out-compete the cancerous ones in a healthy environment. Studies of cell networking and other factors which constitute and regulate living systems can help define what is appropriate to sustain human systems and what natural mandates are necessary for a species to live within the bounds of its' environment. We must have more ability to quantify this to envision what a sustainable future looks like before earth's resources are depleted.

Natural law also can help to inform us what behaviors may constitute adjudicative rights and to possibly curb harmful behaviors before they are culturally accepted and engrained within the culture and institutional systems. Nothing exists in and of itself alone. Every successful species is a result of what has gone before and must fit into at least one sustaining pattern. Natural law in living systems are tradeoffs, they are there to adjust resiliency, provide mechanisms to help sustain and adapt; they can either circle back, refresh systems or not; they may be ever-present or arise only rarely.

Engaging the principles of Natural law and evolutionary dynamics of living systems is occasionally applied in medicine as well as ecology. A new approach in oncology is underway which follows a principle of survival of the fittest as a method for delivering chemotherapy treatment. The new technique makes use of a Natural Law which often governs the distress response in plants of exposure to chemicals. Witnessing how antibiotics can become ineffective in cancer patients with repeated use is similar to how insects develop resistance to pesticides. Metastatic cancers often have been shown to grow back even more aggressively and more chemo-resistant with the traditional chemical-based scourge of cancer. Taking the cue from the ag industry pesticide application, the oncologists use this same recuperative law that circumvents or amends how environments surmount chemicals and become even more chemically resistant to treatments. The Natural law principle of governing "competitive release" has led some oncologists to consider a more moderate and in many cases, a much more effective approach to treating cancer with chemotherapy. The method aims to moderate the destructive impact of chemo treatments by using just enough to prevent the cancer cells from growing and spreading; not enough to eradicate the cancer cells completely but to fall just short thereby reducing the size and number of tumors. Avoiding the "scorched earth" method, the treatments leave a small number of chemo-sensitive cells alive so that the cells remain responsive to chemotherapy. Thus by restricting the use of chemotherapy parsimoniously, the chemo-sensitized cells can then replace the pathogenic cells that destroy living tissues using chemotherapy that is more effective to slow the proliferation of the cancer. Similarly, managing the use of pesticides in the same way has been found to increase crop yields while simultaneously reducing pests by maximizing their sensitivity to the pesticide. It ensures that the pesticide remains a viable control mechanism. (DeGregori, J. and Gatenby, R., 2019) (Somarelli, J.A., 2020)

Recognition of Natural law and implementation in operative systems have been found to be more viable as solutions and have better resiliency when, as in living systems, they are openly shared, adequately supported, receptive, transparent, accountable, and sustainable. Every aspect of living systems are constrained by the environment which, as its nature, is in flux. The problem lies in determining bounds. However, if we imagine the scenario where each of us represents a tiny microscopic cell in a community, all working in conjunction with each other to improve and maintain the health of a species on an individual planet, like in *Horton Hears a Who!* If we are all a tiny part of the earth, then when we dam a river, fell a forest, build a road, dredge a seabed or flood a plain – we should at the very least have a deep understanding of what is lost in doing so -- be it a species, an ecosystem, a livelihood, an institution, or an ancient heritage. The question is: can we set the bounds and restrain our species consistently, and with each breath ask, "Will this action engender more life and biological diversity, or less?

Breath the only real Entitlement

Primordial yogic Movement has been spurred on by several authors, but was given particular impetus by a book from David Suzuki and Peter Knudtson: *Wisdom of the Elders: Sacred Native Stories of Nature*. The authors chronicled the traditions, thoughts and spiritual practices that many indigenous groups around the world use to maintain connection with the natural world. The tribes choose to live as they always have within the biological constraints of the earth. This response is a most fundamental one because it also allows for their successors to do the same. The indigene way of life persists in stark contrast to the Western corporate, private enterprise willingness to erase, eradicate, extract, deplete, dam and damage the biosphere. Those who strive to live in balance within the bounds and rhythms of cyclical balance of natural abundance and scarcity will generally take deliberate care of the *gifts* in the natural world. It is central to their discernment, responsible action and insights. Such perspectives may be an appropriate place to begin where a shift in perceptions are most needed. Perceptions bound by what is and always will be, as it was in the long ago past -- that nature is not to be taken, irrevocably altered or otherwise seen as personally advantageous.

All too often a perception of entitlement pits insiders against outsiders, the wealthy against the poor, and the powerful against the powerless. Politics and institutionalized empowerments frequently permit new claims on rights of ownership and resources, waterways and lands (even of inhabitants) where none had been historically. Whether through regulated, unregulated, or institutionalized as laws – creating, manipulating and implementing rights of entitlement from thin air is an anathema. Yet such contractual tactics are embedded in private enterprise and governing bodies and are widely supported by cultural and economic systems of finance, trade and commerce commodities to render what was "gifted" exclusive, proprietorial status - even when the extractions and profits run dry.

1,786 years ago, in 237 A.D. and early in recorded history, a Roman author known as Tertullian looked around him and predicted:

> *"Our teeming population is the strongest evidence: our numbers are burdensome to the world which can hardly supple us from its natural elements; our wants grow more and more keen and our complaints more bitter in all mouths, whilst Nature fails in affording us her usual sustenance."*

Since that early assessment on the effects of a growing human population, the warning bell has rung time and time again from all walks of life, in every century, and with each new generation. Each time alerting us while some of the most stable, diverse and sustainable living systems fractured, became impoverished and non-sustainable; collapsing under the weight of the single most consequential species on earth.

The 5th Extinction occurring now on the planet is no singular catastrophic moment - no natural geological, astronomical or physics-based event. It is being caused by a single species who think themselves more entitled and more special than all others, even more than the planet to which they were born. An upright, nimble-fingered, rather gangly ape-like animal with a slow moving, bipedal gait, just astute enough to have a capacity for language, a singular attribute which has helped to push them beyond their natural limits. The speed with which we are using and changing the land, including coastal habitats, marine biota and freshwater systems, now impacts over 75% of the land on earth because it is considered "usable" (as a current U.S. slogan states of protected, public lands as "land of many uses"). Our direct exploitation and extraction of natural resources has now reached 60 billion tons a year. (Global Assessment Report on Biodiversity, United Nations, 2022) Individually, we are now consuming 15% per capita *more on average* in plants, animals, fossil fuels, ores, and building materials; and trashing more living systems than just 50 years ago. Consider this fact: the current human population makes up one-third of all mammals on earth. Why only a third...because we breed and control almost all of the remaining two-thirds of the remainder to eat. So, what percentage of mammals remains in the wild? - Nowadays a mere 4 percent, almost negligible. As for the dinosaurs that survived extinction, less than a third of the world's birds fly free. The vast majority are poultry.

We're changing the natural order of most of the life-giving processes on earth and altering evolution itself. Where roads are built and humans move in –habitats diminish, invasive species are introduced, organisms are exploited, and biodiversity deteriorates along with eco-systemic connections and their unique interactions often resulting in the loss of entire, intact ecosystems. The problem is not slowing, 100 million hectares in tropical forests alone were destroyed between 1980 and 2000 and scientists tell us that we are today at the crucial apex that should any more rainforest be destroyed, sustainability of the ecosystem as an intact living system will become too impoverished to function. The world not only will lose the lungs of the planet, but so much more.

Conscious Choices

What began with an appeal to look beyond viewpoint must end with an inward look.

Animals can teach us a great deal about trust, teamwork, daring, enjoyment, courage, caring, forgiveness, friendship and love. We share those attributes but may choose to remove ourselves from generously sharing and opening our hearts to others for a variety of reasons, not the least being equivocation. Our cultural notion of what is acceptable and the human tendency to institutionalize often sway us from intuitive right action. So I ask, if a yogic practice could give you more control over the things you don't like in yourself, would you accept a removal of defenses to try another way of seeing? Possibility of change must be accompanied by openness to change; it's like outgrowing the fit and feel of old shoes. Remember, when old knowledge of the world is shattered and new assimilation is a requirement, it might initially be felt like a moral departure or a disavowal of the past to leave a former way of life behind. And yet when facts cannot be denied, the alternative to letting yourself down - may be to let the world down… to say nothing of future generations. Indeed, there might be forces beyond your direct control; but trust in what you feel on the inside as honest and clear is the one and only thing you can control to give life meaning.

Personal growth in an experiential praxis (PyM or other) meant to realign thoughts and perspectives can direct energies to become more reciprocal in the world. While everyone has a sense of some kind of physical heritage in their physicality, finding that perspective with a longer lens of evolutionary history can lead to receptive, expansive understanding of what is more than human, rather of life itself. It is where Intention uniquely human can lead perspectives to change. Whatever view of the natural world each of us may currently hold, opening to new relationship carries prospect for change. How we relate to a dependent pet, a prey normally seen in the cross-hairs, a meddlesome invasive species, or a calf braying for its mother from across a fence can appear more meaningful in the light of their roles in the world. Reciprocity from unrecognized facets can make one realize how intrinsically beautiful and how equally important others are; or how under attack, oppressed, brutalized, dismissed or undervalued an individual or a species.

Changing perspective is just a first step to shine new light on the worth and similarities with other species, the value to place on biodiversity and on leaving living systems intact, and the morality of caring that can be shared more broadly. It's the only way for evolution to continue to shape other species in the world and through them, human evolution. Sally Kempton, an author of books on meditation, yoga and Buddhism has written: "As you learn how to connect to the soul of the natural world, you can begin to help the planet show us what needs to be done." Perceiving from a different viewpoint is halfway to getting there.

The real effort will be to change the perception of who we are, in how we perceive ourselves; not as the highest lifeform at the end of the evolutionary ladder, but as grateful, steady guardians of munificent creativity. Namaste!

References

Aktipis, A., 2021. Malignant Cheaters, *Scientific American* 324, 1, 62-67.

Arnold, K.E., Owens, I.P.F., 1998. Cooperative breeding in birds: a comparative test of the life history hypothesis. Proceedings of Royal Society London. B.265739–745.

Brinton, M. C., & Oh, E. (2019). Babies, work, or both? Highly educated women's employment and fertility in East Asia. *American Journal of Sociology*, *125*(1), 105-140.

Capra, F., *Web of Life,* Anchor Books, New York, NY.

Challenger, M.(2021). *How to be Animal: A New History of what it Means to be Human*. Penguin Books, London, U.K.

DeGregori, J., Gatenby, R., 2019. Darwin's Cancer Fix. *Scientific American*: August Issue Vol. 321.

Deng Ming-Dao, *365 Tao*, 1992, *Harpers.* San Francisco.

Dunbar, R. I., & Shultz, S. (2007). Evolution in the social brain. *Science*, *317*(5843), 1344-1347.

Flemming, H. C., & Wuertz, S. (2019). Bacteria and archaea on Earth and their abundance in biofilms. *Nature Reviews Microbiology*, *17*(4), 247-260

Flinn, M. V., Geary, D. C., & Ward, C. V. (2005). Ecological dominance, social competition, and coalitionary arms races: Why humans evolved extraordinary intelligence. *Evolution and Human Behavior*, *26*(1), 10-46.

Gill, F. B. (1995). *Ornithology*. Macmillan.

Gintis, B., 2007, *Engaging the Movement of Life*, North Atlantic Books, Berkeley.

Greco, L. (1997). From the neolithic revolution to gluten intolerance: benefits and problems associated with the cultivation of wheat. *Journal of pediatric gastroenterology and nutrition*, *24*, 14-17.

Hawken, P. *(2007).* Blessed unrest: How the largest movement in the world came into being, and why no one saw it coming. *Penguin Books.*

Holekamp, K. E. (2007). Questioning the social intelligence hypothesis. *Trends in cognitive sciences*, *11* (2), 65-69.

IPBES, March 2022, Global Assessment Report on Biodiversity and Ecosystem Services – by the United Nations Intergovernmental Science-Policy task force.
Jones, G. W. (2007). Delayed marriage and very low fertility in Pacific Asia. *Population and Development Review*, 33 (3), 453-478.

Kimmerer, R.W., 2013. *Braiding Sweetgrass*. Milkweed Editions: Canada.

Kittle, A.M., et al., 2015, Wolves adapt territory size, not pack size to local habitat quality, Journal of Animal Ecology, Vol.84, Is. 5.

Lewis-Williams, D. (2011). *The mind in the cave: Consciousness and the origins of art*. Thames & Hudson.

Lovallo, William R., 2005, *Stress & Health*, Sage Publications, California.

Rich, L.N., et al., 2012, Anthropogenic mortality, intraspecific competition, and prey availability influence territory sizes of wolves in Montana, Journal of Mammalogy, Vol. 93, Is. 3.

Freedman, F. B., Gibbs, B., Hall, D., Kelly, E., Monks, J. Smith, J., 2006, *Yoga & Pilates For Everyone: A complete sourcebook,* Hermes House, London, U.K.

Margulis, L., 1998, *Symbiotic Planet*, Basic Books: Perseus Books, New York, NY, USA.

McCartney, James, 1978, *Philosophy and Practice of Yoga,* L. N. Fowler, Essex, U.K.

McCowan, B., Marino, L., Vance, E., Walke, L., & Reiss, D. (2000). Bubble ring play of bottlenose dolphins (Tursiops truncatus): implications for cognition. *Journal of Comparative Psychology, 114*(1), 98.

Paulos, R. D., Trone, M., & Kuczaj II, S. A. (2010). Play in wild and captive cetaceans. *International Journal of Comparative Psychology, 23* (4).

Reader, S. M., & Laland, K. N. (Eds.). (2003). *Animal innovation* (Vol. 10). Oxford: Oxford University Press.

Reid, Daniel, 2000, *A Complete Guide to Chi-gung*. Shambala, Boston.

Schmidt, P.A., Mech, L.D., 1997, Wolf Pack Size and Food Acquisition, The American Naturalist, Vo. 150, No. 4.

Simard, S. (2021). *Finding the mother tree: uncovering the wisdom and intelligence of the forest*. Penguin Books, UK.